FROM PRINCIPLES TO PRACTICE

CH01034953

Knowledge aims to fit the world, and action to change it. In this collection of essays, Onora O'Neill explores the relationship between these concepts and shows that principles are not enough for ethical thought or action: we also need to understand how practical judgement identifies ways of enacting them and of changing the way things are. Both ethical and technical judgement are supported, she contends, by bringing to bear multiple considerations, ranging from ethical principles to real-world constraints, and while we will never find practical algorithms – let alone ethical algorithms – that resolve moral and political issues, good practical judgement can bring abstract principles to bear in situations that call for action. Her essays thus challenge claims that all inquiry must use either the empirical methods of scientific inquiry or the interpretive methods of the humanities. They will appeal to a range of readers in moral and political philosophy.

ONORA O'NEILL, BARONESS O'NEILL of Bengarve, is former Principal of Newnham College Cambridge, sits as a cross-bench peer in the House of Lords and is Emeritus Honorary Professor at the University of Cambridge. She has published widely on Kant's philosophy and her most recent publications include *Constructing Authorities* (Cambridge, 2016), and *Justice Across Boundaries: Whose Obligations?* (Cambridge, 2016).

FROM PRINCIPLES TO PRACTICE

Normativity and Judgement in Ethics and Politics

ONORA O'NEILL

Emeritus, University of Cambridge

CAMBRIDGE
UNIVERSITY PRESS

CAMBRIDGE
UNIVERSITY PRESS

University Printing House, Cambridge CB2 8BS, United Kingdom

One Liberty Plaza, 20th Floor, New York, NY 10006, USA

477 Williamstown Road, Port Melbourne, VIC 3207, Australia

314–321, 3rd Floor, Plot 3, Splendor Forum, Jasola District Centre,
New Delhi – 110025, India

79 Anson Road, #06–04/06, Singapore 079906

Cambridge University Press is part of the University of Cambridge.

It furthers the University's mission by disseminating knowledge in the pursuit of
education, learning, and research at the highest international levels of excellence.

www.cambridge.org
Information on this title: www.cambridge.org/9781107113756
DOI: 10.1017/9781316286708

© Onora O'Neill 2018

This publication is in copyright. Subject to statutory exception
and to the provisions of relevant collective licensing agreements,
no reproduction of any part may take place without the written
permission of Cambridge University Press.

First published 2018

Printed in the United Kingdom by TJ International Ltd. Padstow Cornwall

A catalogue record for this publication is available from the British Library.

Library of Congress Cataloging-in-Publication Data
NAMES: O'Neill, Onora, 1941– author.
TITLE: From principles to practice : normativity and judgement in ethics and politics / Onora
O'Neill Emeritus, University of Cambridge.
DESCRIPTION: New York : Cambridge University Press, 2018. | Includes bibliographical
references and index.
IDENTIFIERS: LCCN 2018011098 | ISBN 9781107113756
SUBJECTS: LCSH: Ethics. | Normativity (Ethics) | Judgment (Ethics) | Practical reason.
CLASSIFICATION: LCC BJ1031 .O535 2018 | DDC 170–dc23
LC record available at https://lccn.loc.gov/2018011098

ISBN 978-1-107-11375-6 Hardback
ISBN 978-1-107-53435-3 Paperback

Cambridge University Press has no responsibility for the persistence or accuracy of
URLs for external or third-party internet websites referred to in this publication
and does not guarantee that any content on such websites is, or will remain,
accurate or appropriate.

Contents

Acknowledgements

In this collection I focus on generic features of practical reasoning and judgement, including ethical reasoning and judgement, which have given rise to persistent disputes for a long time. The papers have been written across many years, and engage with persisting and in many cases recurrent features of ethical debate. However, in this collection I say little about the justification of practical principles, which I have discussed elsewhere.[1] My aim is to consider whether and how practical principles can guide action. If we cannot understand whether and how principles can guide action, questions about their justification will hardly matter, since their practical use and point will remain obscure.

I have puzzled about these questions across many years, and have discussed them with many patient friends, colleagues and students, as well as with wider audiences in innumerable seminars and conferences. I am deeply grateful to those who have shared my sense that questions about the relation of practical principles and practical judgement to action matter, and have helped to clarify what is at stake and how far answers can be given. These questions need answering if action is to be guided by principles, and matter not only for abstract philosophical purposes, but for leading our lives. I thank everyone who has had the patience to listen, to criticise, to encourage and to make fruitful suggestions.

---

[1] Including in Onora O'Neill, *Towards Justice and Virtue* (Cambridge University Press, 1996); *Acting on Principle*, 2nd edn. (Cambridge University Press, 2014); *Constructing Authorities: Reason, Politics and Interpretation in Kant's Philosophy* (Cambridge University Press, 2016).

Introduction: taking principles seriously

Principles are prominent in nearly all contemporary discussions both of the way things are and of what is to be done. Both everyday and scientific claims about the world frequently propose and endorse, discuss and dispute *theoretical* or *descriptive* principles in seeking to establish and justify truth-claims and to explain events. Both everyday and more abstract claims about what to do, including ethical and political claims, frequently propose and endorse, discuss and dispute *practical* or *normative* principles, and see them as central to justifying and to guiding action. And yet it is far from agreed that we must take principles seriously. Indeed, the very idea that we can rely on practical principles, or specifically on ethical principles, either in justifying or in guiding action is repeatedly and widely disputed.

The papers in this collection focus on practical principles and on their uses. They aim to resolve difficulties that are said to undermine all forms of principle-based practical reasoning, including ethical reasoning, but leave questions about ethical justification and about metaethics aside.[1] Nor shall I say much about the many ingenious proposals for doing ethics without principles that have been put forward by philosophical advocates of various forms of intuitionism and particularism.[2] My aim is to address elementary and persisting objections to practical principles, among them ethical principles, to show how they can be met and to spell out some of the connections between practical principles and practical judgement. As I see it, if these generic objections cannot be answered, discussing either the justification or the use of practical principles would have little point.

---

[1] See Onora O'Neill, *Towards Justice and Virtue* (Cambridge University Press, 1996); *Acting on Principle*, 2nd edn. (Cambridge University Press, 2014); *Constructing Authorities: Reason, Politics and Interpretation in Kant's Philosophy* (Cambridge University Press, 2016).

[2] Landmark twentieth-century discussions that see principles as dispensable or even as damaging for ethics, run from G. E. Moore, *Principia Ethica* [1903], Tom Baldwin (ed.), revised edn. (Cambridge University Press, 1993) to Jonathan Dancy, *Ethics Without Principles* (Oxford University Press, 2004). For a penetrating recent account of particularist positions and of the reasons they present for doing without principles see Maike Albertzart, *Moral Principles* (London: Bloomsbury Press, 2014).

Part I   Practical principles and relevant descriptions

The papers in the first part of the collection look at some persistent features of our present cultural landscape which can make it hard to see the connections between principles and practice. The papers in the following three sections focus on the task of connecting principles to practice.

I begin by considering a radical criticism of practical principles, including ethical principles, which was put forward by G. E. M. Anscombe and has often been repeated. Anscombe pointed out that practical principles must contain descriptions of the action to be done, and then suggested that we cannot tell *which* descriptions, nor therefore *which* practical principles, are relevant to particular cases. If this radical criticism were convincing, principles could have no practical use. In Chapter 1, 'Modern moral philosophy and the problem of relevant descriptions', I reconsider Anscombe's criticism of 'modern moral philosophy', in which she argued that principle-based approaches to ethics, including all forms of Utilitarian and of Kantian ethics, are pointless and should be rejected.

As I see it, the problem of relevant descriptions does not bear on the *practical* use of principles. Deliberation takes place *before* action, and it makes no sense to insist that we need to find 'the relevant description' (or even 'a relevant description') of an act that does not yet exist. Unless and until an act is done, there is no act-token to be described – relevantly or irrelevantly, accurately or inaccurately. The fact that practical principles, including ethical principles, contain act descriptions, and that these act descriptions can be true or false of particular acts, does not mean that practical uses of those principles seek to describe particular acts. This objection to principle-based ethics imports a spectator's view of action, in which the task is to describe or interpret what is done – or rather what has been done – rather than to deliberate about what to do. The problems on which it centres do not arise in deliberating, where we seek to fit (aspects of) the world to our principles, rather than trying to apply descriptions or principles to particular acts not yet performed.[3]

It is puzzling that Anscombe should have been so concerned that the problem of relevant descriptions would undermine practical, including ethical, reasoning in this radical way, since she proposed a solution to the problem. In distinguishing between the *directions of fit* of practical and

---

[3] However, the problem of relevant descriptions raises issues for theoretical uses of principles and for retrospective judgement of action already performed. I discuss some these in the papers in Part II, below.

theoretical uses of principles she offers an account of reasons for thinking that the problem of relevant descriptions does not undermine the use of ethical (or other practical) principles. While theoretical uses of principles indeed aim to fit the world, practical uses of principles propose standards to which a part or aspect of the world is to be fitted.

Although Anscombe's radical suspicion of ethical principles misses its target, I believe that it deserves close attention because it reflects a deep and persisting cultural tendency to gravitate towards a spectator perspective when discussing practical questions. Spectator views of action and ethics are often revealed by preoccupation with the context or situation of action, at the expense of a focus on the practical question 'What should be done?', which has been basic to ethical discussion, and in particular to Aristotelian and Kantian approaches to ethics. Anscombe was not alone in the emphasis she sometimes placed on a spectator rather than a practical view of ethical situations. Fortunately this was only an aberration in her otherwise deeply illuminating account of the differences between practical and theoretical directions of fit.

Various other discussions of ethics during the past century have assumed that a rigorous approach to ethics needs to fit the world rather than to seek to change it, and so cannot be adequate unless it aims at truth-claims, indeed on some accounts specifically at empirical truth-claims. It is hardly surprising that such lines of thought have been read by some as showing that ethics cannot secure standards of rigour or objectivity, and that what passes for ethical reasoning is irredeemably subjective, ideologically driven or arbitrary.

The other papers in Part I explore some of the cultural and philosophical positions and assumptions that – overtly or tacitly – assimilate ethical to empirical inquiry by assuming that ethical reasoning must either fit the world or lack justification. My purpose both in Chapter 2, 'Two cultures fifty years on', and in Chapter 3, 'Scientific Inquiry and normative reasoning', is to suggest how and why it can be tempting to deny or to marginalise the role of normative considerations in many areas of life, to fantasise that ethical reasoning must either use empirical methods or fail, and to insist that scientific inquiry ought to be 'value-free' or 'value-neutral'. As I see it, practical or normative reasoning is not some marginal or substandard form of empirical reasoning, but a distinctive use of reasoning that is indispensable for all activity, including practices of inquiry, among them practices of scientific inquiry.

Part II Abstract principles and practical judgement

Part II of the collection turns to less radical but far more popular criticisms of practical, including ethical, principles. A central and much repeated objection to ethical positions that emphasise principles is that difficulties arise not in identifying which practical principles are important or can be justified, but in moving from principles to action. Principles are invariably *indeterminate* or *abstract*, and it is repeatedly said that they must consequently either fail to guide action, or alternatively will regiment action in ways that are likely to be blunt and morally insensitive to differing circumstances. These less radical criticisms of principle-based ethics, and of many other forms of normative reasoning, cannot be laid to rest by distinguishing between theoretical and practical uses of principles.

The first two papers in Part II – Chapter 4, 'Abstraction, idealisation and ideology in ethics', and Chapter 5, 'Normativity and practical judgement' – ask whether these generic objections to principle-based practical reasoning are as damaging as is often supposed. The vast majority of critics of principle-based ethics do not argue that it will be undermined by the problem of relevant descriptions, but that it will be defective for these further reasons. They claim that principles are practically useless because they are *too abstract* or *too indeterminate* to guide action. Reliance on principles, it is said, leads unavoidably either to empty *formalism* or to mindless *rigourism*. Either principles provide no guidance, or they offer rigid guidance that is insensitive to differences between cases, thereby reducing ethical and other practical reasoning to what has at various times been derisively characterised as *superstitious rule worship* or *rule-fetishism*. These widely repeated criticisms of practical principles have been made for more than two centuries, and are still regularly put forward in varied forms, not only by particularists and intuitionists, but by varied historicists, communitarians, virtue ethicists, Wittgensteinians, 'situationists', and by some feminists.

Rather surprisingly many of the objections that these critics repeatedly raise had already been addressed by Immanuel Kant in the eighteenth century, and many of the papers in Part II consider specific arguments that he put forward. Each of the last three papers in Part II – Chapter 6, 'Instituting principles: between duty and action', Chapter 7, 'Experts, practitioners and practical judgement', and Chapter 8, 'Kant on indeterminacy, judgement and interpretation' – looks at some of Kant's central claims and arguments about putting principles into practice. Kant, like many others, claims that indeterminacy and abstraction do not undermine practical, or specifically ethical, reasoning. Practical principles can be action-guiding provided they are coupled with practical judgement.

Yet this conclusion may seem to lead only from the frying pan to the fire unless it can be coupled with an account of practical judgement. How are agents, who are typically committed to multiple practical principles, to work out what to do? As I see it, the very plurality of indeterminate practical principles that Anscombe feared would undermine their capacity to guide action (on the assumption that it was necessary to locate a single 'relevant' principle of action for each case) provides a key to the way practical judgement actually works. We do not enact principles one-at-a-time. Practical judgement of all sorts typically enacts or instantiates a *plurality* of principles, and ethical judgement is supported rather than undermined by the need to shape action so that it enacts or instantiates a *plurality* of ethical principles (as well as of other practical principles).

If we had to consider practical principles, or specifically ethical principles, one-principle-at-a-time the indeterminacy of principles would indeed mean that they offered inadequate practical guidance. But if we take seriously the thought that ethical judgement is a matter of finding a way of meeting the demands of the various practical principles to which we are committed – which may include a great variety of legal, professional, institutional, technical and other practical principles, as well as ethical principles – that indeterminacy can be significantly resolved. If I seek to find a way of acting that is both legal and safe, both honest and kind, both tactful and affordable, compatible both with others' rights and with relevant professional standards, the demands of the several principles to which I am committed will cumulatively constrain my action in ways that help lessen indeterminacy, by narrowing in on ways of enacting principles that are adequately and usefully action-guiding.

A plurality of practical principles cannot, indeed, provide algorithmic guidance that picks out a single required act-token: but that is neither a practical nor an ethical requirement. Both in ethical reasoning, and in areas of specialised and technical practice (for example: medicine, engineering, farming) the aim of practical judgement is achievable provided we see its task as that of enacting or instantiating a plurality of practical principles, of which some may be ethical principles. Any act that meets all of the principles to which an agent is committed satisfies those principles, and there is no reason to assume that the task is to identify an act-token that uniquely meets their demands. This account of practical judgement, I conclude, is needed and sufficient to *supplement* although it does not, indeed cannot, *supplant* ethical principles.

Part III   Means, ends and demands

The papers in Part III set Kantian arguments aside to look at some of the
generic requirements by which normative, including ethical, reasoning can
shape action so that it can be effective in actual situations. In Chapter 9,
'Reason and the resolution of disputes', I argue that – contrary to the
claims of those who seek to anchor all practical reasoning in versions of
rational choice theory – instrumental reasoning is never sufficient, but also
never dispensable, for practical reasoning. Chapter 10, 'Consequences for
non-consequentialists', queries the assumption that instrumental reasoning is or should be peculiarly the concern of consequentialists. While
consequentialists are right to see instrumental reasoning as indispensable,
they are mistaken in supposing either that non-consequentialists try to do
without instrumental reasoning or that it can provide a complete or
sufficient account of practical reasoning. The final paper in Part III –
Chapter 11, 'Demandingness and rules' – addresses the frequently raised
objection that consequentialist ethics, and in particular Utilitarian ethics,
is 'too demanding' because it generates 'an overload of obligations', and
asks whether this objection also arises in principle-based ethical reasoning.

Part IV   'Applied' ethics and practical judgement

The papers in Part IV consider how some of these generic features of
practical reasoning and practical judgement bear on ethical practice, and in
particular on the claims of 'applied' ethics. Both Chapter 12, 'Applied
ethics: naturalism, normativity and public policy', and Chapter 13,
'Practical principles and practical judgement in bioethics', argue that it is
a mistake to think of ethical practice as a matter of *applying* principles to
cases, and consequently that the very term 'applied ethics' is a misnomer.
Theoretical principles can be applied to actual cases, but practical, including ethical, principles are not applied, but rather *enacted* or *instantiated*.

However, while all practical principles must be enactable (in suitable
situations), only some of them are enforceable by others. This final theme
leads back to Kant. In Chapter 14, 'Enactable and enforceable: Kant's
criteria for right and virtue', I explore some of the distinctions Kant drew
between different types of ethical principles and the reasons he offers for
thinking that some important duties, including some significant duties of
justice, are enactable but not enforceable by third parties. The distinction
between duties that are and are not enforceable is far from obvious, yet of
great importance for public and institutional life.

Bibliographical note on references to Kant's work

Quotations from Kant's writings are taken from the Cambridge edition of the works of Immanuel Kant, published by Cambridge University Press from 1996. Where an argument depends on close reading of a passage the German is given either parenthetically or in footnotes. References cite abbreviated titles with the standard volume numbers and pagination of the Prussian Academy edition of the works of Immanuel Kant.

Immanuel Kant, 1781, *Critique of Pure Reason* [*CPR*], tr. and ed. Paul Guyer and Allen W. Wood (Cambridge University Press, 1996).

Immanuel Kant, 1784, *An Answer to the Question: What is Enlightenment?* [*WE*], tr. Mary J. Gregor, in *Kant's Practical Philosophy* (Cambridge University Press, 1996).

Immanuel Kant, 1785, *Groundwork of the Metaphysics of Morals* [*G*], tr. Mary J. Gregor, in *Kant's Practical Philosophy* (Cambridge University Press, 1996).

Immanuel Kant, 1786, *What does it mean to orient oneself in thinking?* [*WOT*], tr. Allen W. Wood, in Immanuel Kant, *Religion and Rational Theology*, ed. Allen W. Wood and George di Giovanni (Cambridge University Press, 1996).

Immanuel Kant, 1788, *Critique of Practical Reason* [*CPrR*], tr. Mary J. Gregor, in *Kant's Practical Philosophy* (Cambridge University Press, 1996).

Immanuel Kant, 1790, *Critique of the Power of Judgement* [*CJ*], including the *First Introduction*, tr. Paul Guyer and Eric Matthews (Cambridge University Press, 2000).

Immanuel Kant, 1793, *On the Common saying: That may be correct in theory, but it is of no use in practice* [*TP*], tr. Mary J. Gregor, in *Kant's Practical Philosophy* (Cambridge University Press, 1996).

Immanuel Kant, 1793, *Religion within the Boundaries of Mere Reason* [*R*], tr. George di Giovanni, in Immanuel Kant, *Religion and Rational Theology*, ed. Allen W. Wood and George di Giovanni (Cambridge University Press, 1996).

Immanuel Kant, 1795, *Toward Perpetual Peace* [*PP*], tr. Mary J. Gregor, in *Kant's Practical Philosophy* (Cambridge University Press, 1996).

Immanuel Kant, 1797, *The Metaphysics of Morals* [*MM*], tr. Mary J. Gregor, in *Kant's Practical Philosophy* (Cambridge University Press, 1996).

Immanuel Kant, 1797, *On a Supposed Right to Lie from Philanthropy* [*SRL*], tr. Mary J. Gregor, in *Kant's Practical Philosophy* (Cambridge University Press,

1996), 8: 425–30. The more traditional title is *On a Supposed Right to Lie from Benevolent Motives.*

Immanuel Kant, 1798, *The Conflict of the Faculties* [*CF*], tr. Mary J. Gregor and Robert Anchor, in Immanuel Kant, *Religion and Rational Theology*, ed. Allen W. Wood and George di Giovanni (Cambridge University Press, 1996).

Immanuel Kant, 1800, *Jäsche Logic* [*JL*] (not in the Prussian Academy edition), in Immanuel Kant, *Lectures on Logic*, tr. and ed. J. Michael Young (Cambridge University Press, 1992), 521–64.

Immanuel Kant, n.d., *Lectures on Ethics* [*LE*], tr. Peter Heath, ed. P. Heath and J. B. Schneewind (Cambridge University Press, 1997). The parenthetic letters (*C*), (*M*) and (*V*) in references to these lectures indicate whether the notes are those by Collins, Mrongovius or Vigilantius.

PART I

Practical principles and relevant descriptions

CHAPTER I

Modern moral philosophy and the problem of relevant descriptions[1]

G. E. M. Anscombe's indictment of modern moral philosophy was full-blooded. She began with three strong claims:

> The first is that is not profitable to do moral philosophy … until we have an adequate philosophy of psychology, in which we are conspicuously lacking. The second is that the concepts of obligation and duty … and of the moral sense of 'ought', ought to be jettisoned … because they are derivatives … from an earlier conception of ethics … and are only harmful without it. The third thesis is that the differences between the well-known English writers on moral philosophy from Sidgwick to the present are of little importance.[2]

The connections between these three thoughts are not immediately obvious, but their influence is not in doubt. Many exponents of virtue ethics take Anscombe's essay as a founding text and have endorsed all three thoughts. Many consequentialists and theorists of justice, who may reasonably be thought the heirs of the 'modern moral philosophy' that Anscombe criticised, have disputed or disregarded all three. Yet I believe that Anscombe's essay is neither as reassuring for contemporary virtue ethics nor as damaging to other strands in contemporary moral philosophy as this snapshot account of its influence could suggest.

Anscombe's diagnosis and virtue ethics

Anscombe diagnoses many modern attempts to do moral philosophy as failing for lack of an adequate philosophy of psychology. As she sees it, we still use a moral vocabulary that once had sense and resonance, but we now have no adequate grip on the philosophy of psychology that supports that

[1] First published in Anthony O'Hear (ed.), *Modern Moral Philosophy*, Royal Institute of Philosophy, Supp. Vol. 54 (Cambridge University Press, 2004), 301–16.
[2] G. E. M. Anscombe, 'Modern Moral Philosophy', *Collected Philosophical Papers of G. E. M. Anscombe, Vol. III, Ethics, Religion and Politics* (Oxford: Blackwell, 1981), 26.

vocabulary. Consequently we use it to say things that are deeply confused, and sometimes morally corrupt. We cannot, on Anscombe's view, substitute 'modern', naturalistic psychology for an adequate philosophy of psychology since it offers no adequate basis for an account either of obligation or of virtue.[3]

This diagnosis of the failings of modern moral philosophy initially had limited influence, but became more widely accepted from the early 1980s. Its widening acceptance can perhaps be traced to Alasdair MacIntyre's much-discussed restatement of many of Anscombe's thoughts some twenty-five years after she wrote, in which he acknowledged a deep debt to her essay. In *After Virtue* he accused not only the 'modern' moral philosophers whom Anscombe names but their Enlightenment predecessors of engaging in "an inevitably unsuccessful project".[4] They fell into confusion by discarding teleological accounts of human-nature-as-it-could-be in favour of naturalistic accounts of human-nature-as-it-actually-is.[5] This left them unable to make coherent ethical claims, since ethics is about making a transition from human-nature-as-it-is to human-nature-as-it-would-be-if-fully-realised. Ethics, MacIntyre wrote,

> presupposes some account of potentiality and act, some account of the essence of man as rational animal and above all some account of the human *telos*. The precepts that enjoin the various virtues and prohibit the vices, which are their counterparts, instruct us how to move from potentiality to act, how to realise our true nature and to reach our true end.[6]

MacIntyre added that this scheme is

> complicated and added to, but not essentially altered, when it is placed within a framework of theistic beliefs … and the precepts of ethics … have to be understood not only as teleological injunctions but also as expressions of divinely ordained law.[7]

Apparently neither Anscombe nor MacIntyre saw any difficulty in combining Aristotelian teleological accounts of human beings and law conceptions of ethics *provided that the law concerned was divine law*. This view is easily read as a familiar Thomist fusion of Natural Law theory with Aristotelianism. A theological framework integrates the claims that God determines the end of man and that the principles He prescribes can guide their pursuit of that end. Anscombe put her conclusion boldly:

---

[3] *Ibid.*   [4] Alasdair MacIntyre, *After Virtue* (London: Duckworth, 1981), 53.   [5] *Ibid.*, 50.
[6] *Ibid.*   [7] *Ibid.*, 51.

> To have a *law* conception of ethics is to hold that what is needed for conformity with the virtues failure in which is the mark of being bad *qua* man … is required by divine law. Naturally it is not possible to have such a conception unless you believe in God as a lawgiver; like Jews, Stoics and Christians.[8]

In her view, any law conception of ethics collapses unless it is set in a theological framework.

So she sees the proponents of modern moral philosophy as attempting the impossible in putting forward a law conception of ethics that was detached from divine law. Anscombe comments on their ambition:

> Those who recognise the origins of the notions of 'obligation' and of the emphatic, 'moral' ought, in the divine law conception of ethics, but who reject the notion of a divine legislator sometimes look about for the possibility of retaining a law conception of ethics without a divine legislator.[9]

She sees this ambition as understandable but unrealisable:

> if such a conception is dominant for many centuries, and then is given up, it is a natural result that the concepts of 'obligation', of being bound and required as by a law, should remain although they have lost their root …
>
> It is as if the notion 'criminal' were to remain when criminal law and criminal courts had been abolished and forgotten.[10]

In failing to grasp this point, the proponents of 'modern moral philosophy' fail to see that the 'moral' use of the notion of 'ought' "has no reasonable sense outside a law conception of ethics"[11] and that the only coherent possibility of such position is a divine law conception of ethics. She concludes that if we want to retain the notion of obligation, we must accept a divine law view of ethics.

Many who accept Anscombe's diagnosis have rejected divine law accounts of ethics, but have argued for supposedly Aristotelian ethical visions, in which obligation and the moral 'ought' play no part, or little part. Most modern virtue ethics detaches virtue from any account of divine law. Its proponents say little about this element in Anscombe's criticisms of modern moral philosophy. They simply reject a morality of obligations, or of moral rules and see a life of virtue as constitutive of human flourishing. However, neo-Aristotelians differ widely in their views of human flourishing and of the true end of man. Some take a relativised or quasi-relativised view of the human good, seeing it as varying in differing societies; others identify the human good with a comprehensive and supposedly universal

---

[8] Anscombe, 'Modern Moral Philosophy', 30.   [9] *Ibid.*, 37.   [10] *Ibid.*, 30.   [11] *Ibid.*, 32.

list of desirable states of being and capabilities, whose status and derivation may be harder to establish without a theological framework.[12]

Anscombe herself held to the divine law view of ethics, but left room for those unwilling to follow her to settle for Aristotelianism without divine law. Yet is this a stable position? Many, indeed most, virtue ethicists reject the thought that conformity with the virtues is or could be *law-like*. They distinguish sharply between an *ethics of rules* and an *ethics of virtue*, and insist that virtue cannot be set out in rules or laws. If they are right, does it follow that Anscombe and MacIntyre were mistaken in supposing that virtue ethics was compatible with divine law? If they are mistaken, should they distance themselves from Anscombe's polemic against forms of moral philosophy that appeal to principles or rules, and that use the vocabulary of obligation without the backing of a divine law conception of ethics? At the end of this essay I shall offer a speculative postscript on this striking gap between Anscombe and some of her followers.

Modern moral philosophy and relevant descriptions

We can perhaps see a little more accurately what Anscombe has in mind by asking what a more adequate 'philosophy of psychology' was supposed to contribute to moral philosophy. She certainly was not lamenting the lack of an adequate scientific or naturalistic psychology. She was markedly hostile to experimental psychology when I was taught by her in the early 1960s; she had no doubt been equally hostile to it a few years earlier; and I suspect that she would have been equally hostile to subsequent empirical work in psychology.

Her use of the term 'philosophy of psychology' is best illustrated by the philosophy of action that we find in Aristotle's *Nichomachean Ethics*, to which she repeatedly refers both in 'Modern Moral Philosophy' and in *Intention*[13] (published a year earlier). An adequate philosophy of psychology would cover topics such as action, intention, voluntariness, wanting, pleasure, weakness of will and self-control – and might even embrace accounts of virtue and of flourishing.[14] I have occasionally seen the term *moral psychology* used to refer to more or less this cluster of topics,[15] but the

---

[12] For an example of the latter approach see Martha C. Nussbaum, *Women and Human Development: The Capabilities Approach* (Cambridge University Press, 2000).

[13] G. E. M. Anscombe, *Intention* (Oxford: Blackwell, 1957).

[14] Anscombe, 'Modern Moral Philosophy', 38 and 41.

[15] For example, in Owen Flanagan and Amélie Oksenberg Rorty (eds.), *Identity, Character, and Morality: Essays in Moral Psychology* (Cambridge, MA: MIT Press, 1993).

term seems subsequently to have been pressed into new and narrower duties in discussions of psychological features of moral education, of the sort discussed by Jean Piaget, Laurence Kohlberg or Carol Gilligan. So I shall stick with Anscombe's term *philosophy of psychology*.

Perhaps the deepest thought linking the many topics that Anscombe would group under the rubric 'philosophy of psychology' is the thought that *action is propositional*. Acts fall under many descriptions; act descriptions may have many instances. Although individual acts – act-tokens – are events in the world, we both think about action and act *under certain descriptions*. We also consent to or reject others' action as described in certain ways, but not others;[16] we hold people responsible for what they do under certain descriptions, but not under others;[17] we classify acts under certain descriptions, but not others. How does this make a difference to the way we do moral philosophy?

In 'Modern Moral Philosophy' Anscombe argues that the fact that we think of action under descriptions is fatal to ethical positions that aim to provide accounts of moral *rules* or *principles*. She criticises both Kantian and Utilitarian ethics – the central versions of 'modern moral philosophy' – on these grounds. She writes of Kant that

> it never occurred to him that a lie could be relevantly described as anything but just a lie … His rule about universalisable maxims is useless without stipulations as to what shall count as a relevant description of an action with a view to constructing a maxim about it[18]

And she writes that

> Mill, like Kant, fails to realise the necessity for stipulation of relevant descriptions, if his theory is to have content. It did not occur to him that acts of murder and theft could be otherwise described. He holds that where a proposed action is of such a kind as to fall under some one principle established on grounds of utility, one must go by that.[19]

The so-called 'problem of relevant descriptions' is the basis of Anscombe's condemnation of Utilitarian and Kantian positions, and is presented as a central source – perhaps the central source – of the alleged failure of modern moral philosophy. The problem can appear both profound and intractable. Any act-token will fall under many true descriptions, hence also under many possible principles of action. Absent a proper philosophy

---

[16] G. E. M. Anscombe, 'Two Kinds of Error in Action', in *Collected Philosophical Papers of G. E. M. Anscombe, Vol. III*, 3.
[17] *Ibid.*, 4–5.   [18] Anscombe, 'Modern Moral Philosophy', 27.   [19] *Ibid.*, 28.

of psychology, she asks, how can we tell which act description is relevant for moral assessment? We will not, for example, know whether to assess an action under the descriptions that an agent intends, or under descriptions others think salient, or under descriptions that nobody has noted. Both Kantian and Utilitarian ethics may have other defects, but if Anscombe is right they founder on this point alone: the many different act descriptions and principles under which any act falls may form the basis for diverging moral assessments, and so to incoherence.

I believe, although Anscombe's text does not make this explicit, that this is why she supposes that 'modern moral philosophy' so readily lapses into some form of consequentialism. For if we have no way of determining under which descriptions we should judge action, we cannot judge acts for their *intrinsic* character – which we cannot know. So we must end up judging acts by their extrinsic features, such as their (expected) consequences. This will lead us away from what Anscombe calls 'the Hebrew-Christian ethic', which prohibits certain acts "simply in virtue of their description as such-and-such identifiable kinds of action".[20] She points to examples of types of action that are intrinsically unacceptable, regardless of consequences:

> it has been characteristic of that ethic to teach that there are certain things forbidden whatever *consequences* threaten, such as choosing to kill the innocent for any purpose, however good; vicarious punishment; treachery; idolatry; sodomy; adultery; making a false profession of faith.[21]

There are several oddities to these claims. In the first place, if the problem of relevant descriptions is so intractable, how has 'the Hebrew-Christian ethic' managed to avoid it, whereas modern moral philosophy has not? I presume that Anscombe's answer to this point would be that the former has an adequate philosophy of psychology, while the latter does not. However, this is by and large an inference from her comments on the moral corruption of modern moral philosophy, and not (I think) something she establishes.[22] Equally, why did Anscombe think that the problem of relevant descriptions was a weakness – a fatal weakness indeed – in Kantian ethics and more generally in 'modern moral philosophy' but not fatal for Aristotelian ethics? The problem of relevant descriptions – *if* it is a

---

[20] *Ibid.*, 34.   [21] *Ibid.*, 34; cf. 39–40.

[22] For example, she upbraids Sidgwick for his simplistic claim that we are responsible for *all* foreseen effects of action, and his failure to distinguish good action that has foreseen but unintended bad effects from bad action, *ibid.*, 35–6; she concludes with splendid certainty that "it is a necessary feature of consequentialism that it is a shallow philosophy", *ibid.*, 36.

problem – will surely affect *all* approaches to ethics except those forms of radical particularism that (purportedly) do not view acts by reference to descriptions under which they fall. Mere claims that some approaches to moral philosophy have access to a philosophy of psychology that resolves the problem, and mere assertions that other approaches do not, are not enough.

Relevant descriptions in Intention

These issues can be clarified to some extent by considering Anscombe's more systematic and extensive discussion of the problem of relevant descriptions in *Intention*. There she asks, "how I am to select from the large number of true statements that I could make about a person".[23] And she suggests that any of us could "say what would immediately come to your mind as a report to give someone who could not see and wanted to know".[24] But if there are large numbers of distinct descriptions of a given action – large numbers of distinct *true* descriptions – why should *just one* immediately come to mind? Might not a number come to mind? Might not the wrong one(s) come to mind?

In fact both problems seem to arise quite often. We may find that we are torn between a number of competing descriptions of an action. In *Intention* Anscombe provided an example that later became well known: a man is moving his arm up and down, thereby pumping water into a cistern, thereby poisoning a water supply, thereby poisoning the inhabitants of a villa, thereby dispatching a group of war criminals. This action can be correctly described in many distinct ways, whose ethical significance differs: and multiplicity of true descriptions is ubiquitous.

Does this raise a problem for *all* ethical judgement? Even if in a given case we settle with conviction on one description of what is done, and that description is true of the case, there will always be other true descriptions. If others think that one or another of the competing true descriptions is more compelling or ethically significant, how are we to reply? We have only to think about the competing act descriptions that have figured in debates about abortion, civil war or other contentious political disputes to realise that a choice of one rather than another act description *might* have momentous ethical implications, and that there are no simple or general ways of choosing which is the most appropriate or relevant description of a given act.

---

[23] Anscombe, *Intention*, 8.   [24] *Ibid.*

So does the multiplicity of true descriptions of any given act create an intractable difficulty for *all* attempts to do ethics? How are we to tell which are the morally significant or most significant descriptions of a given act? How are we to judge the action of those who, as it seems to us, fail to see morally significant descriptions of what they do or of what others do? How are we to know that we are not overlooking morally significant descriptions of what we or others do? Won't any account of practical reasoning, *a fortiori* of ethical reasoning, be stymied at the very start if we have to resolve these problems? To many later writers Anscombe's concerns seem to raise a central problem, perhaps the central problem, for any adequate account of ethical judgement. The worry is acknowledged and addressed both in work in the tradition of 'modern moral philosophy' *and* in the work of those who follow Anscombe in aspiring to virtue ethics.

For example, the leading Kantian writer Barbara Herman has described the problem of relevant description as a serious issue for Kantian ethics, and also proposes a solution for it. She writes:

> The CI [Categorical Imperative] cannot be an effective practical principle of judgement unless agents have some understanding of their action before they use the CI procedure … It is useful to think of the moral knowledge needed by Kantian agents (prior to making moral judgements) as knowledge of a kind of moral rule. Let us call them "rules of moral salience".[25]

But where do these "rules of moral salience" (*RMS*) come from, and how are they to be justified? Herman argues that these rules do not themselves have moral weight, but that

> Typically they are acquired in childhood as part of socialisation; they provide a framework within which people act. When the rules of moral salience are well internalised, they cause the agent to be aware of and attentive to the significance of "moral danger". They are not learned as bits of information about the world, and not as rules of guidance to use when engaged in particular sorts of activities … They constitute the structure of moral sensitivity … They may indicate which actions should not be undertaken without moral justification …[26]

The 'rules of moral salience', it seems, are not *moral rules*, but a sort of *moral early warning system*. As such they are not (on Herman's view) essential to moral judgement, in that an early warning system is not *essential* for applying the Categorical Imperative. But these rules "enable

---

[25] Barbara Herman, *The Practice of Moral Judgement* (Cambridge, MA: Harvard University Press, 1993), 77.
[26] *Ibid.*, 78.

an agent to appreciate what is at issue in hard cases by making perspicuous the morally significant features that make them hard",[27] although they "do not themselves generate duties".[28] The rules of moral salience supposedly provide some answer to the problem of relevant descriptions because they "alter our idea of how an agent perceives situations that require moral judgement".[29]

Herman acknowledges that the rules of moral salience, which she sees as "pre-procedural moral rules"[30] need some foundation [*sic*] that connects them to Kant's moral philosophy. Without such connection she would find herself ascribing an internally incoherent account of practical reasoning to Kant.[31] It seems to me that Herman is torn between the thought that rules of moral salience are an indispensable presupposition of any use of the Categorical Imperative, and an account that makes them not just a *preliminary* but an *independent* basis for moral judgement, and so threatens to make the Categorical Imperative redundant or at least less important. Once we have "rules of moral salience" how much work remains for the Categorical Imperative?

Other writers, who share more of Anscombe's views, have suggested that any solution to the problem of relevant descriptions would be a matter not of *rules* of moral salience but of *capacities* to appreciate the salient features of situations, which we internalise, making any appeal to ethical principles redundant. On such views, we can reach ethical judgements without appeal to principles or rules, guided simply by our sensitised, attentive perception or judgement of the case at hand that calls for ethical response. For example, John McDowell writes of moral judgement or deliberation as "a capacity to read the details of situations"[32] or a "capacity to read the details of situations in the light of a way of valuing actions"[33] or a "capacity to read predicaments correctly".[34]

---

[27] *Ibid.*, 79.   [28] *Ibid.*, 79.
[29] *Ibid.*, 81. Cf. also "To be a moral agent one must be trained to perceive situations in terms of their morally significant features (as described by the *RMS*)", 83; "The role of the *RMS* in moral judgement is to provide the descriptive moral categories [*sic*] that permit the formulation of maxims suitable for assessment by the CI procedure", 84; they "guide the normal moral agent to the perception and description of the morally relevant features of his circumstances", 78.
[30] *Ibid.*, 86.
[31] *Ibid.*, 85. She locates this foundation in the Moral Law itself, and draws on the Fact of Reason passages in the *Critique of Practical Reason* to support her reading. This is not the place to query Herman's reading of those difficult passages. In my view they are about the status of practical reason, and not about judgement. For a different reading of the passages see Onora O'Neill, 'Autonomy and the Fact of Reason in the Kritik der praktischen Vernunft', in O. Höffe (ed.), *Immanuel Kant, Kritik der praktischen Vernunft* (Berlin: Akademie Verlag, 2002),30–41, Klassiker Auslegen 26, pp. 81–97.
[32] See John McDowell, 'Deliberation and Moral Development', in Stephen Engstrom and Jennifer Whiting (eds.), *Aristotle, Kant and the Stoics* (Cambridge University Press, 1996), 23.
[33] *Ibid.*   [34] *Ibid.*, 26.

If either 'rules of moral salience' or 'capacities to read situations' can provide this much, it may seem tempting to cast the full weight of moral judgement onto them, if at the price of flirting with forms of relativism. Yet it is quite unclear to me how either of these approaches could resolve the problem of relevant descriptions. What shows that 'rules of moral salience' or 'capacities to read situations' fasten on the (morally) relevant descriptions of the acts being considered?

Reflective and determinant judgements

I think that Herman was right to hold that Kant needs an account of capacities to judge the nature of cases. I also think that he wrote extensively on the topic. The best-known texts are his discussions of *determining* and *reflecting* judging (often translated as *determinant* and *reflective* judging) in the *Critique of Judgement*. Kant there divides theoretical judgements (note: *theoretical*, not *practical* or *ethical* judgements) as follows:

> If the universal (the rule, the principle, the law) is given, then the judgement, which subsumes the particular under it, is *determining (determinant)* … If, however, only the particular is given, for which the universal is to be found, then the judgement is simply *reflecting (reflective)*. (Kant, *CJ* 5:179)

Both sorts of judgement begin with a case to hand, for example with a particular object, or situation, or an act. Our judgement of a particular is *determinant* if we merely ask whether some 'given' description or category or principle applies. I see a bird and determine whether it is a chaffinch; I find four people playing cards and determine whether they are playing bridge; I write a cheque and determine whether my account will be overdrawn. Determinant judgement *subsumes*. Subsuming may not be philosophically thrilling, but is surely cognitively indispensable. Determinant judging does not offer an answer to the problem – or supposed problem – of relevant descriptions: it is blind to the problem, since it assumes that 'the universal (the rule, principle or law) is given'. However, it is not on Kant's view the only way to judge objects, situations or acts.

Reflective judging is more interesting, and resembles the ways in which both Herman and McDowell approach the task of finding relevant descriptions. Here 'only the particular is given' and 'the universal has to be found for it'.[35] I see a bird, but rather than simply determining whether it is or is not a chaffinch, I try to work out what sort of bird it is. If in the course of

---

[35] *Ibid.*

that task I conclude that it is not a chaffinch, the task is not at an end, as it would be in determinant judgement: there are further possibilities to consider, and the possibilities are open-ended. In reflective judging we do not simply test whether the card players are playing bridge or not, but more ambitiously try to work out what sort of game they are playing. It may be a game that I do not know, and if so I will have to work out how it is played by grasping the rules being followed, and may need to find a new name for it. Or again, if I subject my financial affairs to reflective judging I may consider many matters other than being or not being overdrawn: I may take many different views of a particular payment and its implications for my own and others' financial situations.

When we judge reflectively we consider – or explore – ways in which we *might* describe an object, a situation or an act. There may be some gap between Barbara Herman's idea of (a list of) rules of moral salience or John McDowell's picture of a capacity to read situations, and the more open-ended view of reflective judging of cases that Kant proposes. But they are clearly on the same track. However, none of these approaches offers a particularly convincing way of determining which descriptions are 'relevant' in particular cases.

Practical judgement

Both determinant and reflective judging, as Kant explicates them, and the proposals that Herman and McDowell set out, are types of *theoretical* judging. These types of judging are possible only when a particular case is *there to hand*, as material to be judged; or when some hypothetical case has been adequately specified to be an object of hypothetical theoretical judgement. The outcomes of determinant and reflective judging alike are judgements about what is the case, or is hypothetically the case. The difference between the two is that in determinant judgement the person who makes the judgement also has a specific rule, principle or law in mind, and seeks to determine whether the instance (actual or hypothetical) falls under it or not, whereas in reflective judging the person who makes the judgement doesn't have any specific rule, principle or law in mind, so has to search for ones that might apply to the instance (actual or hypothetical).

But in *practical* judging we are not judging a particular act. The task in practical judgement is to shape action *that is not yet done.* There is no particular act to be judged. The aim of practical judgement is to shape the world (in small part), not to identify some way in which the world is shaped. Action yet to be done can be shaped by ensuring that it satisfies a range of standards, rules, principles or laws that are taken into account in deliberating. There will, of course, often be many ways of satisfying any set of standards, rules, laws or principles, indeed many ways of satisfying a single standard, rule, principle or law. For example, a rule such as 'always check your petrol before driving onto the motorway' could be satisfied by many different acts. I might check the petrol the night before my trip, or as I get into the car, or as I pass a pump – or, alas, as I drive onto a long stretch of motorway without service stations. A principle such as 'keep in touch with your friends' can be satisfied by innumerable different sorts of action. Practical judgements, whether technical or legal, financial or managerial, political or ethical, aim *to guide action* rather than to pass judgement on *acts already done*. Practical judgement, including ethical judgement, does not encounter the problem of relevant descriptions because it is not directed at individuable act-tokens. Determinant and reflective judgement aim to *fit the world* or *some possible world*; practical judgement aims in some measure to *shape the world*, or to *specify how it should be shaped*. The different direction of fit shields practical judgement from the problem of relevant descriptions.

Yet it may seem that practical judgement escapes the problem of relevant descriptions only to encounter one of its near relatives. Granted that practical judgement does not start with a particular act, and that agents do not have to work out how a (non-existent) act should be described. Still, since practical reasoning starts with some rule, principle or law it seems doomed to reach no more than indeterminate recommendations. Yet in the end any act we do has to be fully determinate. For example, starting with the thought that it would be a good idea to buy enough groceries for the weekend, what am I to do when I go into a supermarket and see that there are literally countless ways in which I could act to satisfy this aim or principle? Practical judgement may not leave us unsure about how to describe a case, as reflective judging does; but doesn't starting with any rule, principle or law leave us unsure what to do? This is not Anscombe's problem, but it is a demanding problem.

I think that this problem is in large measure an artefact that arises from considering specific practical rules, principles and laws in isolation. But, of course, that is not how life is. If the sole rule or principle that I sought to satisfy were that of leaving a supermarket with enough food to last the weekend I would indeed feel (and perhaps behave) like Buridan's ass – or worse. However, even in this case selecting *any* bundle of goods that would last the weekend would resolve my asinine problem. But, of course, in what we call real life I enter the supermarket not with a single aim in mind, but also with many other aims and various rules, principles and laws. I not only try to get enough food to last until Monday, but also to do so quickly, without overspending, and without buying food that is unhealthy, or monotonous, disliked by those who will eat it, or produced by methods of which I disapprove. And I will also have regard to legal rules such as refraining from shoplifting, or to ethical requirements such as treating the staff with courtesy or refraining from queue jumping.

Practical judgement is typically a matter of finding some way – at least *one* way – of acting that satisfies *a large number of distinct aims, standards, rules, principles and laws.* The overwhelming indeterminacy that seemed to threaten when we considered the artificially simplified task of choosing an act that satisfies a single rule or principle reduces when we consider the more realistic task of satisfying a plurality of aims, standards, rules, principles and laws. Just as equations can often be solved only when we know a sufficient number of constraints, so questions about how to act are often resolved only by taking account of a number of constraints. (Of course, sometimes groups of rules or principles may make demands that cannot all be simultaneously satisfied; and others may make demands that cannot all be satisfied in certain types of situations. I set aside questions about conflicts between principles of differing types, including conflicts between principles of duty.)

However, even when we can specify the action to be performed to a reasonable degree, the problem of indeterminacy will persist. Even when I meet *all* the constraints set by ethics, law, custom, family budget and food preferences, my supermarket choices do not point to a fully determinate basket of goods. Yet this seems to me to be unproblematic. *Any* basket of goods that meets all these constraints will be an acceptable basket of goods – no matter whether its acquisition reflects obsessive hours of calculation or a flurry of impulse buying. Since practical judgement aims to guide action, it is enough if it does so – and probably illusory in most cases to think that when all demands are met, further calculation to identify some more narrowly specified 'optimal' act is needed or possible. There is no reason for imagining that any ethical rules or principles must be (quasi) algorithms that lead us to very tightly specified act-types – and no possibility that rules or principles of action will lead us to an individual act-token. Those who imagine otherwise are probably suffering from unfulfillable Utilitarian hankerings.

If these considerations are convincing, the difficulty of identifying relevant act descriptions does not tell *for* an ethics of virtue or *against* the positions that Anscombe groups under the heading 'modern moral philosophy'. The problem of relevant descriptions arises in describing or judging a given particular, but not in shaping future action. Describing the world we confront in adequate ways is a demanding task – and every bit as demanding for Aristotelians as for Utilitarians, for Kantians as for Rawlsians. But it is only the background for ethical and other practical reasoning. Those who conflate the appraisal of particular situations with practical judgement take a spectator view of the moral life.

Postscript: divine law and law-likeness

None of this shows that 'modern moral philosophy' escapes Anscombe's other criticisms. In fact, I think that at some points Anscombe comes close to acknowledging that the problem of relevant descriptions cannot be the *basic* problem for ethical judgement. For example, she remarks at one point that "things have to exist to have predicates"[36] – and that simple thought is enough to show that no problem of relevant descriptions can arise for acts that do not exist because they have not yet been performed.

If we set aside the problem of relevant descriptions, what is the most serious of Anscombe's criticisms of modern moral philosophy? It might be her thought that modern moral philosophy has been drawn to ethical terms that are excessively abstract ("Morally wrong" rather than "untruthful", "unchaste" or "unjust"[37]). It might be her thought that modern moral philosophers say too little about intention, or about other topics in the philosophy of psychology, and consequently place too much faith in the project of justifying action by its (expected) results. However, I think that, judging by the amount she says, Anscombe's deepest objection was to the persistent use of the vocabulary of moral requirement, of moral obligation and moral prohibition by those who do not accept a divine law conception of ethics.

As noted, she is not opposed to law conceptions of ethics as such. She believes that Aristotelian ethics, an ethics of virtue, can be reconciled with a divine law conception of ethics.[38] Yet a divine law conception ethics would have to be expressed in principles: if it were not, divine law would not be law-like. (How abstract the act descriptions contained in these principles are or should be is a further consideration.)

---

[36] Anscombe, 'Modern Moral Philosophy', 33.   [37] *Ibid.*

[38] Here she is at odds with many proponents of 'Aristotelian ethics' who treat virtue as the fundamental ethical category but do not embed their account of virtue in a Divine law framework.

It seems to me uncontroversial that any law conception of ethics, including a divine law conception of ethics, must represent ethics as *law-like*. Disagreements between different law conceptions of ethics will be about the *source* and *authority* of the supposed laws, but all will assume that laws must be *law-like* – that they prescribe for all cases within their scope. Yet I am not sure whether Anscombe accepts this point. Her objections to those who advance law conceptions of ethics without accepting divine law appear to be about their views on the *sources* of law. She states that "you cannot be under law unless it has been promulgated to you"[39] and notes that various alternative sources of law, such as positive law or social norms cannot provide a basis for ethical law. She casts scorn on a certain reading of the Kantian idea of self-legislation, insisting that "the concept of legislation requires superior power in the legislator".[40]

I find it hard to resist the thought that in speaking of *law* conceptions of ethics Anscombe in fact had in mind a *command* conception of ethics, and overlooked the formal structure of laws. If I am right – the comments are scattered – then I think we can see why she simply swept aside non-theological law conceptions of ethics with little consideration. There are easy objections to deriving ethics from non-divine legislators; some (for example, Plato in *Euthyphro*) even think that there are problems in deriving ethics from divine legislators, although Anscombe dismisses those worries.[41] I think she may have dismissed them because her view of a divine law conception of ethics far from being Thomist was *radically antinomian*. Divine Law is seen as fiat.[42] Starting from that standpoint, laws are decrees, and what is referred to (rather misleadingly) as Divine *legislation* need not have even the form of law.[43] On this approach it is not at all surprising that Anscombe rejects all use of the vocabulary of moral obligation that is not divinely promulgated. Nor is it surprising that she objects to rules and principles without divine backing. Nor therefore is it surprising that she thought that it was possible to reject positions that argue for ethical rules and principles – and the moral ought – with so little consideration. If this is indeed the background to her blanket criticism of the positions she groups together as 'modern moral philosophy', there may be a lot more to be said.

---

[39] Anscombe, 'Modern Moral Philosophy', 37.   [40] *Ibid.*, 27.   [41] *Ibid.*, 41.

[42] Consider the remark "What obliges is the divine law – as rules oblige in a game", *ibid.*, 41. It seems clear here that it is the *source*, and neither the *form* nor the *content* of law, that is viewed as authoritative.

[43] *Ibid.*, 37.

Two cultures fifty years on[1]

C. P. Snow's Two Cultures

Just over fifty years ago in the Cambridge Senate House C. P. Snow delivered a famous and curious lecture, in which he contrasted the humanities and the natural sciences, and came down strongly in favour of the latter.[2] The argument of the lecture now strikes readers not merely as dated, but at times as perverse. Yet Snow's views of the distance and hostility between some exponents of the humanities and natural scientists, and more broadly between those who admire and respond to each range of work, still resonates. *The Two Cultures* is much more than a bygone academic spat.

Snow was not, of course, the first to pronounce that there was a radical difference between intellectual cultures and practices, but his approach is distinctive and in some ways sharper and more combative than others. He sets out his case for thinking that there are two inimical academic or intellectual cultures by appealing not to claims and arguments about their divergent underlying methods, aims or effects, but to a local example. He contrasts certain Cambridge scientists, most of them physicists, with a particular group of writers and critics who were also prominent in Cambridge in the middle of the last century, whom he refers to as 'literary intellectuals', and (rather inaccurately) identifies with 'the traditional culture'. His most specific targets were the influential critic F. R. Leavis and his (mostly unnamed) allies or disciples, and their claims about 'the great tradition' of English literature. Needless to say, the fact that these critics wrote about 'the great tradition' of English literature did not make

---

[1] Given as the Rede Lecture, 2010, to mark the 50th anniversary of C. P. Snow's Rede Lecture on *The Two Cultures*. Snow's was the 100th lecture in the modern series of Rede Lectures as one-off lectures; in their older version the Rede Lectures reach back to the sixteenth century.

[2] C. P. Snow, *The Two Cultures*, 1959; Canto edn. with introduction by Stefan Collini (Cambridge University Press, 1998).

them the sole or the best protagonists or exponents of that tradition, let alone of traditional culture, or of the humanities – and Snow at times conflated these.

Snow's focus was also in several ways narrower and more fiercely partisan than that taken by well-known earlier writers on these themes, and in particular narrower than the approaches taken by T. H. Huxley in his 1880 lecture *Science and Culture*[3] and by Matthew Arnold in his 1882 Rede Lecture *Literature and Science*.[4] Huxley had defended the natural sciences and Arnold literary studies, but each had shown more understanding and respect for the other academic culture than Snow – both scientist and novelist – chose to display. Perhaps Snow remembered his time in Ernest Rutherford's laboratory: it was Rutherford who perhaps drew the sharpest and most dismissive of all demarcations between (some of) the natural sciences and the humanities, remarking (it is said) that there was physics, and the rest was stamp collecting.

Snow affects even-handedness, yet has almost nothing favourable to say about work in the humanities or in particular about literary studies. His accusations, which he puts in the mouths of unspecified natural scientists, include the claim that 'literary intellectuals' are "unconcerned with their brother men", "in a deep sense anti-intellectual" and all-too-often drawn to fascism and worse. Natural scientists on the other hand may be ignorant – or perhaps merely diffident – about literature, but as Snow sees it

> … they have their own culture … which contains a great deal of argument, usually much more rigorous and almost always at a much higher conceptual level than literary persons' arguments …

Snow sees the 'literary intellectuals' as engaging mostly with one another and producing nothing that counts as knowledge, let alone as useful knowledge. Even more culpably, the 'literary intellectuals' were profoundly ignorant of the exceptional scientific culture amid which they lived, which in Cambridge in those years included a galaxy of Nobel Prize winners in physics, chemistry and medicine.

Snow's accusations were not only sharp, but often sneering:

> A good many times I have been present at gatherings of people who, by the standards of the traditional culture, are thought highly educated and who have with considerable gusto been expressing their incredulity at the

---

[3] T. H. Huxley, *Science and Culture*, 1880, reprinted in his *Science and Education: Essays* (London, 1893), 134–59. Huxley delivered the Rede Lecture on a different theme in 1883.

[4] Matthew Arnold, 'Literature and Science', in R. H. Super (ed.), *The Complete Prose Works of Matthew Arnold*, Vol. X (Ann Arbor: University of Michigan Press, 1974), 52–73.

illiteracy of scientists. Once or twice I have been provoked and have asked the company how many of them could describe the Second Law of Thermodynamics. The response was cold: it was also negative. Yet I was asking something which is the scientific equivalent of: *Have you read a work of Shakespeare's?*

I now believe that if I had asked an even simpler question – such as, What do you mean by mass, or acceleration, which is the scientific equivalent of saying, *Can you read?* – not more than one in ten of the highly educated would have felt that I was speaking the same language. So the great edifice of modern physics goes up, and the majority of the cleverest people in the western world have about as much insight into it as their neolithic ancestors would have had.

In 1962 F. R. Leavis responded in a critical lecture which – intentionally or otherwise – did much to show the justice of Snow's charges, and outdid his sneering tone. Leavis wrote:

> Not only is [Snow] not a genius, he is intellectually as undistinguished as it is possible to be … 'The Two Cultures' exhibits an utter lack of intellectual distinction and an embarrassing vulgarity of style.[5]

Snow was certainly *distinguished*: a research scientist who had held significant public positions recruiting scientific manpower for the war effort; the author of a much read (if also much criticised) series of novels; a leading university and public figure. But clearly he did not count as distinguished in *any* way that Leavis prized. Leavis's response, I think, confirms the truth of Snow's accusation that a troubling cultural distance and mutual disdain divided 'literary intellectuals' and physicists, and perhaps others working in the humanities and the sciences, at least at that time.

Tensions and differences between cultures, including intellectual and academic cultures, continue, and fault lines in the cultural and intellectual landscape can seem like deep crevasses from close up. What we cannot find, I suggest, is a fissure that separates the methods of work in the natural sciences from work in the humanities. In my view, Stefan Collini was broadly right when he wrote in his marvellous introductory essay for the Canto edition of *The Two Cultures* that, in view of the constant sprouting of sub-disciplines and interdisciplinary endeavours across the years since Snow had lectured

> it is largely a matter of emphasis whether one regards these changes as indicating that, rather than two cultures, there are in fact two hundred and two cultures, or that there is fundamentally only one culture.[6]

---

[5] Leavis's lecture was reprinted in *The Spectator* on 9 March 1962, and later (after legal vetting) in book form.

[6] Stefan Collini, Introductory essay to *The Two Cultures*, xliv.

I agree with Stefan Collini that we have long moved away from, indeed probably never inhabited, a world of precisely two intellectual or academic cultures, let alone two that fit C. P. Snow's template. Fifty years later it was all too plain how much Snow's case depended on treating a very specific literary and critical subculture as representative of all non-scientific culture.[7]

Myths about method

And yet … We do, I think, still live in a world in which assumptions about intellectual and academic cultures and about differences between their methods and importance remain, and in which many knowledgeable people think (even if they are too circumspect or mannerly to say so) that those on the far side of certain divides do work that is intellectually suspect or trivial. Recent examples of such attitudes include work in biology and psychology that assumes without much in the way of argument that naturalistic explanations will not add to but wholly supersede cultural and moral, not to mention theological, inquiry. And we still find unthinking and even sneering hostility to parts of the natural sciences among some who claim to be the sole true guardians of alternative lifestyles, holistic medicine and green futures.

I shall say no more about these divisions, and nothing about practical measures, in particular educational changes, that might increase understanding between intellectual and academic cultures – themes with which Snow and many others have rightly been concerned. Instead I shall look at some underlying aims and assumptions said to be fundamental to various types of inquiry, and in particular at those relied on in the natural sciences and the humanities. I shall argue that they have far more in common than Snow supposed, and in particular that empirical work itself in and beyond the natural sciences always also deploys methods that are not empirical.

Interpretation, inference and empirical truth-claims

In trying to say something about the range of types of investigation used by inquiry in the humanities and the natural sciences I shall say nothing about the techniques that they variously use. I take it that different inquiries need and use differing techniques, as appropriate. It is commonplace for work in

---

[7] He more or less concedes this in accepting that it was ill-considered of 'scientists' (not of himself!) to base their political aspersions on the 'literary intellectuals' on selected writers of the period 1914–50.

one discipline to borrow another's techniques. Archaeologists use chemical or DNA analysis when investigating the provenance of artefacts and remains; epidemiologists consult historians in charting the natural history of diseases; climate scientists rely on work done by archaeologists, classicists and historians investigating agricultural and other forms of economic activity which provides evidence about past changes in temperature or rainfall; literary scholars use statistical methods. Techniques are used where they are useful. Rather than discussing techniques, I shall try to say a bit about the broad *cognitive* aims and strategies of different types on inquiry, focusing first on work in the humanities, about which questions are often raised.

It is generally thought that work in the natural sciences has clear aims: it seeks evidence for empirical truth-claims about the natural world, and investigates whether available evidence falsifies or supports them. It deploys both empirical methods and formal analysis. However, a great deal of work in the humanities has aims that parallel those of work in the natural sciences. It too makes empirical truth-claims, and investigates whether available evidence falsifies or supports them. Work in the humanities is distinctive, in making truth-claims about cultural as well as natural objects, ranging from *representations* and *artefacts*, to the *activities* and *ways of life* in which those representations and artefacts are embodied and deployed. Anyone undertaking empirical inquiry in the humanities has therefore also to *interpret representations*, whether words, texts, symbols, images, musical scores; or *artefacts*, whether pictures, manuscripts, tools, furniture or buildings. Much research in the humanities also seeks to interpret *uses* of representations and artefacts as found in action and practices, beliefs and attitudes, *mentalités* and performances, discourse and communication, as well as constellations of these that constitute more abstract cultural objects such as languages, genres, traditions, and what are now called *identities* (and used less confusedly be spoken of as *senses of identity*) – or indeed cultures.

Does the fact that work in the humanities investigates cultural objects and their uses and embodiments mark a deep difference between their aims and those of the natural sciences? Perhaps the humanities are distinctive not because they make no empirical truth-claims, but because many of their truth-claims are about cultural objects, so require them also to engage in *interpretation* and *inference*. Interpretation and inference do not look 'outward' at the ways in which representations or artefacts, or their embodiments, fit the world: they are preliminary to making truth-claims about cultural objects. Putting matters very broadly and approximately, interpretation focuses on specific representations and artefacts, and their uses and embodiments, and considers how they can or should be understood, while inference focuses on connections between differing representations and artefacts, and their uses and embodiments, and the ways in which they can or cannot be linked to one another. Both interpretation and inference are indispensable in making truth-claims about cultural objects.

These points do not, however, support a sharp contrast between the *empirical* methods of the natural sciences (aimed at causal explanation) and the *interpretive* methods of the human sciences (aimed at understanding, meaning and significance). The classical contrast between *interpretation* and *explanation*, between *Erklären* and *Verstehen*, as formulated by Wilhelm Dilthey, Max Weber and many others, sees the two approaches as inimical. But this perspective takes a very specific view of interpretation in the humanities and cognate social inquiry, seeing it as drawing on *empathy* or on a *participatory stance*, so as non-empirical (at least up to a point). But while the humanities – and cognate social inquiry – indeed build on interpretation, claims that interpretation must be based on empathy or a participatory stance are specific and contentious views about how it should be done.[8] Work in the humanities uses *many* sorts of interpretation to formulate claims, including empirical claims, about representations and artefacts, and their embodiments in action and practice. It also uses many sorts of inference to connect different claims.

The evidence for this point is entirely commonplace. It now seems uncontroversial that the study of history, or literature, or civilisations, or art aims at empirical truth, and seeks to respect available evidence, and to reject claims that are incompatible with that evidence. Historians and literary scholars take it for granted that accuracy should not be subordinated to edification or propaganda. Since evidence is often incomplete, and the scope for experiment severely restricted (many claims are about the past; some experimental approaches would misuse or abuse human beings), empirical truth-claims in the humanities can be hard to establish: but it is the mark of good empirical work in the humanities, as of good empirical work in the natural sciences, that where there is reliable evidence against some claim, the claim must give way.

This, of course, leaves plenty of room, in the humanities, as in other inquiries, for conjecture and speculation – provided they are marked as such. No doubt, the disciplines needed for making truth-claims are

---

[8] For discussion of other interpretive methods see Chapter 8, below.

sometimes poorly used, even betrayed, and there is a good deal of persuasion and propaganda in work in the humanities, which asserts or pushes truth-claims not supported by or even incompatible with available evidence. Incompetence and political agendas can surface in all areas of inquiry, and tendentious ways of interpreting evidence can be used to promote tendentious truth-claims. Still, I take it as uncontroversial that a great deal of work in the humanities is every bit as committed to discovering and supporting truth-claims, including in particular empirical truth-claims, as is work in the natural sciences. We cannot formulate truth-claims about cultural objects without relying on interpretation and inference, but when we do so we take a stand on what is the case. Truth-claims in the humanities, as in the natural sciences, aim to fit (aspects of) the world.

Moreover, the humanities are not alone in building empirical inquiry in part on interpretive and inferential moves. The natural sciences and the technologies that build on them do the same. For example, a medical researcher may revise the classification of a range of tumours, arguing that a new classification takes better account of evidence, suggests more promising lines of investigation, or may provide a basis for tailoring more effective interventions for specific conditions. Psychiatric diagnosis relies on classification of mental disorders: here interpretation is evidently a necessary preliminary to diagnosis, treatment or epidemiological work on the incidence of specific mental disorders.[9] Reinterpretations and revisions of scientific concepts – from the basic concepts of physics to more domain-specific concepts such as those of *species*, *gene*, *information* or *statistical significance* – may provide a basis for formulating and testing new empirical claims. And it goes without saying that scientific work relies on inference, and distinguishes adequate from inadequate ways of linking claims.

I do not mean to suggest that interpretation and inference are more fundamental than empirical investigation: they are interdependent. Inquiry into both natural and cultural objects requires consideration of and agreement about the interpretation of the terms of discourse deployed and the inferential moves that are acceptable. Equally, much interpretive work falters or fails without empirical testing of proposed distinctions and

---

[9] For an illustration of the role interpretation plays in scientific work on mental disorders see the systems of disease classification in the *International Classification of Diseases* (*ICD*), produced by the World Health Organization, www.who.int/classifications/icd/en/ or the *Diagnostic and Statistical Manual of Mental Disorders* (*DSM*) produced by the American Psychiatric Association, www.dsm5 .org/Pages/Default.aspx. Both are updated as interpretations change. http://en.wikipedia.org/wiki/ American_Psychiatric_Association.

classifications, and of interpretations and inferences that reveals whether they are usable, robust and perspicuous. Empirical inquiry may be more prominent in the daily practice of the natural sciences, and interpretation in that of the humanities – but neither aspect of inquiry can stand without the other.

The humanities and covert normativity

These lines of thought do not, I suggest, show that nothing much distinguishes work in the humanities from scientific inquiry. But they do show that the differences are not due to some fundamental cleavage between two cultures. Work in the humanities is not the preserve of the 'literary intellectuals' who so vexed C. P. Snow, and we can quite reasonably ask which inquiries in the humanities yield which sorts of new knowledge, what it is useful for, and what it contributes to social and individual life.

The topic that I want to turn to now is not the indirect contribution of work in the humanities to economic life and well-being (which I take to be large, but hard to quantify). Nor is it the indirect contribution of work in the humanities to the vitality of cultural and public life (also large, but hard to quantify). I want to consider whether work in the humanities bears on action not only *indirectly*, as all forms of empirical inquiry do, by providing knowledge of which we need to take account in acting, but more *directly* by offering reasons for pursuing some rather than other lines of action and for fostering some rather than other practices. Do we need to attend to the *normative* as well as to the *cognitive* (variously empirical, inferential, interpretive) claims of the humanities?

Normative and empirical claims differ in the way in which they relate to the world, or (as it is often put) in their *directions of fit*. Empirical claims aim to fit (some part of) the natural or human world; normative claims set standards to which (some part of) the world is to be fitted. Although the distinction goes back a long way, I think that one of the more memorable formulations was given by my philosophy tutor at Oxford, Elisabeth Anscombe. In her compressed, eccentric and brilliant work *Intention* (published very shortly before C. P. Snow's lecture: he would not have liked it!), she imagines a man with a shopping list who is followed by a detective who lists what he buys. The aim of the first list is normative; that of the second is empirical. Anscombe put it like this:

> if the list [i.e. the shopper's list] and the things that the man actually buys do not agree ... then the mistake is not in the list but in the man's performance

(if his wife were to say: "Look, it says butter and you have bought margarine", he would hardly reply: "What a mistake! we must put that right" and alter the word on the list to "margarine"); whereas if the detective's record and what the man actually buys do not agree, then the mistake is in the record.[10]

Empirical truth-claims aim to fit the world, and must be revised, reformulated or rejected if they do not. Normative claims set standards to which aspects of the world are to be fitted, and if the fit is poor, the world should be changed rather than the claim revised, reformulated or rejected. If normative claims do not fit the world, the problem lies not in what is said, but in what is done. We take normativity seriously whenever we set ourselves to do something, so take a view – set a standard – for what would count as success in doing it.

Normativity pervades human life and practice. Yet many have qualms about normative claims both in the humanities and in other forms of inquiry. Suspicion of normativity is often directed at specific sorts of normative claim that may be unconvincing. Yet some normative claims are not merely acceptable but, I shall argue, indispensable for inquiry.

However, some suspicions about normative claims have a basis. Older discussions of work in the humanities – for example Arnold's *Literature and Science* – saw study of the humanities as normatively important (they did not, of course, use the term) because it was morally edifying. Such study, Arnold repeatedly insisted, enables us "to *know the best which has been thought and said in the world*". Unfortunately it is hard to show that study of the humanities – or for that matter of the sciences – improves character and action. The questions are simply too slippery. Do we really know whether certain sorts of music (the Lydian mode? heavy metal?) have bad effects on character? Has anybody shown that studying lots of (the right sorts of) literature improves character (Mr Casaubon? F. R. Leavis?)? Do we know whether studying history is more likely to train the judgement and teach toleration, even statecraft, or to fuel nationalistic sentiments and resentment? Has anybody shown that the study of rhetoric improves capacities to persuade better than a bit of training in marketing and public relations? Has anybody shown that doctors who read in the humanities do better by their patients? Do we even know whether exposure to pornography harms? Some of these questions are, I take it, susceptible to empirical inquiry, but often we find strong convictions supported by more-or-less circular claims that certain sorts of content will harm *if used*

---

[10] G. E. M. Anscombe, *Intention* (Oxford: Blackwell), para. 32.

or presented in the wrong way. My sense of the matter is that *unqualified* claims that the humanities have normative importance because their study is ethically improving are unconvincing, even embarrassing, perhaps no better evidenced than C. P. Snow's extension of his claims about one group of literary intellectuals to the entire 'traditional culture'.

Yet, while such claims may embarrass and are hard to establish, I suspect that they are still widely accepted. Covert moralism lingers even among those who think that inquiry in the humanities should be value-neutral (itself, of course, a normative claim!).[11] The desired ethical conclusions are often reached by claiming (uncontentiously) that normative claims are important *objects* of study, then alleging that the results of such empirical studies are normatively important. I think this move is unconvincing. The study of ethical and other beliefs and attitudes has by itself no practical implications for those who lack those beliefs and attitudes. Only those who explicitly hold subjectivist or relativist views can try to wring normative, let alone specifically ethical, conclusions from empirical claims about actual normative views – and for them *others'* beliefs and attitudes may be irrelevant. Deriving normative claims from the fact that others are committed to them may rely on some version of a naturalistic fallacy, an argument from consensus or authority: these roads do not lead to normative conclusions.

Yet the road-block is surprisingly often ignored. Attempted shortcuts to normative, including ethical, claims lurk in various types of contemporary discussion (perhaps found more in the social sciences than in the humanities) of the beliefs, attitudes, outlooks and opinions, of persons or groups, which are presumed to achieve some sort of standing by the mere fact that they are widely held or believed, and even to provide useful ethical pointers or policy guidance. If democratic process is taken to be desirable (another normative claim), these moves may not be *wholly* unjustifiable in all contexts, but few of us would take democratic endorsement as *unconditional* normative justification – for example, we would not generally assume that majority views trump individual rights or the rule of law. Yet it is not unusual for suppressed normative assumptions, such as conceptions of democratic legitimation, to be used to draw normative conclusions from the empirical findings of surveys of attitudes or opinions. But knowing that certain normative claims are accepted, or accepted by a majority, or by a quite a lot of people, or at least by some people, does not ground any normative conclusions *at all*. Any move from claims about

---

[11] See Chapter 3, below.

what is (widely) accepted to claims about what ought to be done needs hefty additional premises and arguments, if it is not to amount to an instance of a naturalistic fallacy, of an appeal to consensus or authority – or more probably of no argument at all. Empirical studies of views and attitudes ground neither ethical nor other normative conclusions.

Pervasive normativity

And yet, it seems to me, normative claims far from being disreputable are both indispensable and ubiquitous in work in the humanities, and also in work in the natural, social and medical sciences. In saying this I do not mean simply that choices of research topics and decisions by research funders are likely to reflect ethical, political and other norms. Nor do I mean just that the normative commitments of researchers or clinicians will shape the work they choose to do. I mean that inquiry of all sorts *requires* normative assumptions. Yet it is not immediately obvious where or how work in the humanities, let alone the natural sciences, presupposes normative claims.

An obvious first port of call might be to look at work in ethics, political philosophy and cognate bits of jurisprudence, in which the *justification* of quite distinctive normative claims is central. However, I want to bracket questions about ethical and political justification, to comment on normative claims as they are *actually* deployed, whether or not they are or can be explicitly justified.

Everyday normative commitments bear on the choice of standards and judgement of evidence, on metrics and methods, on knowledge and communication. They pervade and support practices of inquiry. For example, when scientists or engineers debate a classification or a metric they have already identified some empirical features of the world, and are proposing how they should be measured or classified. They may rely on a certain scheme of classification or metric for a specific purpose. Such normative claims are not ethical claims, and they are not claims about justice. But they are claims about the standards and requirements – the *norms* – needed for specific sorts of inquiry and activity. Empirical inquiry cannot be detached from normative assumptions.

The very thought that *all* truth-oriented inquiry relies on normative claims may meet some resistance. Are not normative claims 'value judgements', and so something that we should scrupulously exclude from truth-oriented inquiry, and above all from scientific inquiry? That is what we have been telling one another for a long time, and the point is often made energetically by people who reject the logical positivism from which it derives. And yet the claim is false. All forms of inquiry depend on normative claims, and their more sophisticated exponents are aware of this and seek not only to use but to make explicit and to justify the normative claims on which they rely. This is wholly explicit in the very wide range of work on epistemic norms in the philosophy of science.

This thought is in no way original. It was memorably summarised in Wilfred Sellars's slogan that everything is 'fraught with ought'.[12] Still, those who cling to positivist positions may find it preposterous. To make it seem more familiar, I begin by gesturing to some very ordinary examples, still leaving aside the obvious case of work in political theory, ethics and jurisprudence, where a concern to justify specific and particularly demanding normative claims is avowedly central.[13] Inquiry of all sorts routinely deploys normative practices and claims of a quite humdrum sort. These indispensable normative claims set out *standards* and *requirements* and thereby the success conditions – and failure conditions – for specific types of action and practices, including practices of inquiry and practices for formulating truth-claims. There is no way to list norms systematically and exhaustively, but the following groupings are suggestive:

(a) *Linguistic norms* articulate success conditions for speech acts: no account of communication can be built without making normative claims: "The rules for the use of words … are normative rules: they say how words *should* and *should not* be used."[14] Unless we heed lexical, grammatical, syntactical and other linguistic norms, our speech acts will be incomprehensible or misunderstood. Those who flout linguistic norms undermine cognitive and interpretive practice, damage intelligibility, and thereby understanding and communication.

(b) *Epistemic norms.* Linguistic norms are not enough for making truth-claims, or for empirical research, whether in the natural or social sciences or the humanities. Epistemic norms specify conditions for inquiry of all sorts by articulating standards for consistency, coherence and validity, for making claims about probability, for handling evidence, for assessing testimony, and for dealing with examples and counterexamples.

---

[12] Wilfrid Sellars, *Science, Perception, and Reality* (Atascadero, CA: Ridgeview, 1991); Daniel Whiting, 'Is Meaning Fraught With Ought?', *Pacific Philosophical Quarterly*, 90 (2009), 535–55.

[13] The role of normative claims in these areas is widely acknowledged, but commonly criticised on the grounds that the justifications offered are incomplete, or work only given assumptions that are queried. This is true, but since incompleteness of justifications is also a feature of empirical inquiry, including inquiry in the natural sciences, the weight of the criticism is unclear.

[14] T. Crane, 'Fraught with Ought', *London Review of Books* (19 June 2008).

(c) *Norms of instrumental rationality and prudence* are also indispensable for all sorts of action and inquiry, and are not coextensive with ethical norms. They include norms of effectiveness and (where there are suitable metrics) of efficiency for a wide variety situations.

(d) *Norms of communicative effectiveness* for a great variety of contexts. Among these, norms for effective *mediated* communication – not only by the media – are particularly important. They include norms of *intelligibility*, without which content remains inaccessible to supposed audiences, and norms of *assessability* without which audiences cannot judge content that they understand.

(e) *Specialised norms* for specific domains that articulate success conditions for specific types of inquiry, such as norms that define the proper use of notations and units of measurement, specific conceptions of effectiveness or efficiency (for varied contexts, in pursuit of varied objectives) and conventions for acceptable or effective action.[15]

Ethical norms

A claim that we rely on normative assumptions in all activity, including all truth-oriented inquiry, is not, I think, particularly controversial. Yet scepticism about normative claims persists. Sometimes this scepticism is intended more specifically, as scepticism about *ethical* norms or about norms of *justice*, or even specifically about the heady thought that some of these norms are relevant for *all* activity in *all* circumstances. If that were the whole story, then it might seem that all that I have done in arguing that normativity pervades inquiry is to change the subject, while failing to show that specifically ethical norms can be justified or whether they are essential for inquiry in the humanities or elsewhere. I do not propose to open questions about the justification of ethical norms here, any more than I have pursued questions about the justification of linguistic, logical, epistemic or other cognitive norms.

However, I finish by suggesting that the very thought that we can exhaustively classify norms as ethical and non-ethical may be tenuous. If we are in the business of making truth-claims, including empirical truth-claims, we can hardly ignore norms of truthfulness or honesty: which are

---

[15] Many of the norms for felicitous or successful speech acts which J. L. Austin discussed in *How to Do Things with Words: The William James Lectures delivered at Harvard University in 1955*, J. O. Urmson and M. Sbisà (eds.) (Oxford: Clarendon Press, 1962), set standards for the adequate performance of complex acts involving a large element of social convention, such as promising, warning, advising, contracting or marrying. However, reliance on norms is not confined to speech acts of these sorts.

generally seen as ethically important norms. If we are in the business of communicating or debating research findings, we can hardly ignore norms that articulate necessary conditions for successful communication, including norms that must be respected if we are to make content accessible, intelligible and assessable for intended audiences.

The *real* puzzle with many discussions of supposed disciplinary and cultural differences, including C. P. Snow's 'Two Cultures' lecture, is in my view that they often say *almost nothing* about the normative standards required for inquiry of various sorts. *Supposedly* we have long seen through the logical positivist dogma that the only available options are the study of formal systems, the search for verifiable truth-claims, or wallowing in the literally meaningless. *Officially* we have long known that it is wholly unlikely that we can establish a range of value-neutral behavioural or other social sciences[16] that eschew normative claims. Yet suppositions that this is possible have enjoyed a long half-life after their limitations were recognised.

Once value-neutrality is taken to be possible and desirable, it can seem obvious that normative, including ethical, questions need to be explained away, rather than to be taken seriously. Some want to reinterpret them as (unobvious) naturalistic claims, or as expressions or attitudes (emotivism), or as inbuilt cognitive tendencies. Others want to (mis)construe them as an acceptable genre of empirical inquiry by allowing the study of attitudes and opinions to count as settling normative questions. Some, including C. P. Snow in *Two Cultures*, make many normative, including ethical, claims but are entirely silent about their source or justification.

I think we may gain by being more explicit, acknowledging that all academic and intellectual cultures, like wider cultures, have normative presuppositions, and that interrogating and assessing them by intellectually rigorous standards matters. Of course, justifying normative claims is often strenuous, some normative arguments are difficult and others simply do not work. However, critical consideration of normative claims is not a matter of proceeding by hunch or prejudice, and can be demanding. Like empirical arguments, normative arguments do not proceed without making assumptions. Yet normative justification may be no harder than empirical justification.

---

[16] Naturalism in the social sciences is quite often understood in a strong sense as a programme of seeking to explain human life in the same way as we seek to explain the operation of any other natural system, *plus* the assertion that this is the only way to look at matters. At this point it amounts to a version of scientism. Cf. Chapter 3, below.

Scientific inquiry and normative reasoning[1]

Directions of fit: empirical and normative claims

Science is widely seen as inquiry that seeks to establish truth-claims by using argument and proof (as in mathematics), by rigorous respect for empirical methods and evidence (as pre-eminently in the natural sciences, but also in other domains), and by combining these methods. These uncontroversial views are sometimes combined with stronger and more controversial claims that scientific work should use *only* these methods, and should not use or rely on the normative or interpretive methods that are widely used and prized in non-scientific inquiry, and that it should be rigorously 'value-free' or 'value-neutral'. Others have gone still further and have supported forms of *scientism*, claiming not merely that science should be 'value-free' or 'value-neutral', but that these scientific methods should be exported to areas of inquiry traditionally thought of as non-scientific.[2] However, if normative reasoning is required for scientific inquiry, neither 'value-free' science nor (*a fortiori*) scientism provides convincing options.

The practice of science, I shall argue, itself relies on the selection and adoption of appropriate normative standards, and suggestions that science can be, or should be, 'value-free' are mistaken. Any choice to use or to reject standards is a matter of selecting and relying on specific norms, and of rejecting and avoiding reliance on other norms, and these norms cannot be established by empirical methods. Consequently empirical methods are not sufficient for scientific inquiry, which also requires normative

---

[1] This paper extends arguments presented in Onora O'Neill, 'Science, Reasons and Normativity', *European Review*, 21, Supplement S1 (July 2013), 94–99.

[2] I shall say nothing here about the many forms that scientism has taken, about their connections to behaviorisms or to other substantive research programmes in the natural and social sciences, or about the wider cultural landscapes in which they have flourished or continue to flourish. For useful overviews see Tom Sorrell, *Scientism: Philosophy and the Infatuation with Science* (London: Routledge, 1991); J. de Ridder, R. Peels and R. van Woudenberg (eds.), *Scientism: Problems and Prospects* (Oxford University Press, forthcoming).

reasoning (as well as relying on interpretive moves[3]). Moreover, at least some of the norms required for the practice of science are what we normally think of as ethical norms. If these points are convincing, science cannot and should not aspire to be 'value-free' or more specifically 'ethically neutral'. Claims that scientific practice can or should rely solely on logical analysis and empirical investigation, and that all norms (including ethical norms) are irrelevant to the practice of science have no plausibility.

Normative and empirical claims

The distinction between empirical and normative inquiry is a distinction between types of *speech act* rather than types of *speech content*. When we make *empirical* claims we seek to fit what we say to the way the world is, and accept that we must modify or retract our claims if they turn out not to be true of the way things are. This responsiveness to the way things are is fundamental to all empirical claims, including scientific work and inquiry. By contrast, when we make *normative* claims we appeal to or rely on standards that can be adopted and (in suitable circumstances) enacted, thereby articulating a way in which the world could be shaped or reshaped (in some small part) so that it fits those norms. Empirical claims are shaped to fit aspects of the world; aspects of the world are shaped to fit normative claims.

Philosophers now commonly describe this difference as one between *directions of fit*. The distinction between the two directions of fit was aptly illustrated by G. E. M. Anscombe in her short but still influential book *Intention*[4] by an everyday story about a man who is asked by his wife to do the shopping, and who (for reasons about which nothing is said) is followed by a detective who records what he buys. On the shopping list it says *butter*, but the man buys *margarine*. When he comes home his wife complains about his shopping performance saying "Look, it says butter and you have bought margarine." Anscombe points out that he can hardly reply "What a mistake! We must put that right" – and then alter his list to read 'margarine'.[5] By contrast, if the detective makes an inaccurate record, it is

---

[3] I shall say nothing about interpretation here, but offer some reasons for thinking that it is indispensable in scientific and other forms of inquiry in Chapter 8, below.

[4] G. E. M. Anscombe, *Intention* (Oxford: Blackwell, 1957). The term 'direction of fit' had already been used by J. L. Austin, in *How to Do Things with Words: The William James Lectures delivered at Harvard University in 1955*, J. O. Urmson and M. Sbisà (eds.) (Oxford University Press, 1962); however, the distinction is considerably older. See Chapter 2, above, and Chapter 7, below.

[5] Anscombe, *Intention*, 57.

his list that should be corrected. The shopping list is meant to be *norma-tive*[6] for the shopper's performance, not *descriptive* of it, and it is the performance rather than the list that should be corrected if there is a discrepancy. The detective's list is meant to be *descriptive* of the shopper's performance, and it is that list and not the shopper's performance that should be corrected if there is a discrepancy.

Norms come in many kinds, and I shall say little here about many of the differences between ethical and political, epistemic and logical, legal and prudential, technical and social norms which we regularly invoke and follow, defend and reject, both in everyday life and in specialised activities. It is widely accepted that any systematic activity relies on norms or standards of many sorts, and that we can gain no traction by ignoring this fact, or by focusing solely on the descriptive or explanatory aspects of activities and practices, including cognitive activities and practices. The point of contention is the difficulty of justifying norms on which practices of inquiry, including scientific practice, depend. The generic difficulty of justification that we encounter here arises because norms cannot be justified by deriving them from empirical claims about what is the case: any attempt to do so would ignore the classical Humean observation that it is impossible to derive *ought* from *is*, and the difference between the two directions of fit.[7]

However, Hume did not assert that norms cannot be justified, but more narrowly (and plausibly) that they cannot be justified by deriv-ing them from facts. If so, normative justifications must build on other sorts of claims, and in particular on normative claims. And if normativity is ineliminable, the task of normative justification will matter as much as that of empirical justification, and both will be needed for the practice of science. Yet discussions of the justification of some of the normative conditions for systematic inquiry are often reluctant, as if there were something intrinsically disreputable about making or relying on normative claims, and in particular about doing so in the context of systematic empirical inquiry, including scientific reasoning and practice. This reluctance has a long intellectual and cultural history.

---

[6] Anscombe used the less common term *directive*; the wider term *normative* has now become standard. See Chapter 5, below.

[7] David Hume, *A Treatise of Human Nature* [1739], L. A. Selby-Bigge (ed.), revised P. H. Nidditch (Oxford University Press, 1978), III. I. ii, p. 469.

Suspicions about normativity

The term *norm* belonged – in some contexts still belongs – to sociology and other branches of social inquiry, which investigate the standards, rules and norms that others (for example, members of various religious, social, professional or other groups) *actually* accept and put into practice in relevant contexts. Empirical study of others' norms is frequently undertaken by sociologists, historians and sundry social scientists, not to mention by the pollsters and public relations firms whom businesses and political parties pay to discover and tabulate the norms and attitudes held by the public, or by specific 'demographics', at a given time.

Such empirical inquiries focus on whatever norms are *actually* accepted by some group at some time, but need neither accept nor adopt those norms, and need not raise or address questions about their justification or their lack of justification. These inquiries do not ask whether the norms whose incidence they document are good or bad, feasible or infeasible, justifiable or unjustifiable. Since they bracket questions about justification, they need neither endorse, nor adopt, nor reject the norms that they investigate.

Empirical studies of others' norms (unsurprisingly) often document widespread acceptance of norms that both the researchers and many others would consider repugnant, contentious, or worse, such as the cultural norms enacted in religious persecution, regimes of terror, or in everyday prejudice or exclusion, or the epistemic norms that guide superstitious, sloppy or dogmatic truth-claims.

But the fact that some norms lack justification is irrelevant where the aim is to investigate *others'* norms using empirical methods, as in much work in sociology, history and anthropology. Here norms are the *objects* of study, and need have no normative force for the investigators. The study of others' norms does not seek to show which norms *ought* to be accepted, and does not attempt to extract normative commitment or force from the fact that certain norms are actually accepted by some or many people. Such studies use empirical methods, and aim to reach empirical conclusions. It is a further and regrettable matter if some people then use (or rather misuse) these findings for partisan, ideological, superstitious or other questionable purposes, or claim that widely accepted norms are justified by their very acceptance. However, if the aim is not to document others' norms but to consider which norms *ought* to be deployed in scientific practice, claims that the justification of norms is unimportant or impossible are extremely challenging. Requests for justification of the normative aspects of systematic inquiry demand more than an appeal to the happenstantial commitments or 'values' that individuals adopt.

The claim that 'values' are 'merely subjective' and cannot be justified has a moderately long pedigree. For nearly a century it has been particularly associated with logical positivism. Yet the specific view that logical positivists put forward in the 1930s was extremely challenging for the scientific practice that they hoped to support. The logical positivists held not only that scientific claims must be in principle verifiable, and supported solely by logical analysis and empirical evidence, but also and more strikingly that everything that could not be supported by these methods was 'literally meaningless'. Clearly logical positivism, at least in its first fine careless rapture, asserted a more aggressive position even than those advocated by various forms of scientism. Scientism may seek to replace the methods used in fields traditionally thought of as non-scientific, but does not claim that everything that does not use empirical methods, including ethics and aesthetics, theology and metaphysics, is *literally meaningless*. However, the actual practice of science requires normative assumptions. If norms such as commitments to recording data accurately, to modifying or rejecting hypotheses when they are falsified, or to honesty in scientific communication, were no more than the subjective 'values' or preferences of individual scientists, what could be said in criticism of those who invent their findings, make inaccurate or dishonest scientific claims, or ignore evidence?

Subjective 'values'?

Those who think that science should be 'value-free' or 'value-neutral', often claim to doubt, or even deny, that ethical norms can be justified, but console themselves with the thought that this does not matter because rigorous work in the empirical sciences can and should proceed without normative, and in particular without ethical, assumptions. From this perspective, attempts to bridge the gap between *is* and *ought* look dangerous, and to some perhaps dangerously attractive, as if they had to be put out of bounds lest ethical commitments overwhelm 'value-neutrality' and lead to scientific disaster by replacing science with pseudo-science and ideology. This thought has sometimes been supported by further assertions that norms, and in particular ethical norms, *cannot* be justified, so have no place in science or in rigorous inquiry.

Logical positivism flourished for a relatively short period, yet some of its claims about 'values' have survived and are now surprisingly widely held.

'Values' are still often characterised as 'merely subjective', as reflecting no more than arbitrary individual choices, sometimes now called 'autonomous choices' (thereby cloaking arbitrariness with a label that used to have a weightier meaning). Once 'values' are thought of as merely subjective, it makes sense to speak of 'my values' or 'your values', and to think of them as floating free of demands for deeper justification than the mere fact that they have been chosen or adopted by someone, or by some group. Yet the continued use of the term 'value' (rather than of explicitly subjective terms such as 'preference' or 'attitude') suggests that these subjective states are *not* arbitrary and *not* mere reflections of individual choice, but on the contrary weighty and in need of justification that is not merely subjective. The central norms that matter for scientific practice can hardly be matters of happenstantial individual choice: and if they were, scientific claims could not lay claim to universal assent. Scientific practice must respect at least some norms that are more than the 'values' individuals happen to adopt, and must be anchored in norms that can be relevant to all if it is to command an unrestricted audience.

Normative justification and appeals to authority

If the 'values' individuals happen to choose or prefer cannot provide an adequate basis for the normative requirements of scientific practice, what approach to justifying those normative standards is available?

One time-honoured way of answering questions of normative justification is to appeal to the relevant authority or authorities. *In their proper contexts*, arguments from authority often have weight. In a court of law an appeal to statute and precedent has weight. In commercial life appeals to contract have weight. In international diplomacy treaty obligations have weight. Within a Church appeals to the authority of Scripture, or to its authorised interpretation, or to ecclesiastical traditions, may have weight. In professional life appeals to agreed and established standards of professional conduct have weight. In these defined contexts there are recognised and legitimate authorities to which we can appeal. But invoking supposed authorities and their requirements or conventions for wider purposes of normative justification, and in particular for ethical justification, leads to problems. Authorities may themselves be questioned. Are they setting the right standards? Are they promoting norms that are no more than currently or locally accepted conventions or fashion? Are they backing norms that there are good reasons to revise or reject?

Questioning authority is generally seen as fundamental to scientific and other inquiry, where it is taken as a matter of pride and principle that arguments from authority are *not* decisive. So it seems unlikely that the normative commitments that are basic to scientific practice can be justified solely by appeals to authority. However, if we do not think arguments from authority acceptable in science, yet find that practices of inquiry, including scientific inquiry, must rely on at least some normative claims, where else can we turn? Can we even get started unless we accept certain norms as 'given' or authoritative, and appeal to the edicts of supposed authorities to justify norms of scientific inquiry and practice? What justifications can be offered to those whose views of scientific method and practice we think inadequate? What basis would there be for criticising some conceptions of the normative assumptions needed for scientific method and practice, or for adopting others? Is it possible to secure any deeper justification for norms of scientific practice?

These issues have been widely explored in sociological and historical work on the natural sciences, and many have pointed to and even been drawn to the positions in which relativists end up – or (perhaps we should say) the positions that end up in relativism. Many scientists, and many others, find such positions unconvincing, not to mention irritating. Falling back on justifications that are rooted in arguments from authority is widely seen as inadequate, has practical deficiencies, and flies in the face of claims that scientific reasoning has universal scope.

Normative justification and pluralism

Appeals to authority are not only controversial, but also likely to fail where those with very different normative commitments interact and disagree. Disagreements about norms are commonplace, particularly in a globalising world, where no appeal to authority is likely to settle disputes, which are often about the standing of differing claims to authority. This problem has dominated many discussions of the justification of political and ethical norms: Which business practices amount to corruption and bribery? Where does the boundary between public and private life lie? What do norms of truth telling or politeness require and prohibit? To what extent may medical practice go beyond scientific evidence? If we can say *nothing* about the justification of answers to these normative questions, except to assert (or assume) that certain norms and standards are *taken as* authoritative, at least by some people, we are likely to face recurrent and irresolvable conflicts, and to lack ways of resolving them. Cultural and political pluralism have proved a persistent challenge to those who seek to justify ethical and political norms, and may be equally problematic in seeking to justify norms on which scientific practice relies.

One approach to justifying norms that matter for scientific inquiry might therefore be to borrow some of the strategies used by certain political philosophers to address the implications of persistent normative disagreement. Some prominent political philosophers have argued that where we find a diversity of normative commitments, we can still justify certain claims about justice by relying on processes of *public reasoning*. Their hope is that this will offer a way for those who lack a common tradition or culture, so start with normative disagreement, to move towards agreement and avoid the limitations of appealing to the (ungrounded or disputed) authority of the *actual* social and moral norms of some group or other, which outsiders may find unconvincing.

Various conceptions of *public reason* have been put forward as a basis for norms of justice by some of the most prominent political philosophers of the last half century, including Jürgen Habermas and John Rawls, and more recently Amartya Sen. In *The Structural Transformation of the Public Sphere*[8] Habermas set out an account of public reason as emerging during the European Enlightenment, as domination of public life by the power of Church or state declined. Habermas saw this Enlightenment world as moving towards a world that supports participation in debate by all competent persons within (perhaps beyond) states, and as precursor to an increasingly democratic (and ultimately perhaps global) conception of public reason, in which reasoning is free from coercion, which (he claims) will lead across time to convergence and even consensus.

However, Habermas's account of public reason focuses on the *conditions for reasoners to participate* rather than on the *ethical and epistemic norms their reasoning should deploy*. It is premised on norms of freedom, equality and democratic process that allow participation in public discourse, but says less about the justification of the epistemic or ethical norms that should shape and structure that discourse. This focus allowed Habermas to link his conception of public reason with deliberative conceptions of democracy, in which citizens exchange views and seek agreement. However, while the agreement that citizens reach through deliberation in which all may take part can surely count as *democratically legitimated*, it is

---

[8] Jürgen Habermas [1962], *The Structural Transformation of the Public Sphere: An Inquiry into a Category of Bourgeois Society*, Thomas Burger (tr.) (Cambridge: Polity Press, 1989); Jürgen Habermas, 'Reconciliation through the Public Use of Reason: Remarks on John Rawls's Political Liberalism', *Journal of Philosophy*, 92 (1995), 109–31.

unclear why its conclusions should be thought of as *justified*. A consensus may be unacceptable, even dire.

In his later work John Rawls proposed a partially similar account of public reason, which he characterised as taking place among the citizens of a bounded, liberal and democratic political society, who "enter by birth and leave by death" and are willing to accept constraints, provided others too accept and abide by them. Rawls's conception of public reasoning sees it as independent of many of the norms favoured by specific social groups, whose moral, social and religious views and normative commitments may vary. He argues that public reasoning, as he construes it, will yield agreement on basic principles of justice, but that many other sorts of disagreement, including ethical and other normative disagreement, will persist unresolved. That is why Rawls called his later version of liberalism 'political liberalism'. This phrase was not intended to be a tautology, but to indicate that Rawlsian public reasoning seeks to justify the basic normative principles for the political sphere – a theory of justice – but no more. Rawls accepted that it would prove impossible to resolve differences about ethical norms that matter beyond the public domain, and that political liberalism cannot support any comprehensive conception of the good. Moreover, since the justifications he offers are relativised to the specific context of bounded, liberal, democratic polities, they cannot query or justify these framing institutional assumptions. This does not look a propitious model for justifying the basic normative standards required for scientific practice: a context-bound justification of norms of scientific reasoning could not support the universality of science.

Amartya Sen in recent work has taken this line of thought a step further, by removing the assumption that the reasons appealed to in political justifications have to be those of fellow citizens, and proposing that they may come from anyone, anywhere. He thereby weakens the link between his conception of public reason and conceptions either of fellow citizenship or of democracy, and sees public reason more abstractly as guided by norms that might be considered in an open-ended 'conversation of mankind'. Once again the extent of agreement and the assumptions that it presupposes both limit the possibility of justification. It seems that the strategies used by political philosophers to support accounts of justice may not be enough to justify the normative basis of scientific practice.

Normative reasoning in scientific practice

So if we are to justify the generic norms that matter for the practice of science we must dig deeper than any of these accounts of public reason. Normative claims can only be justified by showing how rigorous normative arguments can be built up. Needless to say, such arguments must start from certain assumptions, and in the case of normative reasoning at least some of the premises must be normative.

The distinctive feature of normative reasoning is not that it has no starting point, but that its *direction of fit* is unashamedly the converse of that used in empirical or descriptive investigation that seeks to determine what is true of (some part of) the natural world. Normative reasoning does not aim to be true of the way things actually are, but to specify standards or principles for action and practices, which if adopted may also be formative for the states of affairs to which activity leads. However, the generic normative standards that matter in scientific inquiry cannot simply appeal to individual choice or to individuals' 'values', since doing so would undermine the claim that scientific claims should be fit to reach an audience that is in principle unrestricted.

It is true that some rather *specific* scientific norms can be adequately justified by invoking the authority of agreed practices and conventions. For example, norms that specify standards and units of measurement, thresholds of significance for specific purposes, or requirements for submitting research proposals can assume and rely on the conventions that have the backing of one or another professional, public or other authority. So too can norms that bear on the employment of scientists, the sourcing of laboratory equipment and standards and structures that matter for research funding and peer review. These specific norms can be adequately justified where a relevant authority can be taken for granted.

But the *generic* norms on which the practice of science relies are different. They are standards that must be met if inquiry is to have *unrestricted scope*, and its claims and arguments are to be universally relevant. Here an appeal to some supposed authority or to some actual custom or practice would beg questions. The context of normative reasoning presupposes that *actual* practices could be changed, improved or worsened, and justifications that merely point to accepted standards or to the status quo will not be enough. Only practices of inquiry that are fit to be followed by all, and are open to check and challenge by others, can claim unrestricted scope and can count as science.

The *generic* norms of scientific practice form a central theme in contemporary work in epistemology and the philosophy of science, much of which focuses on the basic epistemic and ethical standards that must be met if the scientific inquiry and findings are to be open for all to consider, to assess – or to reject. These generic norms are relevant to all inquiry, all communication and all practical activity that can count as scientific.[9] They include norms of *consistency* and *coherence*; norms of *honesty* and *accuracy* in seeking, using and communicating evidence; as well as norms of *qualifying, rejecting or revising beliefs* if relevant evidence becomes available. These generic norms are uncontroversially needed for the practice of science; some are standardly seen as ethical norms and others as epistemic norms. (It is also plausible, as well as traditional, to hold that scientific inquiry may rely on some aesthetic norms and standards such as norms of *simplicity* or even of *elegance*.)

Norms for 'open science'

Ethical norms that bear on communication are also among the generic norms needed for the practice of science. They include norms of communicating in ways that are *intelligible to* and *assessable by intended audiences*, which are basic to all adequate communication. However, in the case of science, the intended audience is thought of as unrestricted: the most fundamental feature of scientific communication is that it potentially addresses 'the world at large'. The *openness* of science is not a nice 'add-on' feature that all can enjoy in an era of vastly improved communication technologies, but fundamental to scientific practice. Esoteric claims are not scientific claims.

The openness of scientific communication makes distinctive demands that go beyond mere openness. It cannot be secured merely by *disclosing* or *disseminating* scientific claims. Transparency is indeed an important (as well as a fashionable) norm, and often important for scientific practice. But it sets too low a normative standard for scientific communication. Information can be put into the public domain, thereby achieving transparency, without aiming for (let alone achieving) either intelligibility to or assessability by intended audiences, let alone for an audience that is in

---

[9] See for example C. A. J. Coady, *Testimony: A Philosophical Study* (Oxford University Press, 1992); Miranda Fricker, *Epistemic Injustice: Power and the Ethics of Knowing* (Oxford University Press, 2007); Philip Kitcher, *Science in a Democratic Society* (New York: Prometheus Books, 2011); Hugo Mercier and Dan Sperber, *The Enigma of Reason: A New Theory of Human Understanding* (Cambridge, MA: Harvard University Press, 2017).

principle unrestricted. Although transparency is a sufficient remedy for misplaced secrecy, it is not sufficient to ensure that communication is intelligible to or assessable by an audience that is in principle unrestricted.

Scientific communication therefore requires not mere transparency, but 'intelligent openness' that ensures that communication is in principle accessible, intelligible and assessable for *all* others, so fully open to their check and challenge.[10] The norms of scientific practice must meet the necessary conditions for the possibility of communicating with a potentially unrestricted audience. This is a demanding normative standard that is independent of any appeal to particular public or professional authorities, and is justified by the constitutive aims of scientific practice. These norms of scientific practice *endorse* reliance on empirical evidence where relevant, but their *justification* lies in the fact they are necessary conditions of the possibility of offering scientific claims to 'the world at large', so that anyone can ask whether claims should be accepted or rejected, can check and challenge the evidence presented, and can query the processes by which it was established and the conclusions that are inferred.

During the long post-positivist hangover that afflicted so many discussions of scientific method for much of the twentieth century, the normative demands of scientific practice were often not well articulated, and were sometimes suppressed or rejected. It was often said that science should avoid pseudo-science, and that this required rigorous 'value-neutrality', which could be secured only by systematic *avoidance* of normative and above all of ethical commitments. In that past world, some were also tempted to go further and to embrace forms of scientism, asserting that some or many areas of inquiry that had traditionally been approached in other ways, should be pursued solely by scientific methods and without relying on any normative assumptions, and that this was necessary to avoid pseudo-science and to ensure 'value-neutrality'. Of course, avoiding pseudo-science is important: but it is not a matter of achieving 'value-neutrality'. On the contrary, if we took the idea of 'value-neutrality' seriously, we would undermine the very norms by which we distinguish the universal claims of scientific practice from the defective and less-than-universal claims of pseudo-scientific practice.

[10] See *Science as an Open Enterprise*, Royal Society, 2012, http://royalsociety.org/~/media/policy/proj ects/sape/2012–06-20-saoe.pdf.

PART II

Abstract principles and practical judgement

CHAPTER 4

Abstraction, idealisation and ideology in ethics[1]

Although Burke, Bentham, Hegel and Marx do not often agree, all criticised certain ethical theories, in particular theories of rights, for being too *abstract*. The complaint is perennially popular. It was common in Existentialist and in Wittgensteinian writing that stressed the importance of *cases* and *examples* rather than *principles* for the moral life; it was prominent in Hegelian and Aristotelian flavoured writing during and since the 1980s, and it is ubiquitous in writing on virtue ethics and ethical particularism.[2] Work in all these genres stresses the distinctiveness and particularity of moral vicissitudes and queries the importance of ethical theory. Critics of abstraction are opposed not only to theories of rights, and the broadly Kantian notions with which these are often linked, but also to consequentialist ethical theories. The two types of ethical theories that have been and remain most influential in the English-speaking world were both accused of being 'too abstract'.

On the surface this is a curious complaint: if we take abstract reasoning quite straightforwardly as reasoning that leaves out a great deal, three quite simple defences of abstract approaches to ethics might be offered. First, abstraction is, taken strictly, unavoidable in all reasoning: no use of language can be fully determinate. Second, abstraction is not always objected to in practical reasoning. Accountancy and law both use very abstract types of practical reasoning, yet are widely admired and practised, indeed highly rewarded. Third, only abstract standards are likely to have wide scope: if ethical standards are to be relevant to a wide range of situations or of agents, they surely not merely *may* but *must* be abstract.

---

[1] 'Abstraction, Idealisation and Ideology', in J. D. G. Evans (ed.), *Moral Philosophy and Contemporary Problems* (Cambridge University Press, 1988), 55–69. I have applied these arguments to issues of global justice in 'Ethical Reasoning and Ideological Pluralism', *Ethics*, 98 (l988), 705–22, and in *Justice Across Boundaries: Whose Obligations?* (Cambridge University Press, 2016).

[2] For influential early versions of these claims see Alasdair MacIntyre, *After Virtue* (London: Duckworth, 1981), and Bernard Williams, *Ethics and the Limits of Philosophy* (London: Fontana, 1985).

If reasoning has to be abstract, is often admired for being abstract and apparently gains advantages by being abstract, why should ethical reasoning be persistently and fervently denounced for abstraction? Which issues lie behind the charge of abstraction? Can or should anything be done to answer the charge?

Abstract reasoning and ideal agents

Some complaints that ethical reasoning is too abstract have objected mainly to reliance on abstract views of agents. These complaints form the core of Hegelian and Marxian criticisms of 'abstract individualism', and were ubiquitous in communitarian objections to 'deontological liberalism'.[3] Abstract ethical and political theories, it is said, make assumptions about agency that are not satisfied by, perhaps cannot be satisfied by, human beings. The theories fail because they ignore the social and historical features that are constitutive of human agency, and assume capacities for reasoning and choosing that human agents simply lack.

The target of this line of criticism is not, however, merely abstraction. The objection is not just that much (too much) that is true of human agents is *omitted* in some accounts of agents, but that much (too much) that is false of human agents is *added*. Descriptions and conceptions of agents in much post-Enlightenment ethical and political theory (not to mention economic theory!) are often *idealised*. They are satisfied only by hypothetical agents whose cognitive and volitional capacities human beings lack. We none of us have cardinal and interpersonally comparable utilities, or complete and transitively ordered preferences, or complete information. We lack both infallible powers of calculation and independence from the institutional and ideological context we inhabit. We certainly don't have transparent self-knowledge or archangelic insight into others' preferences.

Many supposed 'models of man' idealise in a second sense. They don't merely posit agents with streamlined, super-normal cognitive and volitional capacities. (Perhaps there are theoretical uses for such idealisations.) They also treat enhanced versions of certain capacities as *ideals* for human action. Rational economic men, ideal moral spectators, utilitarian legislators and the legions of rational choosers have been taken as setting *standards* for human economic or political or ethical action. We are to

---

[3] A widely used term introduced by Michael Sandel, *Liberalism and the Limits of Justice*, 2nd edn. (Cambridge University Press, 1988).

think of idealised agents and their flawless compliance with (supposedly) rational norms as admirable and super-human, rather than as irrelevant to human choosing, let alone sub-human.

Appeals to the choice procedures of hypothetical idealised agents can seem relevant and compelling if we concentrate on domains of life where we might want or admire enhanced cognitive or volitional capacities of specific sorts, such as shopping or gambling. They are less convincing in areas of life where we don't want those capacities overdeveloped or know that they won't and perhaps can't be highly developed. We would not admire medical ethics that posited ideal rational patients, or personal relationships designed for ideal rational friends and lovers.

If all criticisms of abstraction in ethics were criticisms of idealising conceptions of agency, we would at least know where to head in order to deal with them. Plenty of people have headed off in those directions. Rational choice theorists have tried to show how some of their stronger and less plausible assumptions about cognitive and volitional capacities can be weakened and replaced with more plausible premises. Utilitarians acknowledge the approximate character of utilitarian calculation and the importance of 'putting out to sea with the almanac already calculated'. Plausibility is sought at the cost of softening the sharper and more radical implications of felicific calculation. Decision procedures that acknowledge uncertainty, partial information and the constraints of time are advocated. Maximin is preferred to maximising. Human rights theorists emphasise the imperfection of human cognitive and volitional capacities in order to argue from these to 'welfare' rights. They point out that liberty rights are worthless without agency, that human agency is vulnerable to material and other deprivation, and conclude that liberty rights are not taken seriously unless there are also rights to have basic needs met.[4]

Abstract reasoning and formalism in ethics

Ethical and political discussion can do without idealising accounts of agency. This does not, however, show that it can do without abstraction in the strict sense.[5] However, a good deal of criticism of abstraction in

---

[4] This line of thought was developed by Alan Gewirth, *Human Rights: Essays on Justification and Applications* (University of Chicago Press, 1982), and Henry Shue, *Basic Rights: Subsistence, Affluence and US Foreign Policy*, 2nd edn. (Princeton University Press, 1996), and has long since become a standard view.

[5] Formalism and idealisation are linked. Principles that could be relevant both for idealised agents and for varying human agents would have to be particularly schematic and indeterminate.

philosophical ethics suggests that abstraction itself might be dispensable. It is criticism not just of theories that rely on (excessively) idealised views of agency but of the supposed *formalism* and *emptiness* of all practical reasoning that invokes principles or rules. The charge of empty formalism is frequently levelled against Kant, who (it is repeatedly said) proposes in the Categorical Imperative a formal test of principles of duty that lacks determinate implications for action. Mill speaks for many when he alleges that Kant "when he begins to deduce from this precept any of the actual duties of morality ... fails ... almost grotesquely ...".[6] The supposed failure of Kantian formalism was later neatly summarised in Charles Péguy's acid quip "Le kantisme a les mains pures, *mais il n'a pas de mains*."[7] What is the point of 'hands' kept clean by grasping nothing?

However, objections to formalism are not directed only at Kant. All ethics of principles, including theories of human rights, are often charged with formalism whether or not they make idealising assumptions about agency. Formalism is said to be both theoretically and ethically inadequate. A range of interconnected objections is repeatedly raised. I shall consider four of them. Two of these objections are mainly theoretical. It is said, first, that any ethics of principles underdetermines decisions and offers no "algorithm for the difficult case"[8] and, second, that we can never formulate plausible exceptionless or universal moral principles.[9] The other two objections are ethical rather than theoretical. It is said, third, that thinking in terms of principles or rules can blunt moral and human sensibilities, lead to decisions that are taken 'by the book' and fail to consider context, and, fourth, that reliance on abstract or indeterminate principles is self-undermining and self-defeating.

The two theoretical objections are closely connected, and are, I think, true under their standard interpretations. They are also, I shall argue, quite insufficient under that interpretation to show that we either should or can avoid appealing to ethical principles or rules. The two ethical objections to abstraction are, I shall argue, unsustainable generalisations from ways in which principles or rules can be misused. I shall consider these objections in turn.

---

[6] J. S. Mill, 'Utilitarianism', in A. Ryan (ed.), *Utilitarianism and Other Essays* (Harmondsworth: Penguin Books, 1987), Ch. 1, 275.

[7] C. P. Péguy [1910], *Victor Marie, Comte Hugo* (Paris: Gallimard, 1934).

[8] A phrase that may first have been used by Annette Baier, *Postures of the Mind: Essays on Mind and Morals* (Minneapolis: University of Minnesota Press, 1985), 226, but which has gained appeal with the widening use of algorithms to structure online content.

[9] *Ibid.*, 216–17.

Principles and algorithms

It is true that principles underdetermine decisions. This is hardly news for those who have advocated ethical theories that make principles or rules central. Kant, for example, insisted that we can have no algorithm for judgement, since every use of a rule would itself need supplementing with further rules (cf. Kant, *CPR* A133/B172).[10] Yet some of the reasons often given for rejecting reliance on principles or rules appear to be based on no more than an assumption that they would have to be algorithmic – i.e. that they would have to determine complete answers for all cases that fall under them, so that particular decisions would be given by and indeed deducible from rules.

If no principle or rule can determine every detail of its own application or instantiation, even the most highly specified rule can be implemented in varied ways, and there can strictly be no algorithms of action. However, this move would be too easy a rebuttal of the view that ethical principles should be algorithms for action. There is a quite reasonable, if non-technical, sense in which *some* rules of action can be algorithmic: there are algorithms for multiplying and for reaching a draw when playing noughts and crosses, although these algorithms do not determine every move of every muscle or every aspect of action of agents who follow the algorithm. The significant point is not that there are strictly no algorithms for aspects of action, but that there is no reason to think that ethical principles are algorithmic or have been thought to be so by their advocates.

The view that principles or rules must be algorithmic in the wider sense has sometimes been combined with the stronger and stranger view that any ethical theory that centres on principles ought to provide a universal practical algorithm for agents. Not only must each principle or rule provide an algorithm for the cases it covers: the set of principles and rules taken together must cover all cases. On such a view, an ethic of principles would enable us to calculate what is ethically required and what is permitted in every situation: it would be an algorithm not just for some tasks or situations but for life.

The only ethical theory that purportedly offers a life algorithm is classical Utilitarianism. Here a set of abstract (and idealising) assumptions is used to define a procedure to identify an 'optimal' act in each situation. All 'available' options are to be listed, their expected consequences

---

[10] For textual references and commentary on Kant's distinctions and arguments see Chapters 5 and 8, below.

reckoned and evaluated, and the option with maximal expected utility identified. Actual decision makers can go through none of these steps. Since they lack complete information about what is possible and cannot individuate options exhaustively, they cannot list all available options. Since they lack a comprehensive science of society they cannot foresee all expected consequences. Since they lack cardinal and interpersonally comparable knowledge of utilities they cannot select the option with maximal expected utility. The 'rules of thumb' that would-be utilitarian agents have to fall back on are not algorithmic: they augment or replace calculation with judgement. Classical Utilitarianism did not aspire to be an ethic of principles. It purported to rely on strong idealising assumptions about agency to ground its claim to provide an ethical algorithm. Without implausible idealisations, Utilitarianism's calculating aspirations cannot be fulfilled. By contrast, any usable Utilitarianism depends on judgement to identify options for action, to predict and evaluate their likely results and to rank those results using a relatively low-definition decision procedure. This reduces the appeal of calculating Utilitarianism: how valuable is high precision calculation in handling low definition materials?

Some critics of abstraction have seemingly accepted the aspirations even if they reject the content of classical Utilitarianism. They apparently think that *if* there are ethical rules or principles, they *must* be algorithmic. As a corollary they suggest that those who propose an ethics of principles must be eager to shuffle off the burdens of responsibility by finding rules that will 'decide for us'. Advocates of ethics of principles can hardly recognise themselves as the targets of these criticisms. Kant reminds us as forcefully as Sartre later did that the thought of 'delegating' hard decisions to 'authorities' or 'codes' tempts, but is a symptom of immaturity or bad faith (cf. Kant, *WE* 8:37ff.). Algorithmic rules for conduct, let alone life algorithms, are fabulous: they belong in the fairyland of felicific calculation.

Exceptionless principles

The second complaint that critics of abstraction commonly level against ethics of principles is closely connected to the first. It is that we can find no plausible exceptionless or universal ethical rules or principles. This is a more sweeping objection than the complaint that there are no algorithmic rules. Algorithmic rules would have to be exceptionless; but not all exceptionless rules need be algorithmic, since some may fail to specify what is required or forbidden in each situation except in the broadest terms.

'When in doubt, do something' is exceptionless, but not much of an algorithm. However, exceptionless rules can cut quite a lot of ice, even if they are not algorithms, provided they constrain action in significant ways. Kant's Categorical Imperative, for example, requires that we reject action on principles that cannot even be adopted (not enacted!) by all, although it does not purport to identify a correct act for each situation. It provides what Kant terms 'negative instruction'. Many people think that theories of rights constrain action but provide no algorithms for action, let alone life algorithms. Even if we find the complaint that ethical rules provide no algorithms beside the point, the charge that there are no plausible exceptionless ethical rules or principles would tell against a wide range of theories that do not claim to offer algorithms for action but do propose exceptionless principles of action. Is the charge true? If so, must we or had we better do without ethical theories, principles or rules?

The claim that we can find no plausible exceptionless rules or principles is often put as an objection to setting aside context and circumstance in making decisions. Failure to take context and circumstance into account, it is said, makes a fetish of rules or principles. It leads to rigourism in ethics; in and out of utilitarian circles it amounts to "superstitious rule worship".[11] The objection of rigourism is often made plausible by pointing to examples (in life as well as in theory) of over-rigid reliance on certain rules.

Within a classical utilitarian context of debate, where we supposedly have access to algorithmic calculation about particular cases, the charge that adherence to exceptionless rules would be superstitious is well taken – unless the rules build in all the indicated exceptions, which makes the charge vacuous. Outside the classical utilitarian context it is not obvious what the critics of abstraction expect an 'exceptionless' rule to be. The objection is presumably not that we cannot state plausible ethical rules or principles that are formally universal. It is rather that these formulations are not complete. There may be exceptions even to principles that we take seriously such as 'don't lie' or 'don't kill'. Why is this deep criticism? That we understand such principles as qualified by *ceteris paribus* clauses is no reason to think that we do not take them seriously, or that they do not constrain action. Principles and rules must be indeterminate, so cannot

---

[11] A phrase coined in the early post war period by J. J. C. Smart in criticising rule utilitarianism from an act utilitarian standpoint. "The restricted [=rule] utilitarian regards moral rules as more than rules of thumb for short-circuiting calculations of consequences … Is not this a form of superstitious rule-worship (easily explicable psychologically) and not the rational thought of a philosopher?", J. J. C. Smart, 'Extreme and Restricted Utilitarianism', *The Philosophical Quarterly*, 6 (1956), 344–54, at 348–9.

specify all the boundary conditions or all the details of their own application in varying contexts. We cannot deduce their applications. Why should it be a criticism that we cannot? What image do those who criticise the supposed lack of 'exceptionless' rules have of ethical principles or rules? Do they assume that any exceptionless rule or principle would have to be algorithmic? Do they expect ethical rules to tell them what to do, although they do not expect rules of language to tell them what to say?

The claim that there cannot be exceptionless ethical rules would constitute a general criticism of ethics of principles only if 'exceptionless' rules and principles had to provide algorithms for action. However, we have seen that there is no reason for thinking that ethics of principles must consist of algorithms, and good reason to think that they cannot consist of algorithms, even in the broader sense in which there can be some algorithms of action. Moreover, the criticism simply does not apply either to Kant's ethics, or to theories of rights or of obligations, which stress the incompleteness of principles or rules, and deny that they are sufficient for determining decisions. Advocates of ethical principles standardly deny that rules or principles are or can be complete, and insist that they must be supplemented by deliberation if we are to apply (necessarily incomplete) principles to cases. The charge that advocates of ethics of principles fail to provide plausible exceptionless rules is implausible unless it is understood as the charge that they have failed to provide plausible exceptionless rules *from which decisions can be deduced*. That charge is true, but has little point; those who advocate various ethics of principles don't claim to provide such principles.

For the charge to seem plausible, any ethics of principles has to be interpreted as philosophically backward. The results are often textually grotesque. For example, Kant's cases of dutiful action in *Groundwork* have been taken as deductions from rather than as illustrations of the Categorical Imperative. Kant did not see his examples in that way; and anybody who has looked at *The Doctrine of Virtue*, or read Kant's *Groundwork* with care, can see that Kant (although he held some rigid ethical views) knows and indeed insists that principles of duty alone don't and can't tell us what to do. He could hardly think otherwise given his well-known insistence on the importance of judgement. Contemporary human rights theorists also assume that the interpretation and application of rights is an intricate and demanding business. Nor is 'applied' ethics a matter of deducing decisions from principles. It requires judgement and additional premises because rules are *not* algorithms, because the application of rules to cases is not a mechanical operation, because we need to work out what it would take to institutionalise or instantiate certain rights, and to allocate corresponding obligations, in various circumstances.

The need for deliberation or even for casuistry – for procedures by which principles are connected to situations and can guide action – is taken for granted by most utilitarians as well. Mill clearly holds that deliberation is needed to apply the principle of utility: although (as he said) nobody would go to sea without the almanac already calculated, nobody would expect the almanac to make the skipper's judgement redundant. Kant and Mill and their respective successors don't disagree that principles and rules are necessary, that they are incomplete and that their application needs deliberation. Their disagreement is over the weight ethical reasoning should place on desire and preference.

Sheltering behind rules

The third and fourth criticisms of abstraction in the strict sense point to ethical rather than theoretical deficiencies in ethics of principles. Abstract ethical reasoning which relies on principles or rules can, it is said, blunt moral and human sensibilities, so lead to decisions that are taken 'by the book' and take too little account of context; it may also be self-undermining and self-defeating in deep ways. I believe that there is some, but only some, truth behind these claims. This limited truth may be misinterpreted as evidence that ethics of principles are committed to algorithmic rules, so are theoretically flawed.

Appeals to rules and principles have often been offered in supposed justification of wrongs. The standard examples of disastrous wrongs done by agents who appeal to rules or principles to justify their decisions are not examples of appeals to ethical principles. A classic twentieth-century theme is that of officials who shelter behind roles, official rules and the authority of orders, and try to use these to 'justify' wrong-doing. These wrongs can be petty, or ghastly – as in the much-discussed case of Nazi bureaucrats. What do such cases tell us about an ethics of principles? Only a little, I suggest. In the first place, both the rules to which bureaucratic wrongdoers usually appeal and the assumption that these rules outrank other principles of action may lack ethical weight. Secondly, all but the lowest level rules on which bureaucrats rely are far from algorithmic. Postal workers may not have discretion about how much postage to charge for letters with a given weight and destination, but even junior officials have some discretion in the application of rules; while powerful officials – Eichmann, for example – are constrained but not determined by the policies they implement, and can reveal their commitment (or partial dissent) from the policy by the judgements they make about implementing it. Except in the smallest matters, following orders does not determine action closely: even in small matters it does not fully determine all aspects of action. Only if all rules were algorithmic could they make judgement redundant. Standard bureaucratic excuses such as 'I was only applying the rules' or 'I was only carrying out orders' are nearly always disingenuous; they rest on pretence that all rules are algorithmic.

It is not only bureaucrats who try to shelter behind rules. Sometimes specifically ethical rules or principles are invoked in defence of ethically questionable action. Peter Winch once used the example of Ibsen's character Mrs Solness,[12] as a case in which ethical principles are misused to 'justify' bad and offensive action. Such bogus 'justifications' do not convince. To do so they would not only have to invoke ethical rules that have weight, but to offer reasons for relying on that particular rule or principle in this particular situation and for applying it in a specific way. Our experience is not much like that of ideal-typical petty bureaucrats. Situations do not come handily pre-classified for subsumption under one and only one ethical rule or principle, which prescribes rigidly determinate action. Before we apply rules we have to construe the situation we face; when we have done so we may find more than one pertinent rule, and every relevant rule will underdetermine action. Ethical rules and principles offer remarkably little shelter outside ideal-typical petty bureaucratic roles.

Still, rules and principles offer minimal shelter, and are often thought to offer rather more. The truth behind the claim that appeals to abstract principles are ethically blunting is, I think, that such appeals are quite often made by ethically blunt agents. Some agents assume (falsely) that the problems and cases we confront are uncontroversially candidates for subsumption under one and only one rule or principle, which can determine fully what ought to be done.

A similar limited truth lies behind the claim that (ethical) principles and rules are self-defeating. Those who need to refer explicitly to rules in guiding their action may do so in blunt and insensitive ways, just as those who constantly need to refer explicitly to rules of grammar may speak or write in blunt and insensitive ways. Some cite abstract principles yet distance themselves from actual situations; they pay lip-service to impeccable principles that never incommode them. Others undercut their own performance by excessive scrutiny of the principles they take

---

[12] Peter Winch, *Ethics and Action* (London: Routledge & Kegan Paul, 1972).

themselves to follow. There are often strong reasons to sustain ways of life in which we neither parade nor perform explicit reasoning about matters like trust, or kindness, or spontaneity, or the pursuit of happiness. Too much concentration on rules or principles can mar performance. This does not show that principles or rules cannot guide reasoning in these matters, but rather that they do so best when deeply absorbed and internalised, as the rules of a language must be deeply absorbed and internalised for effortless and precise speech. In both cases explicit focus on rules and principles may be self-defeating. Yet there are also cases where it is important to refer explicitly to rules and principles. These may include 'hard' cases, aspects of the education of children and cases where important principles are confused or flouted. Here the greater danger may lie in failure to formulate and follow rules and principles explicitly.

The indispensability of principles

Both the theoretical and the ethical criticisms of abstraction in ethics are unconvincing. They depend upon misconstruing principles or rules as precluding rather than requiring deliberation. The advocates of various sorts of ethics of principles do not claim that there are principles from which specific decisions or requirements can be deduced. They take ethical principles and rules as non-algorithmic, and assume that their application requires deliberation; yet they have been persistently read as taking a different view.

The important point about rules and principles is not that the morally insensitive try to exploit them for shelter, but that even the sensitive cannot dispense with them. Once we reject the view that rules and principles of action must be algorithmic we can see why any plausible view of reasoning about conduct must give principles and rules an important role. Although some critics of abstraction and theory in ethics suggest that deliberation could dispense with rules, and fall back on sensitive articulation of situations, this is as implausible as the thought that principles or rules by themselves could make decisions.

There are two reasons why articulations of situations alone are ethically inadequate. First, descriptions are neither unique to cases nor uncontentious. Cases no more determine unique descriptions than rules pick out fully determinate actions. Reasons have to be given for preferring one rather than another description of a situation; and these reasons lead straight back to more general principles. Secondly, even if a certain description of a situation can be justified, it is by itself inert. It is only when we see situations *of that sort* as requiring action *of this type* that knowledge of some description of a situation can be connected to a practical principle that can guide action. Principles enable us to navigate among descriptions of situations. Fortunately we do not always have to keep our principles in the forefront of consciousness: we have much of the almanac not only calculated, but in our bones. That we make our moves directly, intuitively, spontaneously no more shows that we do not need principles than the rapid inferences we draw without explicit laying out of arguments show that we don't rely on principles of inference. In each case reliance on principles has become an ingrained – but not a redundant – habit. Without these habits we would be wholly at sea.

'Facts' and cases

Do these arguments show that the entire critique of abstraction (as opposed to idealisation) in ethics has been groundless? It seems to me unlikely that so strong and persistent an intellectual current could be superficial. What then are the deeper sources of perennial concern about abstraction? I suggest that abstraction worries us not because some writers maintain that ethical reasoning requires only principles or rules, but because nearly all writers, whether or not they advocate ethical principles, have offered too meagre and cursory an account of deliberation or judgement. Perhaps the illusion that all the work in ethical debate is to be done by the major premise has arisen because we are unsure how the minor premise is to be found and used.

It is not enough to suggest that the minor premise is just a matter of establishing 'the facts'. Situations have no unique descriptions. What we see under one true description as an urgent crisis or problem may appear under another as mere and trivial routine. Ways of reasoning that assume that 'the facts' of human situations can be uncontroversially stated are likely to be dominated by established and often by establishment views. Without a critical account of the selection of minor premises, ethical reasoning may avoid formalism only to become hostage to local ideology. This is not an idle worry. Writing in applied ethics has to work with some account of the topics to be handled. Neither the selection of topics nor their description is neutrally given. Could any of us demonstrate that contemporary applied ethics is more than the scholasticism of a liberal tradition? What explains the particular agenda of 'problems' that dominates the literature at a given moment?

Those who dispute the relevance of principles in ethical reasoning have, it seems to me, failed to offer an adequate account of how we are to describe the situations we find. For example, a lot of Wittgensteinian and related writing on ethics, and some work in virtue ethics, has suggested that examples carry the whole burden of ethical deliberation, and that the articulation of examples, although subtle, is possible because we can determine 'what we do want to say'. But what we want to say depends much on who we are, and how we understand the world. Outside closed circles there are real and deep controversies about the articulation of cases and examples; even well-established descriptions may be evasive, self-serving or ideologically contentious.

Of course, we may choose to retreat to closed circles, which we define by the possibility of agreeing on the articulation of cases and an agenda of ethical problems. This strategy is likely to push us not merely into relativism, but into circles that are smaller than those we actually inhabit. Even within the confines of the Athenian *polis* – a classical image of a moral community – there was dispute about the articulation of examples, and no guarantee that disputants could agree on cases: Does failing to return a knife to its frenzied owner count as failure to give each his due? *Every* articulation of a situation privileges certain categories and descriptions, and is incomplete and potentially controversial even among those who inhabit the same circles. Those who don't live in the same circles may find that disagreement amounts to mutual incomprehension.

This suggests that we need to think more about the means by which understanding, and perhaps agreement, can be sought, and less about the conditions under which they can be taken for granted. We might ask: what are the minimal assumptions we must make for there to be ways of seeking to come to a mutually comprehensible and perhaps agreed-upon account of the minor premises of ethical reasoning? What does deliberation require?

Relativism and multilingualism

It is difficult to discuss this point without entering into debates about relativism. For present purposes I shall bracket conceptual relativism of the sort that would trap us in permanent conceptual and social isolation. I offer only gestural reasons for doing so.

First, conceptual relativism suggests that we cannot even discuss matters with those in different traditions because we lack a common conceptual framework. The reality of ethical and political conflict, however, suggests that when we are in dispute we do not entirely misunderstand. It is *because* we understand (pretty well) what the other lot mean and are up to that we are in furious dispute. Those who are separated by ethical and political disagreements are more like those who speak different languages. Multilingualism is possible even if perfect translation is not. If we can be ethically and socially as well as linguistically multilingual, we may find more than one way of articulating a situation so as to make it accessible. Many people, I suggest, are at least partly ethically multilingual.

The second reason for bracketing conceptual relativism is practical. If we do not bracket relativism, we have only two options for dealing with those whose ways of thought and life we do not understand. Either we can cut ourselves off and retreat to the cosiness of 'our' shared outlook; or we can seek to impose our ways on others. If we are to have options other than quietism and imperialisms (violent or merely paternalistic) we must bet against relativism. Silence and violence are possible, but not the only possibilities.

Betting against relativism

What would it be to bet against relativism? Rather than accepting that there is nothing rational to do in the face of deep misunderstanding and disagreements, we would have to look for ways to reach wider mutual comprehension and perhaps some resolution of disagreement. This search cannot be just a blind groping for minor premises that all will understand and perhaps accept. If it is to count as a bet against relativism it must be more than this: indeed, it must be guided by principles.

There is a possibility – welcomed by some – that we can make no bets against relativism. It may be said, for example, that we can do no more than accept that the conversation of mankind will lead us and others to new perceptions and descriptions, which will sometimes permit wider under-standing and agreement. If this is our situation we can draw no generally acceptable distinction between consciousness raising and consciousness lowering. While we will not think of ourselves as trapped in timeless conceptual capsules, the sense we come to make of others' ethical reasoning will depend on the way we drift with the tide of history. Since the conversation of mankind sometimes takes a distinctly nasty turn, we have reasons to balk at and bet against this moderated relativism.

If we balk, one consolation that may be offered us is the claim that all change will at least enlarge horizons, since 'the tradition' retains a com-prehension of its past formations. We can understand the Athenians, even if they would have found us baffling. There are two difficulties with this position. The first is that it embodies a worrying ethnocentrism – specifically Eurocentrism – in assuming that there is only one tradition. The second is that even when we are talking about pasts that are ancestors to our own present there is an implausible optimism in assuming that transitions always happen without loss: it may merely be that when there is loss we may not experience it as such. The present categories of any tradition are always the categories of the rewriters of its history. Historicised relativism appeals to ethnocentrism and optimism as strategies for bridging non-comprehension.

If we are to take seriously the thought that others may not understand our very articulations of situations, or if they understand may think them pointless or evil, what can we do? Which principles must we follow if we bet against relativism? How can we work towards rather than assume acceptable minor premises? I shall do no more here than gesture towards lines of inquiry that require accounts of practical reasoning to address questions of ideology.

First, in practical reasoning that is not predicated on relativism we must accept that others may not share our views of situations and problems and that we may have to discuss and mediate disagreements. Our first task may be to enable communication. If so, the most fundamental ethical principles may be those by which we question our own and others' perceptions of situations and seek strategies for securing communication, and where possible some agreement on the appropriate minor premises for ethical reasoning.

The beginning of a bet against relativism may be action on principles of tolerating and mediating discursive differences. Such toleration would not be mere indifference to others' views and voices. It would rather be a matter of straining to follow the terms of others' discourse and to grasp their assumptions and their starting points. Such moves towards multilingualism may fail where others are deeply alien and separated from us by impassable conceptual gulfs. There is no guarantee that all bets succeed. However, there is no reason to be sure that this bet must fail: there is little evidence of impassable conceptual barriers between human beings who have not suffered traumatic breakdown.

The principles required to guide a quest for mutual accessibility can be thought of as requiring strategies of decentring, and of seeking to enlarge our horizons and understand other standpoints.[13] However, trying to

---

[13] This brief discussion draws both on Kant's account of shifting horizons and of the *sensus communis* in the *Critique of Pure Reason*, the *Critique of Judgement* and in his *Logic*, and on Gadamer's rather different use of the metaphor of the horizon.

communicate with others whom we initially cannot understand needs more than a shift of our own horizon. A shift of horizons would not constitute a bet against relativism if it were only a conversion, during which our own former starting point dropped below a new 'horizon'. Attaining multilingualism is not a matter of forgetting one's native tongue. The objective of building understanding between those who do not initially share terms of discourse requires a strategy of seeking to grasp both perspectives, not the loss or suppression of some original bearings.

The strategy of seeking multilingualism could be articulated in Kant's terms as a matter of acting on three principles. Those who seek to enlarge their horizon must preserve their own view or voice; they must seek to share others' views; they must strain to render consistent the constantly revised set of views to which action on the first two principles of the strategy may lead (see Kant, *CJ*, 5:293–4). If such a strategy works – there is no guarantee that it will always do so – those who transform their understanding may become conceptually multilingual, and may find their views of the problems they confront and their possibilities for action changed.

But won't multilinguals suffer schizophrenia? Enlarged horizons, in the sense just explained, don't guarantee an integrated viewpoint or a clear basis for action. It is a myth that horizons fuse. Perhaps multilingualism can lead to a sort of breakdown and moral paralysis, or to extreme fragmentation of moral life. However, multilingualism need not disable. It might be continuous with the experience of 'monolinguals', who also find that their one language allows multiple and dissonant possibilities for describing situations. Even within the horizons with which we grow up, we experience conceptual and ethical hiatuses. Enlarged horizons do not offer our first glimpse of ethical conflict. However, if we are looking only for *strategies* for seeking, and not for *algorithms* for selecting, the minor pre-mises to which we are initially drawn, we do not need a guarantee that every use of a principle of seeking to bridge disagreement about particular situations will bear fruit. We need only to bet that it is not ruled out that a strategy of acting on such principles can work for at least some cases. The strategies to which I have gestured may seem slender weapons for con-fronting entrenched ideologies and dominant articulations of the problems to be addressed. Yet betting on these strategies may be the best we can do if we refuse to be relativists or to rely uncritically upon some locally entrenched account of 'the facts'.

CHAPTER 5

Normativity and practical judgement[1]

Norms and practical reasoning

Norms are apt for reasoning because they have propositional structure and content; they are practical because they aim to guide action, rather than to describe aspects of the world. These two features hold equally of norms construed sociologically as the norms of specific social groups, and of norms conceived more practically as principles of action. On either view, norms are indeterminate, while acts are not merely determinate but particular. Consequently norms cannot fully specify which particular act is to be done. Are they then not genuinely action-guiding unless supplemented by practical judgement? Yet accounts of practical judgement are often thin, sometimes seeing it as no more than blind, unreasoned 'picking' of one rather than another enactment of a norm. However, on another view practical judgement can carry the substantive task of seeking ways of acting that satisfy a plurality of norms, which can be both reasoned and practical.

Discussions of normativity and practical reason often focus on reasons for adopting, or for rejecting, specific norms. This focus is useful for addressing questions about the nature and justification of norms and their division into various modal types (requirements, prohibitions, permissions, recommendations, etc.). And it is also the right focus for raising questions about the nature and justification of ethical norms and their division into various modal and other types (ethical obligations, prohibitions, permissions, recommendations, etc.). Yet a focus on reasons for adopting specific norms, or for adopting specific ethical norms, does not seem to be enough to guide action. Norms are always indeterminate; acts are always particular and so determinate. A given norm can always be

[1] First published in *Journal of Moral Philosophy*, 4.3 (2007), 393–405; reprinted in Thom Brooks (ed.), *Ethics and Moral Philosophy* (Leiden: Brill, 2011), 77–92.

satisfied by a plurality of possible acts. So it seems that there will always be a gap between norm and act, and that while practical reasoning may be able to justify specific norms, it will not by doing so show which particular acts are required. Moves from a specific norm to one or another particular enactment of that norm are generally seen not as instances of reasoning, but rather as 'applications' of that norm. Yet the use of the term 'application' is more obscure than it seems: action that changes the world to fit a norm is quite different from cognition that fits or applies a concept to the way the world is.

This gap between indeterminate norms and their particular enactments is not confined to the domain of morality. It arises for norms that bear on many different aspects of action, including norms thought of as social or legal, grammatical or technical, epistemic or cultural, as well as ethical norms. It arises for norms that prescribe with varying modalities, including those that we see as expressing requirements, obligations and permissions, and those that we see as formulating recommendations, advice or warnings. In all cases, reasons for adopting a specific norm will not yield reasons for selecting one rather than another act that instantiates that norm.

Can we then think of practical reasoning as justifying acts as well as norms? In order not to prejudge this question I shall rely on an ample – I hope at least non-excluding – view of practical reasoning, once formulated by Philippa Foot when she suggested that practical reasoning is what you have if you are "good at making the kinds of practical choices that arise for human beings, given the material circumstances of their existence".[2] This very broad characterisation strikes me as sufficiently ample to avoid begging questions. Being good at making choices is not just a matter of being good at choosing norms. Some people who adopt, indeed seek to live by, admirable norms make a poor fist of enacting them. These are the people whom we think of as having poor judgement. Now it may be that practical reason can offer no guidance to practical judgement, and that reason can reach no further than the justification of norms. But we should not reach this conclusion by adopting too limited a view of practical reason. *A fortiori*, we should not restrict our account of practical reasoning to those aspects of reasoning that lend themselves to quantification, such as those formalised in models of rational choice. Norms may incorporate quantitative

---

[2] Philippa Foot, 'Morality as a System of Hypothetical Imperatives', in her *Virtues and Vices* (Oxford: Blackwell, 1978), 157–73.

requirements or considerations, but need not do so. Whether or not they do so, it is still an open question whether practical reasoning can tell us anything about the move from adopting justifiable norms to enacting those norms.

That being said, we need to say something preliminary about the way in which a focus on norms can help us to understand how practical reasoning bears on norms, while leaving it open how it is to bear on acts that instantiate those norms. There would be no point in speaking of practical reasoning unless we can see why it offers a basis for saying that some norm is or is not a reason for doing some action of type A. Norms pick out types of action that fall under specific act descriptions: it is their propositional structure and content that makes norms apt for reasoning. However, by the same token the fact that a norm picks out a *type* of action, means that it can offer no more than *a reason for doing some type of action*, and not *a reason for doing a particular act of that type*.

Since practical reason seeks to guide action it must be future oriented, rather than directed at particular acts that have not been done and cannot be individuated. We can, of course, formulate definite descriptions of future acts. For example, I can use definite descriptions to specify the types of acts I intend to do at some future time: the walk that I intend to take after lunch, the drink that I hope to enjoy at a certain pub, the meeting at the pub that I shall arrange with friends. But this is not to say anything about the particular acts that I will do, beyond stating of what types they will be, and that with some generality. The definite descriptions do no more than specify the types of act that are to be done. Although they individuate the agent by whom and the occasion on which action is to be done, they do not distinguish between the innumerable ways in which the specification of action might be met. It may seem then that the gap between norms (for which reasons may be given) and enactments of those norms (for which no complete reasons can be given) marks a limit of practical reasoning.

Taking a relaxed view of norms

So the optimistic thought that norms are apt for practical reason because they combine propositional structure and content (making them apt for reasoning) with a capacity to guide action (making them practical) is too quick. This might suggest some problem with reliance on the idea of a norm. The term has a chequered history, and may seem in some ways to be too narrow and in others too broad to provide a useful focus for practical reasoning. However, I do not think that the difficulties lie specifically in the use of the term *norm*, rather than of other terms for practical propositions that combine propositional structure and content with claims to be action-guiding (such as *principle, rule, standard, law*). We should not and we need not be the prisoners of past uses of the term *norm* (particularly now that the term *normative* is used in a much broader way). As I see it, there are reasons for being rather relaxed in our understanding of both terms, and rather self-conscious about their relations to other terms that serve cognate purposes. Indeed, the only feature of norms that it seems to me essential to retain is the thought that their use is to guide the way action changes the world rather than to describe the way the world is. A focus on direction of fit suggests four issues that might arise if we relied on traditional, more restrictive understandings of norms. I shall discuss these in turn and suggest that there is nothing particularly problematic about centring discussion of practical reasoning on norms.

1. *Norms and other directives.* One set of considerations that might lead us to wonder whether norms offer *too narrow* a focus for practical reasoning, in that there are other practical uses of propositions that we would not usually view as norms, which also incorporate act descriptions to which the world is to be fitted and which are taken to guide action. For example, there are *intentions* and *instructions*, and other practical uses of propositions that are sometimes termed *directives*, which we might be reluctant to think of as norms, although they function like norms in that they are intended to guide action rather than to fit the way things are. In each case we think of ways in which action can be shaped to fit one proposition rather than another, and contrast this with uses of non-normative principles, that aim to fit a proposition to the way the world is or will be – including the way certain actions are or will probably be.

This wider range of practical uses of propositions is the focus of Anscombe's classic work *Intention*, and the action-guiding aspect of the practical uses of propositions she discusses are vividly encapsulated in her example of the man whose wife complains of his shopping performance saying "Look, it says butter and you have bought margarine", who would get things very wrong if he replied "What a mistake! We must put that right" – and altered the list to read 'margarine'.[3] The shopping list is

---

[3] G. E. M. Anscombe, *Intention* (Oxford: Blackwell, 1957), 57 and discussed in Chapter 1, above.

intended to be normative for the shopper's performance, rather than predictive of it: the mismatch calls for different shopping, not different listing, i.e. for changes in action rather than for changes in theory. In my view the fact that we would not traditionally speak of an instruction or intention to buy butter as a *norm* is not a deep problem. Instructions and intentions function normatively, and there is no reason to be squeamish about thinking of them as norms (in a moment I shall allude to some historical reasons why we may mistakenly think that we should be squeamish).

The same relaxed view of norms will allow us to think of other types of 'directive', such as intentions, vows and promises, orders and requests as normative, although they might not traditionally have been called norms. Norms in a traditional, sociological sense of the term are perhaps a subclass of 'directive', which not merely guide action but are thought of as having an authority that is not traceable either to individual decisions or commitments (as are intentions, vows and promises), or to second and third person impositions (as are orders, instructions and requests). To put matters vaguely, norms, in the traditional sociological usage of the term, are *impersonal directives*, often seen as backed by social, legal or other authority. Norms in this narrower sense may be ethical, grammatical, social or legal and are often domain specific (*norms of international behaviour*, *norms of economic rationality*, etc.). However, we do no harm in classifying a fuller range of uses of practical propositions as norms, provided that we realise that we have broadened the traditional understanding. What is common to all these, and many other, practical uses of propositions is that they set out standards to which the world should be adjusted, rather than aspects of the way the world is.

2. *Norms and modality*. A second rather different caveat is that some propositions that function normatively are not accurately characterised as 'directives', in that they do not specify *requirements* for the aspects of action for which they are normative. Propositions can have other practical uses. They can be used to formulate advice or warnings, recommendations or guidance, or Kantian 'counsels of prudence', none of which strictly speaking *requires* or *directs* action of a specific type. But once again it seems to me that we can take this point lightly and extend the term *norm* to cover this wider range of practical uses of propositions: like requirements and prohibitions they function normatively to specify ways in which the world should be changed. Examples of norms that do not require but rather recommend or warn against specific types of action are very common in

self-help manuals, good practice guidance, proverbial wisdom and traditions of virtue.

So it is, I think, useful to adopt a capacious use of the term *norm*, that
covers uses of practical propositions of all sorts, regardless of their source
(first, second or third personal, or impersonal), or the modality of their
prescription (requirement or prohibition, warning or advice). Taking this
elastic view of norms is not only acceptable but advantageous, because it
reconnects norms with contemporary understandings of normativity.
However, if we accept this broadened understanding of norms two further
points follow.

3. *Socially embedded norms.* A long tradition in sociology, often
reflected in ethical writing, assumes that the crucial feature and advantage of focusing on norms in discussions of practical reasoning is that
(unlike 'abstract' principles and rules) norms are socially embedded or
entrenched. There is, of course, a lot of history here. Some strands in
that history urge us to think that norms provide a uniquely suitable
focus for practical reasoning precisely *because* they are socially
embedded, *because* they are the norms of this or that group at this or
that time, and that this is what makes them important, practical and
motivating. Others have seen the understanding of norms as socially
embedded as a great deficiency of a sociological understanding of
norm-based practical reasoning. If norms are seen as practical propositions that are entrenched in the lives of some group, the objection
runs, they offer a highly problematic focus for practical reasoning, and
in particular for ethical reasoning. Some embedded practical propositions may provide poor reasons for action – and the fact that they are
embedded adds only the questionable weight of an argument from
authority. (We need only think of appeals to entrenched norms of
revenge, honour killing or female genital mutilation.) By contrast,
'abstract' principles of action that at a given time are not well
embedded may sometimes offer significant reasons for action.

However, letting go of the traditional, narrower sociological understanding of norms as embedded is not problematic. In fact, I suspect that
current usage of the term has long since distanced norms and normativity
in discussions of ethics and practical reason from the older sociological
conception of norms as socially embedded, although there are pockets of
lingering confusion.

4. *Norms as motivating.* And there is a fourth point that follows
from accepting a relaxed view of norms. An explicit rejection of the
older sociological conception of norms as social embedded

undermines the psychological corollaries of such views, and requires us to set aside the assumption that norms are invariably motivating. There is no doubt a complex story to be told about the ways in which norms come to be accepted, understood, rejected and modified, and about the emergence of particular norms in the lives of individuals and societies. There is also no doubt a story to be told about what Sabina Lovibond once called 'the animal precursors of practical reasoning'.[4] However, if we accept a broader understanding of norms as practical propositions *that may or may not* be embedded in the life of this or that group, we will also have to accept that they have no automatic psychological or motivational role. This may be an advantage. It may be that – as with theoretical cognition – the best account of the development of the emergence and embedding of specific norms in agents or in groups would not be given in terms of the norms. The embedding of norms may be better explained in terms of the entrenching of lower level routines, habits, inhibitions and tendencies, and of the exposure of suggested norms to check and challenge. The most psychologically effective way of living up to some norm may not make it an explicit focus of practical reasoning. For example, if I seek to live up to a norm of law-abidingness, I may do best to be conformist and inconspicuous, rather than to check my compliance with the statute book with high frequency. More generally, morally responsible ways of living may not depend heavily on explicitly moral reasoning or motivation, any more than cognitively responsible ways of living need depend on explicit efforts to conform to epistemic norms. As A. N. Whitehead memorably put it

> It is a profoundly erroneous truism, repeated by all copy-books and by eminent people when they are making speeches, that we should cultivate the habit of thinking of what we are doing. The precise opposite is the case. Civilization advances by extending the number of important operations which we can perform without thinking about them. Operations of thought are like cavalry charges in a battle – they are strictly limited in number, they require fresh horses, and must only be made at decisive moments.[5]

Explicit thought about norms is needed when we address questions of justification, but in acting on norms and in thinking about motivation we

---

[4] Sabina Lovibond, 'Practical Reason and its Animal Precursors', *European Journal of Philosophy*, 14 (2006), 262–73.

[5] A. N. Whitehead, *An Introduction to Mathematics* (London: Williams and Norgate, 1911), 45–6; reissued by Google books. For discussion of wide-ranging evidence for this claim see Malcolm Gladwell, *Blink: The Power of Thinking Without Thinking* (London: Penguin, 2005).

may often do better to rely on shortcuts, habits and heuristics – or indeed on nudges.[6]

Indeterminate norms, determinate acts

With these preliminaries on one side, we can ask with fewer ambiguities how exactly norms – of any sort – are supposed to guide action. This is not the same as asking which norms can be justified, for which contexts – uncontroversially a central task of practical reasoning. Yet the question of whether and how norms (justified or not) can guide action seems to me a more fundamental question than those about the justification of norms, or about the relation of justification to motivation. If we cannot understand *how* norms can shape action, an account of their justification may be of little practical use.

On the surface norms seem defective guides to action. Norms, taken in the relaxed sense I have suggested, are abstract entities with propositional structure and content to which action is to conform. A norm formulates some standard or requirement, some recommendation or permission; action is then supposed to be guided or shaped by that standard, requirement, recommendation or permission. However, while norms are indeterminate, the acts done in living up to them – or in failing to live up to them – have to be determinate in all respects. How then can norms guide action? Isn't the temptation to think of practical matters, including morality, as a matter of being guided by certain norms an illusion, because norms are *never* enough to shape action?

There is some temptation to think that this issue could be avoided if only the important norms were algorithms that provide wholly definite instructions for each context and could *specify exhaustively* what must be done in living up to them. This thought seems to me highly implausible – and particularly implausible for the case of ethically important norms:

> An algorithm is a finite procedure, written in a fixed symbolic vocabulary, governed by precise instructions, moving in discrete steps … whose execution requires no insight, cleverness, intuition, intelligence or perspicuity, and that sooner or later comes to an end.[7]

---

[6] Cf. Richard H. Thaler and Cass R. Sunstein, *Nudge: Improving Decisions about Health, Wealth, and Happiness* (New Haven, CT: Yale University Press, 2008).
[7] David Berlinski, *The Advent of the Algorithm: The Idea that Rules the World* (New York: Harcourt, 2000), p. xviii.

Strictly speaking algorithms are therefore possible only within formal systems, where contexts and moves can be exhaustively specified. We can provide an algorithm for multiplication or for preventing the other player winning at noughts and crosses even if they have the first move. But when we multiply or play noughts and crosses in real life, we need more than algorithms: multiplication can be done 'in one's head' or aloud, or in writing, and the order of the multiplicands can be varied. Noughts and crosses can be played on paper, on a blackboard or on the sand, using varied marks, and various implements to make them, and so on. There are no true algorithms for action.

This may seem surprising. Does not Benthamite Utilitarianism ostensibly aspire to provide an algorithm for morality, supposedly allowing us to calculate which act is optimific? The formal structure of utilitarian reasoning may look algorithmic. The instructions for utilitarian calculation tell us to list all options; to reckon the probable outcomes of each; to calculate and sum the expected utilities of these outcomes for all parties; and finally to maximise. In practice, as we all know, utilitarian calculation cannot even approximate the underlying algorithm: we can specify only selected options; we are often unsure about their probable outcomes; our calculation of expected utility for anyone (let alone everyone) is pretty gestural. Only the maximising looks even close to algorithmic – however, on reflection we see that it too is not wholly tied down and could be done in various ways.

On second and more cheerful thoughts, it may not be important if norms are not algorithmic. For they can at least formulate constraints on or advice for action, and perhaps all that matters is that we choose *some* act that meets the constraints set by or the advice offered by a norm that we are seeking to respect. Yet how are we meant to do this? A standard answer is that it is a matter of judgement. But this is not wholly reassuring. Invoking judgement without explaining how it is to work seems to leave us no clearer about what we need to add to norms if they are to offer practical guidance. Yet perhaps practical reasoning can take us no further.

Writing of theoretical rather than practical judgement, Kant commented that reason could not take us all the way; the same point has repeatedly been made by later writers:

> if one wanted to show generally how one ought to subsume under rules, i.e. distinguish whether something stands under them or not, this could not happen except once again through a rule. But just because this is a rule, it would demand another instruction for the power of judgement, and so it becomes clear that although the understanding is certainly capable of being

instructed and equipped through rules, the power of judgement is a special talent that cannot be taught but only practised. (Kant, *CPR* A133/B172)[8]

Does an analogous problem arise for the case of practical judgement? Or can we say something about how practical judgement is to go beyond norms and select one rather than another enactment of a norm?

Picking and choosing

One minimalist answer to this problem would be that practical judging is no more than a matter of lighting on *some* act that fits the norm under consideration. For example, if we are aiming to live up to a norm of promise-keeping we need only find *some* act that meets the terms of the promise previously made. Any such act will do, and there are no significant differences between the various acts by which a given promise might be kept. Or if we seek to keep to a norm of parsimony, we need only find *some* way of living that is (adequately) parsimonious. And so on.

On such views, practical judging is simply a matter of *picking* some act that satisfies the relevant norm, and it does not matter which of many differing available congruent acts is chosen. A possible problem with this account is illustrated by the predicament of Buridan's ass, who could not find any reason for preferring one over another bundle of equidistant hay. Here, some writers want to say, choosing gives way to mere picking. As my hand hovers over an array of equally accessible tubs of margarine, do I really *choose* one rather than another? Or is this a case of mere picking?[9] This seems an apt enough characterisation of the particular case. There is no reason to think that the choice of one rather than another tub of margarine from a number that are equally accessible, equal in price, and indistinguishable in quality and appearance is more than a matter of picking. It is not a matter of choice because there is (*ex hypothesi*) no basis for choice and so no better reason for choosing one rather than another such tub.

But this example of mere picking is, I think, a limit case which we cannot take as a model for thinking about all cases in which a variety of discernibly different acts would satisfy the constraints set by some norm.

---

[8] Here Kant is writing specifically about *subsumptive* or *determinant* judgement, the form of theoretical judgement that assumes a particular item to which concepts are to be applied. See Chapter 8, below.

[9] See E. Ullmann-Margalit and S. Morgenbesser, 'Picking and Choosing', *Social Research*, 44 (1977), 757–67, for the distinction. They illustrate picking with the case of selecting among tins of soup, rather than tubs of margarine, from a supermarket display. I have stuck with margarine, in deference to Anscombe.

Most choosing is not a matter of mere picking. Indeed, some would argue that Buridan cases are degenerate examples of choosing, precisely for this reason. As Leibniz puts it in *Theodicy*, "In things which are absolutely indifferent there can be no choice because choice must have some reason or principle."[10] Even if we regard mere picking as a limit case of choice, it at least seems plausible that reasoned choice must (at least implicitly) refer to some norm. Moreover, there is often reason to think that the various ways of meeting the claims of a norm are not equivalent, and that some are better than others. So it seems that we are after all not dealing with mere picking, but rather are making some form of reasoned judgement. If so, practical judgement may generally be more than mere picking, and there may be grounds for thinking that, in a given situation with given norms, one judgement may be better or worse than others, and more generally that some persons' judgements may be better or worse than other persons' judgements. This thought returns us to the problem of understanding how practical judgement works.

Practical judgement and multiple norms

Is practical judgement an aspect of practical reasoning, or is it only a pompous term for acts of picking, by which we instantiate an indeterminate norm with some determinate act that fits the norm? If so what is it that we admire in acts and persons that we think of as exhibiting good judgement? What makes one way of instantiating a norm an exercise of good judgement and another an exercise of poor judgement?

Much of the literature on ethical judgement offers astonishingly little help here. Often this is because work that purports to be relevant to ethics and practical judgement is in fact about (one type of) theoretical rather than about practical uses of judgement, and in particular about the distinctive problems that arise for theoretical judgement when it is unclear which concepts or standards should be applied. Kant divided theoretical judgement into determinant and reflective judgement, on the basis that

> If the universal (the rule, principle, or law) is given, then the judgement which subsumes the particular is *determinant* … If, however, only the particular is given and the universal has to be found for it, then the judgement is simply *reflective*. (Kant, *CJ* 5:179)

---

[10] Proposition 1 of Leibniz's 4th letter in R. Ariew (ed.), *G. W. Leibniz and Samuel Clarke: Correspondence* (Indianapolis: Hackett, 2000).

In both cases theoretical judgement presupposes that a particular aspect of the world is there to be judged. Where the judgement is determinant the task is to see whether a certain concept or description applies; where it is reflective the task is to see which of many possible concepts or descriptions is appropriate. Neither is relevant to practical judgement, where the task is not to apply a concept or description to an act (which does not yet exist), but to enact some norm or principle.

A large amount of writing on ethics (some of it Wittgensteinian in flavour) assumes that practical judgement is a form of reflective judgement, and so that it must address some version of the problem of relevant descriptions. For example, Peter Winch, John McDowell, David Wiggins, and at times Bernard Williams, depicted judgement as the crux of the moral life, yet have focused not on practical judgement but on judgement of the context or situation in which action is undertaken. They have often described ethical judgement as a matter of *appreciating* or *appraising* or *attending to* what is *salient* about situations and cases of ethical significance.[11] Yet the analogy between practical judgement and reading texts or appreciating situations is unconvincing. When we act we may as a *preliminary* matter have to decide how to view the situation in which we already find ourselves, and in which we seek to act: here reflective judgement may indeed be needed. But even when reflective judging is completed, and we have determined how to view the situation, we will still need to decide what to do: and that is where practical judgement does its work. A focus on reflective judging will not reveal whether or how practical judging works.

If we think about action that conforms to a single norm there seems to be little that we can say about practical judgement. Any act that meets the relevant norm – that satisfies the standard or constraint it sets – seems to be as good as any other, and there is no room for distinguishing better from worse judgement. In this case we are indeed reduced to picking one of many possible acts that enact a practical principle. However, the thought of seeking to meet the constraints of a single norm is highly artificial. We constantly need to act in ways that meet multiple constraints and standards. In buying margarine I need to fit the purchase to the shopping list,

---

[11] See John McDowell, 'Deliberation and Moral Development', in Stephen Engstrom and Jennifer Whiting (eds.), *Aristotle, Kant and the Stoics* (Cambridge University Press, 1996), 19–35, esp. 23 and 26. This spectator's view of moral judgement has been well entrenched: see David Wiggins, 'Deliberation and Practical Reason', in his *Needs, Values, Truth: Essays in the Philosophy of Value* (Oxford: Blackwell, 1987), 215–37; Bernard Williams, 'Persons, Character and Morality', in his *Moral Luck* (Cambridge University Press, 1981), 1–19.

and to do so without breaching a large range of other norms that are also relevant to shopping. I will probably take care to meet norms of not stealing, not assaulting the shopkeeper, and not offering counterfeit coin; as well as norms of domestic life, such as taking the purchased margarine home, rather than (for example) feeding it to the pigeons or taking it back to the shelf where it was displayed.

Action on multiple norms can be challenging. If I have to break some bad news in a way that is honest, does not undermine the confidence of the person hearing it, and yet is not so shrouded in euphemism that the message does not get across, then the choice of words, tone and way of communicating may begin to present a real challenge. If I have to bring in a building project on time and on budget and to the standards specified in the project documents, a lot will be demanded. Practical judgement, I suggest, is not something different from acting on norms: rather it comes into play *where and because numerous norms have to be simultaneously taken seriously and observed*. Hence practical judgement can indeed be reasoned, because it is norm guided, and norms are apt for reasoning.

If this account of judgement is correct, it follows that in the end there is always a point at which mere picking has to take place. When all steps have been taken to conform to the full range of norms – ethical and other – that an agent sees as relevant, there will still be a range of possible acts that fit all these requirements. Here reason giving has to stop, and here it is not needed. Picking comes into the picture when *but only when* the differences between the possibilities from which the agent selects are indeed a matter of indifference. It is typically 'below the level of reason giving'. We do not need to cite norms or give reasons to pick one rather than the other of two coins of equal value in giving change, or to place one rather than another tub of margarine in one rather another equally suitable position in the shopping basket. Typically many of the aspects of action that fall below the level of attention or of intention are *picked* rather than *chosen* for reasons that are formulable in norms.

In offering this picture of practical judgement as reasoned I have said nothing about the justificatory arguments that might be given in favour of some norms or against others. I have made no assumptions about the quality of arguments that we may be able to offer in favour of specific norms that are important in specific aspects of life, or about the possibility of offering arguments in favour of wholly general, unrestricted norms of ethical importance. My question has been only whether *if* we had such arguments we would still find that norms were impotent to guide action, and I have argued that we would not provided we had reasons to think that a plurality of norms that are apt for reasoning make their demands, but that we could not expect those norms to guide us 'all the way down' to one rather than another particular act.

Some conclusions

Practical judgement, I have argued, is a matter of finding acts (and policies) that meet the constraints of a plurality of norms that specify requirements and recommendations of a variety of types. However, the way that we deploy a plurality of norms is not best thought of as matter of 'balancing' one against another. There is no metric for balancing or trading-off different types of norms, and there are no reasons for thinking that high success in living up to one norm will generally compensate for failure to respect another. Great success in keeping a business afloat will not exactly compensate for handling stolen goods, or failing to supply goods that are fit for purpose; great success in surgery will not compensate for performing the wrong operation on a patient ('I've done a very good tonsillectomy, although I didn't take out your grumbling appendix'). Practical judgement is an aspect of practical reasoning because it aims to integrate rather than to prioritise or trade off a plurality of norms. This task can be done better or less well, and there are good reasons for thinking of some people as having good and others poorer judgement. But even those with the most intelligent and careful capacities for practical judgement will in the end have to pick among possible acts between which there is, as we say, nothing to choose. Provided picking is used only for this unavoidable task and not prematurely where respect for a range of norms has to be integrated, there will be no deficiency in practical judgement.

If follows that practical judgement will be at its most demanding when agents seek to respect multiple norms whose requirements are in tension, or even contingently[12] incompatible. Two strategies may be relevant here. The first is a matter of forward planning and avoidance. We know a lot about the circumstances and actions that are likely to create conflicts between the requirements of different norms, and can try to avoid those situations. Those who make excessive or conflicting undertakings

---

[12] If two norms are *intrinsically* incompatible they cannot both offer reasons for action. The defect then lies in claims that both are justified, and is not resolvable by practical judgement aimed at their enactment.

(bigamists, fraudsters) will not be able to honour all their commitments. Those who impose excessive or incompatible demands on others are likely to face them with impossible demands, which no exercise of practical judgement can integrate (the worst excesses of the target culture). By contrast, foresight, care and good institutional structures can do a fair amount to avert such problems, by forestalling, reducing and averting contingent conflicts between principles, so easing the tasks of practical judgement.[13]

But individual foresight and social reform have their limits. Often there is no way of acting that satisfies all the norms that an agent would wish to respect, and nothing that could have been foreseen or done to avert the potential for conflict. The most extreme examples are 'dirty hands' problems, where institutions, practices and prior action make it hard or impossible for those who have to act to meet all the norms to which they are committed. Even when nothing is so deeply awry, we may often find that the background of institutions and practices, of habits and customs, of virtues and failings, of skills and incompetence, of capabilities and vulnerabilities within which action is performed, may all hinder attempts to live up to multiple principles. In making practical judgements it is often pointless, indeed misleading, to assume these realities away. It may be true that had institutions and practices been better, or had agents made better decisions in the past or been more competent, less conflict would have arisen. But in the world as it is, agents may be unable to avoid a degree of failure, including moral failure, because no amount of thoughtful practical judgement enables them to integrate and live up to all the norms to which they are committed in the situations that actually arise.

Where realities force hard choices it may simply be impossible for agents to respect all the norms that they seek to respect. The most that they can then do is to recognise the claims of unmet, contingently unmeetable, requirements and recommendations. But the fact that a norm proves contingently unmeetable in some situations will not wholly cancel its claims. Unmeetable norms may leave 'remainders' that call for attitudinal responses such as expressions of regret or remorse, or for more active responses such as apologies, commitments to reform, to compensation,

---

[13] Cf. Ruth Barcan Marcus's comment: "we ought to conduct our lives and arrange our institutions so as to minimise predicaments of moral conflict", 'Moral Dilemmas and Consistency', *Journal of Philosophy*, 77 (1980), 121–36, at 121.

restitution and other forms of making good.[14] The importance of active foresight and institution building and of an active approach to dealing with remainders in the wake of practical conflict between norms does not show that norms are redundant or useless. It shows that living up to them can be hard and demanding. Taking norms seriously is a matter of working towards practical judgement, expressed in action that seeks to enact requirements and standards and to make good where failure has not been avoided.

[14] Cf. B. Herman, 'Performance and Obligation', in her *The Practice of Moral Judgment* (Cambridge, MA: Harvard University Press, 1993), 159–83.

CHAPTER 6

Instituting principles: between duty and action[1]

Much discussion of the practicality – or conversely of the formalism – of Kant's ethics has concentrated on the capacity of the Categorical Imperative to discriminate principles of duty from other practical principles. Yet even supposing that principles of duty can be identified, they will still not fully answer the question 'What ought I do?' Any principle can be enacted or embodied or instituted in many different ways, among which agents have to choose.

Kant makes this point emphatically in the *Metaphysics of Morals* for the case of duties of virtue. A typical claim in the second part of this work, titled *The Doctrine of Virtue*, runs as follows:

> if the law can prescribe only the maxim of actions, not actions themselves, this is a sign that it leaves playroom (*latitudo*) for free choice in following (complying with) the law, that is, that the law cannot specify precisely in what way one is to act and how much one is to do by the action for an end that is also a duty. (Kant, *MM* 6:390)[2]

Seemingly the situation is easier in the case of duties of right, for the immediately preceding section is explicitly titled in capitals: ETHICS DOES NOT GIVE LAWS FOR ACTIONS (*IUS* DOES THAT), BUT ONLY FOR THE MAXIMS OF ACTIONS (Kant, *MM* 6:388). So we apparently have two cases: in *ius* (right) the law prescribes actions; in ethics the law prescribes maxims of ends, which can be expressed by various

---

[1] 'Instituting Principles: Between Duty and Action', in Mark Timmons (ed.), *Kant's Metaphysics of Morals: Interpretative Essays* (Oxford University Press, 2002), 331–47. Wherever possible citations have been revised to use the Cambridge translations of Kant's works. Quotations and references to Kant's works are parenthetic, using the conventions set out in the bibliographical note. Parenthetic letters after references to the *Lectures on Ethics* (*C, V, M*) identify that a passage occurs in the notes by Collins, Vigilantius, Mrongovius.

[2] There are numerous more specific versions of the same claim: "there is no law of reason [for cultivating one's own perfection] for action but only a law for maxims of actions" (*MM* 6:392); "The law [of beneficence] holds only for maxims, not for determinate actions" (*MM* 6:393); "ethical obligation to ends … involves only a law for *maxims* of actions" (*MM* 6:395).

sorts of action. However, the distinction is more complex, and not clarified
by the fact that our understanding of the division between ethics and right
has changed since antiquity.[3]

However, the similarity between the two cases is more significant than
this difference. In each case the law prescribes only a type or pattern of
action, in short a principle, law or rule (which can be incorporated into an
agent's maxims at or through some time): and principles of all sorts are
indeterminate. However, conformity to or neglect of principles of duty is
ultimately a matter of doing or refraining from particular, determinate
acts, and in the case of duties of virtue particular patterns of action. The
difference between the cases lies in the type of principle at stake: principles
of right prescribe *types* of act; principles of virtue prescribe *types* of end.
Neither sort of principle can be used to pick out an act-token or a particular
way of realising an end.

The conventional response to this gap is to point out that Kant holds
that it must always be a matter for judgement by particular agents just how
they will conform to a particular principle, or just how they will pursue a
particular end. An account of principles of duty is not *supposed* to tell one
exactly what to do or how to pursue an end. It is meant simply to show
what type of action should be done, what type of ends should be pursued.
One must look to accounts of judgement for a view of the way in which the
gap between principle and particular act, or pattern of action, is to be
bridged.

Surprisingly, many discussions of ethical judgement are wholly unhelpful in showing how the gap between principle and act is to be bridged: and
say nothing at all about practical judgement. Many broadly anti-Kantian
writers of the last forty years including Peter Winch, John McDowell,
David Wiggins, and at times Bernard Williams, have seen judgement as the
crux of the moral life, yet have focused not on practical judgement but on
judgement of the context or situation in which action is undertaken. They
have tended to see ethical judgement as a matter of *appreciating* or *appraising* or *attending to* what is *salient* about situations and cases of ethical
significance. This focus is often linked to certain types of Wittgensteinian
and Aristotelian views, and emphasises the ethical importance of perception and sensitivity to particular situations. A typical formulation was
offered by McDowell, when he characterised judgement or deliberation

---

[3] Kant comments on the changed meaning of the term *ethics*. In antiquity it covered both duties of
right (including justice) and duties that are not a matter of right (duties to self; duties of virtue);
modern usage contrasts *ius* and *ethica*, duties of right and duties of virtue, *and often classifies only the
latter as ethics* (*MM* 6:379).

as "a capacity to read the details of situations" or a "capacity to read the details of situations in the light of a way of valuing actions" or a "capacity to read predicaments correctly".[4]

Accounts of judgement as sensitivity to circumstances or cases are accounts of a type of *theoretical* judgement. This can be seen in two ways. First, such judgements are essentially third personal: appraisals or readings of a situation are as open to spectators as they are to agents. It is a common literary device to ascribe good judgement of situations not to protagonists but to bystanders – the chorus, the confidant, the faithful friend. The onlooker may even be the first to realise that what is going on in the playground is not play but serious bullying, or that what is going on at a party is not idle chatter but flirtation that is turning to infidelity, or gossip that is turning into slander.

Second, this type of judgement focuses on a *particular situation that is already present to be judged*. By contrast practical judgement is agents' judgement deployed in producing or shaping a particular act or pattern of action that is yet to be done. Practical judgement cannot presuppose that the particular act that is to be done is there to be judged.[5]

The appraisal of situations, and of their details, is of course of great ethical importance – if we do not notice the bullying we cannot consider whether to desist (or, if spectators, to intervene); if we do not notice that flirtation is turning to infidelity, or gossip to slander, we can hardly consider whether to desist (or, if spectators, to deflect the conversation, to turn away or to encourage it). But noticing and appraising a situation is not practical judgement: having noticed the bullying we still need to decide whether to desist or to intervene, and if so to judge which approach will be most likely to work rather than to worsen the victim's lot; having noticed

---

[4] See John McDowell, 'Deliberation and Moral Development', in Stephen Engstrom and Jennifer Whiting (eds.), *Aristotle, Kant and the Stoics* (Cambridge University Press, 1996), 19–35, esp. 23 and 26. See also David Wiggins, 'Deliberation and Practical Reason', in his *Needs, Values, Truth: Essays in the Philosophy of Value* (Oxford: Blackwell, 1987), 215–37; Bernard Williams, 'Persons, Character and Morality', in his *Moral Luck* (Cambridge University Press, 1981), 1–19. This emphasis on judgement of ethically significant situations is not unique to writers who are opposed to principles and to theory. For example, Barbara Herman states in her powerful papers on Kant's ethics that "the rules of moral salience constitute the structure of moral sensitivity" and that they "guide the normal moral agent to the perception and description of the morally relevant features of his circumstances", Barbara Herman, 'The Practice of Moral Judgment', in her *The Practice of Moral Judgment* (Cambridge, MA: Harvard University Press, 1993), 73–93, esp. 78; see also her 'Making Room for Character', in *Aristotle, Kant and the Stoics*, 36–60.

[5] Could not this sort of judgement be applied to merely envisaged or imagined possibilities or options? The difficulty is that what we conceive or imagine cannot be fully determinate: a response to or reading of an abstract possibility cannot fully guide action.

the incipient infidelity or slander there is still the practical question whether to try to check it.[6]

Indeterminacy in theoretical and practical judgement

These considerations show, I believe, that awareness of indeterminacy and a gesture towards the ethical significance of judgement cannot by themselves tell us much, or at any rate not enough, about practical judgement. The problem is not simply that the moral law, and maxims of duty, and especially those of duties of virtue, are 'too indeterminate'. Kant notes the indeterminacy of concepts and of principles in many contexts, and classically in the Schematism of the *First Critique*, where he points out that general logic can contain no complete rules for judgement

> because if it sought to give general instructions how we are to subsume under these rules that could only be by means of another rule. This in turn for the very reason that it is a rule, again demands guidance from judgement. (*CPR* A133/B172)

But this general point about indeterminacy is common to all judgement. In practical as in theoretical judgement agents deal with concepts and principles that are inevitably indeterminate. (This is not to say that they will be *empty*, as certain commentators have thought in their more enthusiastically anti-theoretical moments: concepts, descriptions, rules, maxims and principles are simply and unavoidably *indeterminate*.)

To get beyond this general point we need to take account of the fact that indeterminacy raises quite different problems for theoretical and for practical judgement. In theoretical judgement the particular is given, and *the principle or rule may or may not be given*. Kant divides theoretical judgements into *determinant* and *reflective* judgements:

> If the universal (the rule, the principle, the law) is given, then the power of judgement which subsumes the particular under it … *is* **determining** [**determinant** in other translations] … If, however, only the particular is given and the universal has to be found for it, then the judgement is simply **reflecting** [**reflective** in other translations]. (*CJ* 5:179)

Theoretical judgement *of both sorts* begins with some particular situation or action, and asks either whether a certain description or principle applies (the case of determinant judgement) or which of many possible

---

[6] See Onora O'Neill, 'The Power of Example', in *Constructions of Reason: Explorations of Kant's Practical Philosophy* (Cambridge University Press, 1989), 165–86, and Chapter 8, below.

descriptions, and indirectly which of many possible principles, is appropriate (the case of reflective judgement). This direction of thought – from particular to description or principle – is assumed in the accounts of ethically significant judgement favoured by McDowell and Wiggins and many others. Their concern is with what Kant calls reflective judging, where the appropriate description or principle is not given antecedently, so has to be sought or found. Their focus on the difficulties of reflective judging underpins their scepticism about the relevance of moral principles, and supports their scepticism about obligations. Reflective judging is no doubt important if we are to think and act discerningly: but it is not the same as practical judgement.[7]

In practical judgement the problems created by the indeterminacy of principles are quite different, and in some ways deeper, because *a particular which is to exemplify the principle, description, rule, law (or maxim) does not (yet) exist* (and may never come to exist). The problem which Kant raises in the sentence quoted at the start of this chapter, and in many other passages, is that of an agent who has some maxim(s), whose content is some principle(s) with component act description(s), and aims to act – not that of someone who has an act, so to speak, and strives to find whether a given description applies, or to find the 'right' or appropriate description and so the appropriate principle which should be adopted as a maxim. The agent's stance is practical, or prescriptive.[8] The practical problem for such an agent is not that of finding (one of many) descriptions or principles that apply (to what?) and incorporating them into a maxim, but that of moving from (one or more) principles which have been incorporated into some maxim(s) towards action.[9] Acts have to be produced, or instituted, or enacted by the agent. Here it does not even make sense to speak of the task of judgement as that of 'subsumption under principles' or 'application of principles', or even as that of finding the relevant (salient) description or principle: all of these notions presuppose that a particular is given. The practical task is different: it is to satisfy or contribute to satisfying a maxim, and thereby the principle(s) that maxim incorporates.

---

[7] Kant discusses the principles on which reflective judgement proceeds in many passages on interpretation; see in particular his discussion of *purposiveness* as a principle of interpretation at *CJ* 5:181–6.

[8] For an account of Kant's maxims as *prescriptions* rather than as objects of *introspection* or of *ascription* see Onora O'Neill, 'Kant's Virtues', in Roger Crisp (ed.), *How Should One Live? Essays on the Virtues* (Oxford: Clarendon Press, 1996), 77–97, esp. 92–7.

[9] We do not 'have' a particular act – an act-token – until the deed is done or not done: and then the practical problem is over. Kant sometimes speaks of a particular act already performed as a deed (*Tat*), at other times as that which has been done (*factum*), *MM* 6:227; 6:230, note k; 6:371, note u; his term for an act-type is *Handlung*.

The distinctive task of practical judgement is not confined to ethically significant practical judgements. I may have decided to do something which I take to be merely and obviously permissible, and do not think of as raising any significant ethical questions – to buy the groceries on Tuesday, not Wednesday; to make a cake; to find out about politics in Morocco – but each decision leaves open many different possible actions and patterns of action. The most mundane decisions, like the most morally significant maxims, are adopted before an act is done or adhered to in acting: in either case they underdetermine action, in that they specify act-types or end-types; but what is done will be an act-token, or a pattern of action. If an act or pattern of action is to achieve what I set myself to do, I must select act-tokens or patterns of action that satisfy the principle or decision. Seemingly a principle can offer no complete guidance about choosing one rather than another of the many act-tokens or patterns of action by which it might be satisfied. Neither highly abstract nor relatively specific principles can "specify precisely in what way one is to act and how much one is to do" (*MM* 6:390). Neither determinant nor reflective judgement can help here, for both of these are forms of theoretical judgement, usable only where particulars are available to be judged.

How, one may ask, has so much writing in ethics come to concentrate on a form of theoretical judgement, rather than on practical judgement? Is it due to a problematic view of ethics as a spectator sport, or (more elegantly) as a matter of moral connoisseurship? Or does it perhaps derive from the false assumption that all ethical judgement is retrospective judgement of deeds already done? The theoretical focus can seem appropriate if one imagines that all ethical judgement aims to assess what has already been done (one's own acts or another's), for then the particular is already given, and the need may be to pass retrospective judgement on it.

Kant does not overlook the role of retrospective, theoretical judging of acts already done. One sort of retrospective judgement which he often discusses is that of a judge passing judgement on a case; another is that of agents retrospectively passing judgement on their own deeds and misdeeds: an activity of conscience. Kant discusses this retrospective conception of conscience in many passages in his writings on ethics, often using judicial metaphors to emphasise the parallel. In the *Lectures on Ethics* he is reported as speaking of conscience as "a faculty of judging ourselves according to moral laws" (Kant, *LE* (*V*) 27:351); in *The Critique of Practical Reason*, he speaks of "the judicial sentences of that wonderful capacity in us which we call conscience" (*CPrR* 5:98); in the *Metaphysics of Morals* the juridical metaphors, and with them the retrospective perspective of the agent accused and beset by a guilty conscience, are once again predominant.[10]

Even this retrospective use of theoretical judgement to assess deeds already done (that is, where the particular is given) is demanding. Kant uses examples of retrospective, determinant judgement (the simple case!) in the Schematism passage where he points out that it is not enough to have good (practical) principles. He notes that

> A physician therefore, a judge, or a statesman can have many very fine pathological, juridical, or political rules in his head, of which he can even be a thorough teacher, and yet can easily stumble in their application either because he is lacking in natural power of judgement (though not it under- standing), and to be sure understands the universal *in abstracto* but cannot distinguish whether a case *in concreto* belongs under it, or also because he has not received adequate training for this judgement through examples and actual business. (Kant, *CPR* A134/B173)

The problem here is evidently not that the task of judgement is practical in the sense of guiding action: Kant is imagining that both rule and particular are given, and that the task is that of determinant judgement.[11] He thinks of the judge not merely as having certain 'excellent rules' but as having a case to judge, of the physician as having both excellent rules and a patient (it is less clear what the ruler is judging). In these examples the task of judgement is clearly theoretical, although it may be followed by a task that needs practical judgement.[12] Once the judge has reached a guilty verdict, sentencing may follow; once the physician has a diagnosis, treatment may be prescribed. The quandary attributed to the inadequate judge or physi- cian, for whom the retrospective and theoretical task of determinant judgement of cases proves defeating, is due to their lack of that "peculiar talent which can be practiced only, and cannot be taught … [whose] … lack no school can make good" (Kant, *CPR* A133/B172). But the

---

[10] This conception of conscience as retrospective is predominant but not invariable in Kant's writings, and there are some passages in which he writes of conscience as active where nothing has yet been done. For example, "the human being thinks of conscience as *warning* him (*praemonens*) before he makes his decision" (*MM* 6:440).

[11] This use of determinant judgement can make ethical judgements about what has been done, but because it is not apt for practical judgement cannot be used to shape action ethically. See for example "We have a faculty of judging whether a thing is right or wrong, and this applies no less to our actions than to those of others. This faculty resides in the understanding" (Kant, *LE* (*V*), 27:297).

[12] Kant's picture of the theoretical aspect of judicial and medical judgement may of course oversimplify.

Schematism has *nothing* to say about the quite different task of practical judgement.

Does Kant need an account of practical judgement?

Let us return to practical judgement. One quite appealing thought about practical judgement might be that we don't need any account of it because it does not matter which of the many actions that exemplify a maxim of duty is done. Suppose that we have a duty not to deceive: will not any non-deceiving action fulfil the requirement? Or suppose that we think that it is a duty not to be indifferent to others: will not any way of living that adequately expresses a maxim of rejecting indifference fulfil the requirement? Seen in this way the *latitudo* of maxims of virtue, is just that they leave things open: any act or pattern of action which satisfies the maxim is as good as any other. Equally the indeterminacy of maxims of right is simply a lesser form of latitude which is indifferent as between any act-tokens of the required type. There are countless ways of satisfying any maxim adopted, and we should not get bothered about the lack of an account of how to judge between ways of living virtuously or acting rightly. However, this does not seem to be quite what Kant has in mind.

Immediately after his characterisation of the latitude of wide duties Kant remarks that this should not be understood as

> permission to make exceptions to the maxim of actions but only as permission to limit one maxim of duty by another (e.g. love of one's neighbour in general by love of one's parents), by which in fact the field for the practice of virtue is widened. (*MM* 6:390)

It is clear enough that the issue is not one of making exceptions, yet the idea of limiting one maxim of duty by another does not look likely to help clarify the activity of practical judgement. How can the fact that we adopt and are bound by a plurality of maxims of duty help, as opposed to complicate, practical judgement?

The thought that conflicts of obligations constitute a *reductio ad absurdum* of any ethic of rights or obligation, of the very notion of moral requirement, has been widely canvassed in writing on ethics (quite often by writers who assimilate ethical judgement to reflective judging). More pointedly, are not close relatives of the two maxims of duty that Kant cites, those of civic and of familial duty, a canonical instance of a moral dilemma that has been discussed by countless writers from Cicero to Sartre? How can such examples be expected to help us understand how we are to limit one maxim by another? More ominously, isn't the problem of moral dilemmas or conflicts between duties one of the notorious quagmires in Kant interpretation?[13]

It seems to me that, on the contrary, the remark about 'limiting one maxim by another' may shed useful light on Kant's conception of practical judgement. On Kant's account the Categorical Imperative identifies a number of principles of duty, *each* of which is relevant in *many* contexts. A plurality of principles of obligation is and a plurality of maxims (or a single complex maxim) should be the *invariable* context of dutiful action. Practical judgement is *always* a matter of finding a way of achieving a range of aims and objectives while satisfying a plurality of principles of duty, and of doing so while taking account of the varied realities and vulnerabilities of human life.

Practical judgement and moral conflict

So if an adequate account of practical judgement is to be found, it is important to consider how acting under multiple requirements, with the possibility that they will lead to ethical conflict, can be approached. The short passage in the *Metaphysics of Morals* in which Kant writes about moral conflict has been much discussed, and I apologise for returning to it. I have divided it into two parts so as to consider its two claims in turn.

Both in the German and in the liberally interpolated Latin in this paragraph Kant introduces distinctions that are not easy to grasp. The passage begins:

> A *conflict of duties* (*collisio officiorum s. obligationum*) would be a relation between them in which one of them would cancel the other (wholly or in part). But since duty and obligation are concepts that express the objective practical *necessity* of certain actions and two rules opposed to each other cannot be necessary at the same time, if it is a duty to act in accordance with one rule, to act in accordance with the opposite rule is not a duty but even contrary to duty; so a *collision of duties* and obligations is inconceivable (*obligationes non colliduntur*). (Kant, MM 6:224)

This part of the passage, up to the claim that a collision of duties is inconceivable, is not (I think) hard to interpret. For it does not say that

---

[13] And does not Kant immediately make the problem worse by reminding us that "a human being cannot see into the depths of his own heart" (*MM* 6:392), so suggesting that a requirement to enact a plurality of maxims may be stymied not only by the indeterminacy of the maxims, but by agents' uncertainty about their own maxims?

there can be no moral conflict. It makes a modal claim about principles: 'two rules opposed to each other cannot be necessary at the same time'. There cannot, for example, be pairs of rules requiring that people be open in all dealings and wholly secretive in all dealings, or rules commanding both honesty and deceitfulness, both beneficence and indifference. The first part of the passage simply proposes a *consistency constraint on principles of obligation* (that is on *rationes obligationum* or *rationes obligantes*): it insists that there cannot be incompatible principles (*rationes*) of obligation, that is principles of obligation which could not hold 'at the same time', so could never be jointly satisfied. This point has been widely accepted in writing on duty and obligation[14] as a welcome constraint on any theory of ethical (or other) requirements. However, the first section of the passage does not assert that there cannot be moral conflicts or dilemmas, or that aspects of an agent's maxim cannot be incompatible: it says nothing about maxims.

In some, indeed in many, cases Kant's fundamental principles of obligation clearly can be jointly instantiated 'at the same time'. So they are at least compatible in this rather weak sense: they are not *intrinsically incompatible*. His view may be not simply that these principles are compatible, that is jointly satisfiable in *some* circumstances, but more strongly that they are *intrinsically compatible*, in that there are no circumstances in which they are not jointly satisfiable. The basic principle of all duties of right is simply "so act externally that the free use of your choice can coexist with the freedom of everyone according to a universal law" (*MM* 6:231). Arguably the universal law demanding respect for external freedom is that of non-interference, and dutiful non-interferers will find that their multiple conformities to the fundamental principle of right cannot conflict in *any* circumstances. The fundamental principle of negative perfect duties, such as those of refraining from suicide and refraining from promising falsely, also cannot come into conflict. Conflict can arise only when one or more duty demands positive action.

The underlying principles of duties of virtue, by contrast, often require positive action, but since they are principles of *imperfect* duty, they do not

[14] Ruth Barcan Marcus, 'Moral Dilemmas and Consistency', *Journal of Philosophy*, 77 (1980), 121–36; Barbara Herman, 'Performance and Obligation', in her *The Practice of Moral Judgment*, 159–83; T. E. Hill Jr., 'Moral Dilemmas, Gaps and Residues: A Kantian Perspective', in H. E. Mason (ed.), *Moral Dilemmas and Moral Theory* (Oxford University Press, 1996), 167–98; Onora O'Neill, 'Duty and Virtues', in A. Phillips Griffiths (ed.), *Ethics* (RIP supplementary volume 35) (Cambridge University Press, 1993), 107–120, esp. 115–18; Onora O'Neill, 'Principles, Institutions and Judgement', in John Tasioulas (ed.), *Law, Value and Social Practices* (Aldershot: Dartmouth, 1997), 59–73; Onora O'Neill, *Towards Justice and Virtue: A Constructive Account of Practical Reasoning* (Cambridge University Press, 1996).

have to be fulfilled on every occasion. If there is difficulty or impossibility in being beneficent on one occasion, action may legitimately be postponed until opportunity arises. The principles of virtue can therefore both be *intrinsically consistent* with one another and *intrinsically consistent* with the non-interference required by the fundamental principle of right.

However, problems can arise if we have a particularly urgent case of imperfect duty requiring present action that would breach some perfect duty: this case troubles Kant and is the theme of *On a Supposed Right to Lie from Benevolent Motives*[15] (Kant, *SRL* 8:425–430), while at some points he suggests that a simple priority rule such as 'observance of perfect duty always trumps observance of imperfect duty' is needed. Such a rule would achieve intrinsic consistency among all fundamental principles of obligation, at least for a very wide range. Even without it, Kant's principles of duty are not intrinsically inconsistent, in that they are jointly satisfiable in some (indeed in many) situations.

By contrast, multiple principles of *perfect* obligation which required *positive action* might not only be contingently incompatible (incapable of joint satisfaction in some situations), but intrinsically incompatible (incapable of joint satisfaction in any situation), or in constant tension (incapable of joint satisfaction in most situations). However, Kant's principles of right and of virtue look as if they should be not merely compatible, but intrinsically compatible.

All this, however, tells one little enough. Even if Kant's fundamental universal principles of obligation cannot conflict, this does not show that we will not experience moral conflict. Many human duties are special duties arising from the specific circumstances and institutions with which we live, the particular roles and responsibilities we have assumed, the attachments and relationships we have nurtured. We are always faced not only by the abstract principles of universal duty, but by webs of special duties which should (but may not) be aligned with these fundamental principles, and which link us in complex ways to others. The *Metaphysics of Morals* develops systems of requirement from the fundamental principles of duty, but it offers no guarantee that all the component duties of a system of right or of a doctrine of virtue will be compatible in all situations. Our special duties may include obligations to obey the law, obligations to keep promises and contracts made, obligations to support dependants. There is

---

[15] The Cambridge translation has changed the title of *On a Supposed Right to Lie from Philanthropy*, which can mislead because the contemporary meaning of *philanthropy* is narrower than Kant's term *Menschenliebe*.

little doubt that these special obligations can turn out not to be jointly satisfiable 'at the same time'. Moreover, since some special duties *require* performance 'at the same time', the 'imperfection' which renders fundamental principles of virtue consistent with one another (and with principles of right) cannot guarantee that all duties will be consistent. Our maxims will constantly incorporate reference to special duties, which can be in conflict. Which brings us back to the second part of Kant's comments on moral conflict.

> However, a subject may have in a rule which he prescribes to himself, two *grounds* of obligation (*rationes obligandi*), one or other of which is not sufficient to put him under obligation (*rationes obligandi non obligantes*), so that one of them is not a duty. When two such grounds of obligations conflict with each other, practical philosophy says, not that the stronger obligation takes precedence (*fortior obligatio vincit*) but that the stronger *ground of obligation prevails* (*fortior obligandi ratio vincit*). (*MM* 6:224)[16]

The difficult part of this passage lies in the obscure notion of *rationes obligandi* (in the singular *ratio obligandi*). This phrase is standardly translated 'ground of obligation' following the etymology but I think losing the sense of the German word *Verpflichtungsgrund*. This standard rendering makes the *rationes obligandi* appear even grander and more abstract than the *rationes obligantes*. However, I do not think it is a convincing translation, for several reasons. First, it simply loses the linguistic parallels Kant offers between differing *rationes* (reasons, principles) (or in the passage from the *Critique of Practical Reason*, *CPrR* 5:159, between differing *leges*). Secondly, the reading loses sight of the fact that the *rationes obligandi* are described as features not of laws or principles of obligation in the abstract, but of 'the rule a subject prescribes for himself', that is of a maxim. Since the *rationes obligandi* are elements of maxims, they are particular to situations and occasions. But what are they?

Let me at least offer a translation, which I think is truer to the text. I would render *rationes obligandi* as *obligating reasons*, which preserves the linguistic parallels of the text, takes on board the point that the gerundive is

---

[16] There are also brief but useful discussions of moral conflict in the *Lectures on Ethics*, and in the *Doctrine of Method* of the *Critique of Practical Reason*. One passage in the latter runs "… the method [of moral instruction] takes the following course. *At first* it is only a question of making appraisal of actions by moral laws a natural occupation and, as it were, a habit accompanying all our free actions as well as our observation of those of others, and of sharpening it by asking first whether the action objectively *conforms with the moral law*, and with which law; by this, attention to such law as provides a *ground of obligation* is distinguished from that which is in fact *obligatory* (*leges obligandi a legibus obligantibus*)" (*CPrR* 5:159).

often used for a more specific modal demand (*obligating reasons* can be those of a particular agent in a particular context; *principles of obligation* cannot), and so brings out the agent-related character of these reasons. All of this fits with Kant's insistence that these reasons are internal to "a rule which he [a subject] prescribes to himself", that is internal to maxims.

But what makes *rationes obligandi* reasons? It is simply, I think, that these are the various aspects of a maxim which incorporate or specify either *rationes obligationum*, that is to say fundamental reasons or principles of obligation, or special duties that have been acquired by an agent. Kant does not deny that agents can find themselves seeking to meet ethical demands that may (contingently) conflict. His claim in the disputed passage is only that this is due not to any intrinsic conflict between fundamental principles of duty, but to contingent conflict in a particular case between the many *rationes obligandi* an agent incorporates or has reason to incorporate into a maxim.[17]

Let us now return to the idea that practical judgement involves 'limiting one maxim by another'. How can this task make sense if maxims can incorporate multiple *rationes obligandi*? We can begin with the easy case, without difficult conflict. However, the task of practical judgement can be helped rather than stymied by this plurality of demands. For practical judgement is the task of finding some particular act or pattern of action that meets the requirements. This task is more clearly specified if it is a matter of finding some way of acting that meets a plurality of requirements. So in asking what I should do, I find that my task is to find a way of avoiding injury which does not involve lying, a way of living beneficently which does not involve self-abasement, a way of refraining from theft which does not require indifference to others. And so on. In most cases *guidance is provided by the task of limiting one maxim by another*: we identify acceptable forms of beneficence by ruling out beneficence that relies on theft, or on deception, or on doing violence to others and so on; we identify acceptable ways of avoiding deception if we rule out as beneath consideration or unacceptable those that injure, are cruel, involve self-abasement and so on. With good fortune we can manage much of our lives pursuing quite varied plans and goals, without injuring or perjuring or lying or stealing, and also without indifference or self-stultification or self-

---

[17] I am therefore unpersuaded by Barbara Herman's suggestion that the *rationes obligandi* are "*facts* of a certain sort [that] have moral significance because they are defining features of our (human) rational natures that limit what we can rationally will", although I agree with her conclusion that moral conflict is "*in the agent*, in her maxim of action". See her 'Obligation and Performance', in *The Practice of Moral Judgment*, 169.

abasement. In each context of action, duty – as well as self-interest – makes multiple demands, *but this is generally useful rather than damaging in working out how to shape action and lives.*

Two analogies may be helpful here. The first is mathematical. Just as certain equations can be solved only if we know a sufficient number of constraints, so certain questions about how we ought to act are more readily and better resolvable if we take account of the constraints of multiple principles of obligation. But a more helpful analogy may be that of the equally practical judgement of the designer or craftsman or poet, who has to discover or find *some* way of making that meets *multiple* demands. Imagine that you have to design a wheelbarrow. It has to roll smoothly, to be light enough even for feeble gardeners, to be durable enough for rough use, to be made of available and affordable materials. A clay wheelbarrow won't do; nor will one made of lead. The multiplicity of demands is not a demonstration that there can be no satisfactory wheelbarrows, but it constrains and thereby shapes the activities of those who make wheelbarrows. So with the ethical constraints which action faces: the task of practical judgement about what we ought to do is to find some act which satisfies multiple *rationes obligandi.*

Conflict and casuistry

Of course, not every equation has a solution, and not every design problem can be solved. Equally, practical judging cannot always find a way of meeting all moral demands. Agents will sometimes find no act or pattern of action can fully satisfy all the *rationes obligandi* which they accept and seek to incorporate into their maxim. (Nor, of course, can we always find ways of attaining, or even pursuing, all our projects or desires.)

It is reasonably clear that Kant accepts this point. The most prominent evidence lies, I think, in his multiple discussions of 'casuistical questions' in the *Metaphysics of Morals* and throughout the *Lectures on Ethics.* There is also suggestive evidence in his numerous allusions to the problem of right action in the face of tyranny that are scattered in many different texts.

Kant often comments on casuistry with conventional hostility, labelling it both Jesuitical and hair-splitting.[18] However, many of his examples of

---

[18] In the *Lectures on Ethics* see for example: *LE (C)* 27:356 which depicts casuistry as dealing with small scruples and as concern about trivialities; *LE (M)* 29:615 which depicts casuistry as a 'micrology' and as done by Jesuits and remarks that "It is so called because it has to do with specific and particular cases"; *LE (V)* 27:557 which once again depicts casuistry as dealing with trifles, but notes that sometimes small failings lead to large ones: a child with a habit of hitting may become a murderer.

casuistical questions are by no means hair-splitting or trivial. They are examples of important moral dilemmas which can arise in particular cases. They include the following: Is killing oneself to save one's country or to help mankind suicide or heroism? (*MM* 6:424) Is conventional politeness a form of lying? (*MM* 6:431) Is miserliness mistaken thrift or slavish subjection of oneself to material goods? (*MM* 6:434) Can self-respect and proper pride become arrogance? (*MM* 6:437) Is paternalism by the powerful beneficence, or violation of others' freedom? (*MM* 6:454) How much of our resources should we use "in practicing beneficence"? (*MM* 6:454) Might the world be better with full compliance with the requirements of justice but no social virtues? (*MM* 6:458) Questions like these, with appropriate switches in vocabulary, have raised burning issues generation after generation.[19]

What does Kant think that we should do when we cannot find a way of satisfying multiple *rationes obligandi* such as those invoked in the casuistical questions? If he has no answer, will not his account of dutiful action fail us where we most need help, in the hard cases? Kant certainly does not provide any step-by-step let alone algorithmic method for answering the casuistical questions (presumably his hostility to 'Jesuitical' casuistry is because he thinks it aspires to such methods). He comments in the *Doctrine of Method* of the *Metaphysics of Morals* that taken properly casuistry is not a *doctrine but* a *practice*:

> *Casuistry* is … neither a *science* nor a part of a science … not so much a doctrine about how *to find* something as rather a practice in how *to seek* truth. So it is *woven into ethics* in a *fragmentary way* … and is added to ethics only by way of a scholia to the system … (*MM* 6:411)

Clearly we should not expect to be offered an algorithm or even a recipe for practical judgement that could resolve moral conflict.[20] However, as with mathematics and design, the lack of a comprehensive method for resolving all problems does not cast question on the entire field of endeavour. Here too progress may be possible: if we can identify some of the sources of

---

Nevertheless Kant sometimes hankers for a complete system of casuistry, for example at *LE* (*V*) 27:619, and always regards it as educationally useful; see for example the *Doctrine of Method* of *MM* and *LE* (*V*) 27:702.

[19] Some of the lists of casuistical questions trail off into trivia – and sometimes Kant comments wryly on the point; but all the lists begin with significant conflicts.

[20] The aspiration to algorithms is strictly speaking inappropriate outside formal systems: the indeterminacy of concepts and principles precludes true practical algorithms. Indeed, we should probably not expect to find even 'quasi-algorithms', except for very minor aspects of action such as doing multiplication or putting the right postage stamps on letters.

contingent incompatibility between principles we may be able to reduce them.

If I have only stone-age technology to hand, I will fail to produce a wheelbarrow. If I have only nineteenth-century technology I will fail in my attempt to design a television. Equally, if the institutions that are to hand are unjust in deep ways, or there has been prior wrongdoing, whether another's or my own, then it is more likely that I may find that the *rationes obligandi* which I accept or believe that I ought to accept cannot all be satisfied in some cases. Unjust institutions and prior wrongdoing can make moral conflict common and recalcitrant.

At this stage a very few illustrations must suffice. One that surfaces again and again in Kant's writing is the conflict between the (special) duty to obey rulers (*MM* 6:320) and the terrible deeds they may demand. A less political version of the problem arises when powerful wrongdoers demand that one join them. We are asked to consider the predicament of

> an honest man whom somebody wants to induce to join the calumniators of an innocent but otherwise powerless person (say, Anne Boleyn, accused by Henry VIII of England) (*CPrR* 5:155; cf. 5:158–9)

or of someone of whom a would-be murderer demands information about his intended victim's whereabouts (*SRL* 8:425–30). We are also often asked to consider the implications of promising falsely and thereby entering into special duties which may prove incompatible.

Such examples are not distant from the most discussed examples of moral conflict in the modern world, which are often depicted as arising out of unjust institutions. Sartre's student cannot combine filial and patriotic duty because of the constraints created by the Nazi occupation; Sophie's cruel choice is imposed by the same murderous tyrants; Vaclav Havel's depiction of daily collaboration in falsehood presupposes a regime that demands such collaboration.[21] In such cases we can see quite readily what it would take to eliminate the conflict, even if we are powerless to do so.

In cases of conflict there is then often little to be done, as it were, on the spot. Both Barbara Herman and Thomas Hill have argued that a Kantian approach to obligation is fully compatible with, indeed requires, serious attention to the aftermath of failure to meet all requirements when there is conflict, and that in such circumstances remorse, regret, restitution or

---

[21] Vaclav Havel, 'The Power of the Powerless', in *Living in the Truth*, J. Vladislav (tr.) (London: Faber and Faber, 1986), 36–122, esp. section III.

other remainders and residues may be owed.[22] Unmet *rationes obligandi* are not simply wiped off the map, as (on some readings) unmeetable *prima facie* duties are wiped away: they maintain their claims on us. Kant makes this point more explicitly than he does in the passages Herman discusses in the *Lectures on Ethics* when he writes:

> Now we can never say here that it is absolutely impossible to fulfil both duties, and the duties remain even though they are not fulfilled; for, as we have said, laws and rules can never contradict one another; there is, rather, a contrary action of the ground of one duty against those of another, and this brings it about that the two cannot co-exist. (*LE* (V) 27:537)

The demands of unmet and *contingently* unmeetable *rationes obligandi* are often seen as requiring emotional and attitudinal responses: we pay the price of unmet demands in residues and remainders such as regret, agent regret and remorse. But where the sources of conflict lie in unjust institutions, the most appropriate responses may have to be more active. They might take the form of efforts to bring about institutional changes which put an end to or reduce the sources of conflict. Agents who face a conflict among their obligating reasons can seek to eliminate the sources of (recurrent) conflict. They can seek to establish a well-ordered society, a system of right expressed in the institutions of a republican state and a cosmopolitan world order, and non-corrupt law enforcement, whose special duties are not so prone to generate conflict. Yet, even in a well-ordered society within a cosmopolitan world order, special duties that are taken on without wrongdoing, indeed with all due care and attention may, in the event, turn out to conflict or not to be compatible with other obligations. Political, economic and social institutions can never eliminate all possibility of conflicts among obligating reasons.

A parallel set of longer term responses to moral conflict may be relevant in the domain of virtue. Since prior wrongdoing is one of the sources of moral conflict, its reduction would also help reduce (recurrent) conflict between obligating reasons. In this case the task is partly also one of constructing better social institutions but mainly (in Kant's view) one of forming or reforming characters. It begins with the tasks of moral education, of self-knowledge, of self-improvement. On each Kant has a great deal to say. He emphasises the ways in which children may be brought to awareness of their duties, to hatred of ill-doing, to distinguish advantage

---

[22] This conclusion rejects the thought that obligations are merely *prima facie* up to the point at which they are shown to be actual, and that they have no continuing claim if they cannot be made actual. See also Barbara Herman, 'Obligation and Performance', in *The Practice of Moral Judgment*.

from morality. He emphasises the importance of seeking self-knowledge and self-discipline throughout our lives, and the dangers of being beguiled by excessive, enthusiastic conceptions of total virtue, as if ordinary virtue were not hard enough. He emphasises the importance of securing the regulative virtue of courage, the importance of 'ethical ascetics',[23] and the need to construct a social order in which virtue is supported – the ethical commonwealth of *Religion within the Limits of Reason Alone*. Above all he emphasises that progress towards virtue is a task that does not come to an end:

> Virtue is always *in progress* and yet always starts *from the beginning*. It is always in progress because, considered *objectively*, it is an ideal and unattainable, while yet constant approximation to it is a duty. That it always starts from the beginning has a *subjective* basis in human nature which is always affected by inclinations because of which virtue can never settle down in peace and quiet with its maxims adopted once and for all but, if it is not rising, is unavoidably sinking. (*MM* 6:409)

The construction of just institutions and of good characters are both of them unending tasks, and such success as we may have will never eliminate moral conflict entirely. But in seeking both we make active and constructive, as well as amending, responses to claims of duties that would otherwise go under where obligating reasons conflict.

---

[23] "Ascetics is that part of the doctrine of method in which is taught not only the concept of virtue but also how to put it into practice and cultivate the *capacity for* as well as the will to virtue" (*MM* 6:412).

CHAPTER 7

Experts, practitioners and practical judgement

Experts and practitioners

In the opening section of his 1793 essay *Theory and Practice*, Kant distinguishes two ways in which experts may fail as practitioners. He describes experts as knowing "a sum of rules, even of practical rules" which "is called *theory* if those rules are thought as principles having a certain generality, so that abstraction is made from a multitude of conditions that yet have a necessary influence on their application" (Kant, *TP* 8:275).[1] The sense in which practical rules may be called 'theory' is evidently broad: such theories are abstract or indeterminate, but they are not *theoretical* in a narrower sense that is contrasted with *practical*, in that their use is intended to change rather than to fit the world.

In the same short paragraph Kant describes practice as a matter "effecting an end which is thought as the observance [*Befolgung*] of certain principles of procedure [*des Verfahrens*: of the activity] represented in their generality", that is to say as a matter of living up to (observing, conforming to, enacting) principles or theories. Experts not merely have a grasp of (more or less) abstract or theoretical principles: they are often practitioners who seek to deploy or put their expertise to use.

The first and well-known way in which experts can fail as practitioners is when they lack capacities for judgement "by which a practitioner distinguishes whether or not something is a case of the rule" (Kant *TP* 8:275). Incompetence in judging whether something is a case of a rule or principle

---

[1] The German reads "Man nennt einen Inbegriff selbst von praktischen Regeln alsdann Theorie, wenn diese Regeln als Prinzipien in einer gewissen Allgemeinheit gedacht werden, und dabei von einer Menge Bedingungen abstrahiert wird, die doch auf ihre Ausübung notwendig Einfluß haben." Here Kant makes it clear that the emphasis is on theory guiding action, by using the word *Ausübung* (*enactment*, *instantiation*) rather than the general term for application, which is *Anwendung*. Nisbet's translation marks but does not illuminate the difference by rendering *Ausübung* as *practical application*. For further comment on the difference between application and enactment see below, p. 115.

cannot be remedied by invoking additional rules or principles. Here more theory is not enough:

> judgement cannot always be given another rule by which to direct its subsumption, for this would go on to infinity. (Kant, *TP* 8:275)

Such incapacity is illustrated by the case of "physicians or jurists who did well during their schooling, but who are at a loss when they have to give an expert opinion" (Kant, *TP* 8:275). This sort of failure, in which somebody masters a body of theory but fails when called upon to use it, is common enough. Kant had already used similar examples to illustrate the impossibility of supplying complete rules for *subsumptive* (or *determinant* or *determining*) judgement in the Schematism of the *Critique of Pure Reason*, and elsewhere (see Kant, *CPR* A132–4/B171–4). However, in *Theory and Practice* he sets this familiar source of expert failure in judgement aside.

His interest in *Theory and Practice* is in cases where failure occurs in practice although "a natural talent [for judgement] is present" (Kant, *TP* 8:275). In these cases of failure, as Kant sees it, the problem is rather that "a theory can be incomplete" (Kant, *TP* 8:275), so that there is a "deficiency in premises" (Kant, *TP* 8:275) that undermines or hinders practical judgement. So it appears that in practical judgement having more rules *may* be useful, even indispensable. When this occurs, Kant claims robustly that

> in such cases it was not the fault of theory if it was of little use in practice, but rather of there having been *not enough* theory … Thus nobody can pretend to be practically proficient in a science and yet scorn theory without declaring that he is an ignoramus in his field … (Kant, *TP* 8:275–6)

Rather than dismissing theory as impractical, we should look for a more complete theory, incorporating a greater number of principles that can help steer action with greater specificity.

Kant initially illustrates this second type of failure with technical examples. An artilleryman who criticises the relevant theories (mechanics, ballistics) because their relation to practice is approximate rather than precise, rather than augmenting these theories with more specific theories, for example of friction and air resistance, fails in practice only because his theory is defective. A more complete theory would enable him to predict the trajectory of projectiles more accurately and to aim them better.

This account of failure in practice as due to lack of (sufficient) theory, rather than to incapacity to judge, is evidently meant to apply both to *explanatory* and to *prescriptive* uses of theories. The only exception that

Kant allows is that of highly abstract mathematical or philosophical theories, which may genuinely lack instances. In this case, but only in this case, the common saying that something may be "correct in theory but of no use in practice" may have a point, if only because nothing counts as application or as practice for such theories (see Kant, *TP* 8:276).

Technical and moral judgement

The broad scope of Kant's claims about the importance of theory for practice, which exclude only certain mathematical and philosophical theories, is evident from his initial characterisation of theory as "a sum of rules, even of practical rules" (Kant, *TP* 8:275), and from his discussion of examples of technical and moral judgement. In the introduction of *Theory and Practice* he focuses on theories that have a technical use, so can be used both to explain or predict and to guide the practice of technical experts. Such theories provide a basis for explanation and for expert practice in areas such as medicine, agriculture or engineering. However, in these cases expert practice is *conditional* on adopting certain aims: the theory has practical relevance only for expert practitioners with defined aims such as the physician, the agronomist or the engineer (or artilleryman).

In the subsequent sections of *Theory and Practice* Kant turns to those prescriptive theories that are intended to guide practice *unconditionally*, regardless of any practitioner's specific aims. Such unconditional, *morally practical* theories differ from *technically practical* theories, in that they have no explanatory use. Unconditional practical principles are principles of duty, and Kant discusses the three domains of duty – morality, domestic justice and cosmopolitan justice – in the successive sections of *Theory and Practice*.

It is not immediately clear whether the claim that (given adequate powers of judgement) failure in practice arises from a lack of theory will hold for the case of the unconditional practical principles of morality and justice. Explanatory theories can be applied to cases that arise in experience. They are intended to fit the world, and so should be rejected, amended or improved if they fail to do so. By contrast, prescriptive theories do not have to fit the world as it happens to be, but rather aim to guide practice in the task of fitting (some small part of) the world to the theory. The salient difference between explanatory and prescriptive or normative theories is that the former assume that particular cases are there to be judged, but the latter assume that what is to hand may have to be altered to make it fit the theory. Some of Kant's comments on the ways in which expertise may fail in practice seem to fit explanatory uses of theory better than they fit normative uses, including in particular the unconditionally normative claims of Kant's ethics.[2]

Technical experts who put their expertise into practice draw on a body of empirical theory, which they apply to cases that are ready to hand in order to achieve certain desired or required ends, which are typically seen as the proper ends of professional activity. Such cases are exemplified by a patient with certain symptoms, a criminal case with certain evidence, an artillery piece with certain specifications, and so on. Here the picture of expertise as failing despite capacities for judgement, because there is not enough (or not good enough) theory is plausible enough. Physicians who lack a theory of infection; lawyers who lack a grasp of legal principles, process or statute; agronomists who lack an understanding of the interaction of plants and growing conditions may all go wrong in practice even if their judgement is good. In this case Kant's claims that if only *more* theory were added, these technical theories "would accord very well with experience" (Kant, *TP* 8:276) is plausible. Here practice may fail because expertise fails, because of insufficiencies in theory. And the mark of failure may be either poor explanations or botched practice – or both.

But the situation might be different for the case of unconditional prescriptive theories, such as "a theory based on the concept of duty" (Kant, *TP* 8:276). A theory founded on the concept of duty, as Kant views it, consists of practical rules that are used to shape the world in ways that are not governed by pursuit of ends that are external to the theory, such as the proper ends of some technical or professional activity, self-love or ideological commitments. He states clearly that "a theory of this kind only is at issue in the present treatise" (Kant, *TP* 8:277) and it is practical rather than intended to accord with experience.

How then can Kant's examples of professional expertise coupled with defective practice illuminate the case of moral failure? Or does the comparison mislead? If it misleads, why should we conclude that in shaping the world to fit unconditional prescriptive rules, defective practice by those with competent powers of judgement arises either from defective theory, or from lack of theory? Might it not have other sources?

---

[2] *Theory and Practice* provides evidence that it is the terminology rather than the idea of direction of fit that dates from the mid-twentieth century. See note 4 in Chapter 3, above.

Duty and direction of fit

Kant offers a number of considerations to show that theories of duty cannot be correct in theory yet "invalid in practice" (Kant, *TP* 8:277). Basically his thought is that in the case of moral and legal duty "the worth of practice rests entirely on its conformity with the theory underlying it" (Kant, *TP* 8:277): *there can be nothing else that guides moral action*. This conclusion assumes that practical reasoning and practical judgement do not aim to fit the world, and cannot be derived from examples, then infers that (this being the case) there is nothing but theory – concepts, rules, principles – to guide moral action. In contemporary terms, this amounts to a claim that practical judgements must be principle or theory led, and not world-directed like empirical judgement. What we need if we are to judge practically is not fewer but more principles or standards. And a theory of duty would be undermined by requiring its principles to fit empirical reality.[3]

This point is one that we meet many times in Kant's writings. He had already articulated the distinctive relation of theory and principles to particular cases in morality nearly a decade before the publication of *Theory and Practice*, when he wrote in the *Groundwork of the Metaphysics of Morals*:

> Nor could one give worse advice to morality than by wanting to derive it from examples. For, every example of it represented to me must itself first be appraised in accordance with principles of morality, as to whether it is also worthy to serve as an original[4] example, that is as a model; it can by no means authoritatively provide the concept of morality. Even the Holy One of the Gospel must first be compared to our ideal of moral perfection before he is cognized as such ... (Kant, *G* 4:408)

This passage too in effect asserts the impossibility of picking out particular cases of action as morally significant, or worthy, or dutiful, or just, without *presupposing* "a sum of rules, even of practical rules [which is] called a theory" (Kant, *TP* 8:275). Morality, and with it justice, must *begin* with standards or principles – with 'theory' (in the broad sense); it cannot be derived from experience, or from particular cases.

---

[3] Here Kant and Anscombe take the same approach: ironic given her fierce opposition to Kant's moral philosophy. See G. E. M. Anscombe, 'Modern Moral Philosophy', *Collected Philosophical Papers of G. E. M. Anscombe, Vol. III, Ethics, Religion and Politics* (Oxford: Blackwell, 1981); for comments on her reading of Kant see Chapter 1, above.

[4] I.e. guiding example.

However, while the point may be familiar, and one that Kant argued for and relied on elsewhere, the formulation of these issues in the introductory section of *Theory and Practice* is a particularly clear articulation of the distinction between the two directions of fit. As Kant sees it, here

> The worth of the practice rests entirely on its conformity with the theory underlying it; and all is lost if the empirical and hence contingent conditions of carrying out the law are made conditions of the law itself, so that a practice calculated with reference to an outcome probable in accordance with *previous* experience is given authority to control a self-sufficient theory. (Kant, *TP* 8:277)

If moral and political judgement is a matter of seeking to shape the world to certain standards, we cannot coherently derive those standards from the way the world already is. Empirical evidence of what has been done, or normally done, does not tell us what ought to be done. Arguments from custom or habit, from religion or ideology, from experience or public acceptance, are morally impotent – although they may be highly influential. What actually happens or is done, or was done, even what is commonly done and widely respected, may be instances either of right action or of moral failure. Morality cannot be derived from examples.

Judgement and particulars

Asserting the priority of theory or principle (in the broad sense) in matters of morality and justice leaves us with some unclarity about the very idea of a *case* or *instance* of dutiful or just action, and about the task of practical judgement.

When we act we are faced by a specific situation that *already* exists, although our grasp of that situation may be incomplete or defective. So we have to begin by judging what the situation is. This preliminary judgement is a theoretical as opposed to a practical judgement. It aims to fit the world, rather than to make the world fit or live up to theory or principle. The theoretical judgement of the situations in which we act may call on capacities both for *subsumptive* (*determinant* or *determining* in other passages) and for *reflective* (or *reflecting*) judging. Both of these are types of theoretical judgement that can be used only when 'the particular is given'. Kant distinguishes them in *The Critique of Judgement* as follows:

> The power of judgement in general is the faculty for thinking of the particular as contained under the universal. If the universal (the rule, the principle, the law) is given, then the power of judgement, which subsumes

the particular under it … is *determining*. If, however, only the particular is given, for which the universal is to be found, then the power of judgement is merely *reflecting*. (Kant, *CJ* 5:179)[5]

Both determinant and reflective judging are forms of theoretical judgement that can be used when a particular is given: but they have no role when no particular is (yet) given. No amount of theoretical judgement will help us when the task is practical, and we have to judge what to do. So theoretical or non-practical judgement has only a *preliminary* role in the enactment or instantiation of principles of duty, or of justice. Both determinant and reflective judgement will be needed in identifying the situation that we face, in understanding the context of action, but they cannot guide action. *For here it is in the nature of the case that the particular is not given.*

Some well-known contemporary accounts of moral judgement have, I think, gone astray in construing it as a version of theoretical judgement that seeks to fit the world. For example, those who see moral judgement as a matter of 'situational appraisal', or of 'reading' a situation that confronts us, construe practical (and specifically moral) judgement as what Kant terms *reflective* judging, where the particular is given and the task is to find some way of describing or construing it.[6] Appraising or reading situations can be an important *theoretical* preliminary for practical, including moral, judgement: but it is only a preliminary. The whole point of action-guiding, practical judgement is that it has to be done *when the particular is not given*.

These points seem to me both fundamental and distinctive. Kant's point in *Theory and Practice* is not that we often lack clear insight into the moral character of action that we have already taken. He certainly holds that this is the case, and thinks that it is due to our limited capacities for retrospective theoretical judgement of our own maxims – or of others' maxims – rather than because moral or other practical judgement is reflective. Once action is past, the particular *is* (by then) given, and the only sort of judgement that can be relevant will be theoretical judgement (whether determinant or reflective), for which our evidence is often (perhaps always)

---

[5] The translation here is taken from the older translation by Meredith, rather than that by Eric Matthews. The pagination is the same in both. Cf. Bibliographical note, p. 7. For further discussion of the passage see Chapter 8, below.

[6] See John McDowell, 'Deliberation and Moral Development', in Stephen Engstrom and Jennifer Whiting (eds.), *Aristotle, Kant and the Stoics* (Cambridge University Press, 1996), 19–35; David Wiggins, 'Deliberation and Practical Reason', in his *Needs, Values, Truth: Essays in the Philosophy of Value* (Oxford: Blackwell, 1987), 215–37. For some comments on problems that arise if practical judgement is construed along these lines see Chapter 6, above.

limited and partial. But this is not a point that bears on practical judgement or prospective action.

Kant thinks retrospective judgement of action problematic not because theoretical judgement is generally problematic, but for much more specific reasons. He thinks that we often – perhaps always – lack insight into our own principles of action, and hence into our own moral worth. He emphasised our lack of self-knowledge, and its radical implications for judging the moral worth of our own past action in the *Groundwork* (see esp. ch. 1 and beginning of ch. 2). He reiterates the point in *Theory and Practice* in the words "I readily grant that no one can become aware with certainty of *having performed* his *duty* quite unselfishly" (Kant, *TP* 8:284). Here, as elsewhere, he dramatises this thought. He states that "Perhaps no one has ever performed quite unselfishly ... the duty that he cognizes and also reveres; perhaps no one will ever succeed in doing so however hard he tries" (Kant, *TP* 8:284–5). Arguably this opacity is a straightforward corollary of Kant's arguments against self-transparency in the Paralogisms of the *Critique of Pure Reason*, and also reflects human tendencies to look for flattering accounts of their own past action. The opacity that limits our knowledge of our own – and indeed of others' – past motives, maxims and action is probably an overdetermined element of Kant's position.

However, the point at issue in *Theory and Practice* is more fundamental, and is quite independent of the fact that we are opaque to ourselves. It too can be put dramatically, by noting that *even if we were self-transparent*, even if we did have insight into the moral character of acts we had already done, this would not help us to judge what to do. In practical judgement the particular is *not* given: we cannot work out what to do by discerning what we will have done at some later point. Practical judgement is not a matter of self-prediction.[7] So it appears that in practical judgement, including moral judgement, *all* that we have is normative (including moral) principles, combined with (more or less adequate) understanding of the context of action based on theoretical judgement – determinant, reflective, or both – about the particular situations we face.

This suggests that when we talk about the 'application' of explanatory and of prescriptive or normative theories we are talking about two quite different things. Explanatory theories are applied to given particulars: if they fit, explanation may be furthered or achieved (to some degree). If they don't, then the theory is defective and needs to be extended, amended or rejected. By contrast, prescriptive or normative theories must be used

[7] Cf. Kant, *G* 4:448.

without waiting for a particular to be given: they are not so much *applied* as they are *enacted* or *instantiated, conformed to* or *satisfied*.

Prescriptive or normative theories, as discussed above, come in two kinds. Technically practical theories are backed by some explanatory theory, and become practical only when agents adopt defined ends or objectives that make that theory relevant for them. In this case deficiencies *in the theory* call for extension, amendment or rejection of the theory. However, even technically practical theories are not self-applying, for here too no particular is given prior to action. The farmer who seeks to apply his technical knowledge of agronomy, the physician who seeks to apply his technical knowledge of medicine, will also find that theory underdetermines their choice of action in particular cases. A good grasp of technical theories will not by itself tell a practitioner which crop to plant in a given field in a given year, or which drug to prescribe for a given patient.

In deciding how to act, practitioners *reduce* the indeterminacy with which technical theories leave them by making assumptions about the ends or objectives of expert practice. The farmer aims to have a good harvest of a useful crop – not to grow a colourful crop of weeds, or a crop that does not ripen before winter. The physician aims to improve the patient's condition – not to induce colourful hallucinations or to use the patient as a guinea pig for research of no therapeutic benefit. But this reduction in indeterminacy cannot wholly determine the course of action to be taken. Technical practice too requires practical judgement.

The fact that a prescriptive theory underdetermines what should be done is even clearer in the case of theories of duty. For in this case we cannot assume additional aims or objectives without undermining the unconditional nature of duty. Yet in acting agents have to perform one or another particular action. This may seem to leave us with a gap between expertise and practice, and no understanding of practical judgement to fill the gap. Does Kant's insistence on the priority of theory (rules, principles and laws) in matters of duty simply lead us back to the old criticism of empty formalism?

Practical judgement

As Kant sees it, theories of duty can all be derived from a single principle – the Categorical Imperative – that provides the basis for deriving a plurality of more specific principles. The derivation of more specific principles of duty from the Categorical Imperative raises a large set of issues, which I shall not discuss here. I shall take it that once we make reasonably plausible background assumptions, a range of principles of duty can be identified. In my view these background assumptions include the thoughts that we act as one of a plurality of agents; that each agent's action may bear on other agents; and that each agent's capacities for action are determinate, limited and vulnerable. One can think of these as assumptions about the *plurality, connectedness* and *finitude* of human (or other rational) agents. If any of these assumptions did not hold, we might find that we could not derive many – or any – more specific principles of duty. If we were to assume only a single agent, we could at most offer an account of duties to self (even this might raise problems). If we were to assume a plurality of agents who could not affect one another (for example, because they live on different planets or in different epochs) similar limitations would follow. If we were to assume a plurality of agents with unlimited powers to affect one another, other incoherencies arise.

Assuming that theories of duty comprise a 'sum of (practical) principles', and that practical principles are not applied to given particulars, how do we use such principles to guide action? What is practical judgement? Is it enough to say that moral practice is activity that *conforms to* or *lives up to* (*enacts, instantiates*) moral theory? Or that moral practice is simply a matter of acting in some way or other that *satisfies* principles of duty? Or that just action is simply a matter of acting in some way or other that *satisfies* principles of justice?

At first thought, these claims may seem to suggest that principles of duty and of justice must be radically indeterminate, so can guide action only if supplemented with further assumptions about ends to be sought or objectives to be achieved. If so, Kant's entire view of morality and justice must fall apart, and his distinction between technical and moral principles will falter. A theory seemingly does not take us far towards acting if it merely demands some action that satisfies a core moral principle, such as a principle of not injuring or one of not coercing. Yet introducing additional assumptions – for example, assuming some end such as the pursuit of happiness or self-love, to supply the dearth of premises in theories of duty – are moves Kant thinks unacceptable in matters of duty.[8] Equally, introducing assumptions about self-love (or other forms of heteronomy) will not resolve the indeterminacy of moral theory, although it will undermine its justification. Splicing duty with heteronomous considerations is doubly unappealing.

---

[8] Cf. Kant, *TP* 8:286–7. See also Bernd Ludwig, 'Kant, Garve and the Question of the Motives of Moral Action', *Journal of Moral Philosophy*, 4.1 (2007), 183–93.

Kant argues that the practical advantage therefore lies with theories of duty rather than with heteronomous ethics:

> The concept of duty is incomparably simpler, clearer, and, for practical use, more readily grasped and more natural to everyone than any motive[9] derived from happiness, or mixed with it … [it is] far *more powerful*, forceful, and promising of results than all motives[10] borrowed from the latter, selfish principle. (Kant, *TP* 8:286)

He even claims that somebody tempted to embezzle funds entrusted to him will find that

> if he asks himself what *his* duty is in this matter, he is not at all perplexed about what answer to give, but certain on the spot what he has to do. (Kant *TP* 8:287)

What is the argument for these bold claims? The text can seem rather unhelpful, in that it can be read merely as asserting that it is wholly plain that we can never be sure whether embezzling will lead to happiness, but that we can be crystal clear that it would be wrong to embezzle. As Kant extols the clarity and forcefulness with which duty speaks, it is all too easy to think that his claim is dogmatic and unconvincing.

However, we know that his thought in *Theory and Practice* is that practical difficulties arise where there *is not enough theory*. Why should he think that in this case there is *enough theory*? Perhaps his thought is simply that once we have reason to think that refraining from embezzling is a principle of duty, we can reach the practical conclusion 'so I won't embezzle' without further effort. On this reading, practical judgement is *only* a matter of *satisfying* or *conforming to* theory. All that it takes for practice to live up to a theory of duty is that it satisfy the principles of that theory – in this example, the principle of refraining from embezzling. Practical judgement, as suggested by the introductory paragraph of *Theory and Practice* is not a matter of the *application* (*Anwendung*) but of the *enactment* (*Ausübing*) of theory.

How far can practical judgement guide action?

This, I think, is correct, but also puzzling. Practical judgements often seem to those who make them far from simple or clear, and a range of questions

---

[9] Kant here uses the term *Motiv*. The term is not one he often uses and it is reasonable to assume that he uses it here because it is the term used by Garve in a passage he has just cited.

[10] Kant here uses his usual term *Bewegungsgrund*. Arguably it does not mean the same as *Motiv*, and the seeming parallel is an artefact of the translation.

can be raised about this stripped down account of practical judgement. I shall consider several of them, by offering some quite limited comments on the later sections of *Theory and Practice*.

First, how well can we reconcile this minimalist account of practical judgement with the parallels drawn between explanatory and prescriptive theories at the beginning of *Theory and Practice*? I think that there may not be much problem here, provided that we distinguish the *application* from the *enactment* of principles. In *applying a principle* to a given case, the particular must be given, as when we apply explanatory theories or principles to the world. But in practical affairs this is not where we find ourselves. In *enacting* or *conforming to a principle*, a particular is produced or realised rather than given, and only in retrospect will we be able to apply principles to whatever has been enacted, since it is only then that there will then be a 'given' particular. Kant, I think, made it harder to see both the difference and the analogy between *application* and *enactment* by introducing his discussion with examples taken from the case of technical judgement. Here the background theories are in the first instance theoretical (in both the narrow and the broad sense) so *can* be applied to given particulars, but the experts who put them to practical use in their professional practice do not *apply* but rather *enact* their principles.

Secondly, if moral judgements based on principles of duty are simply enactments of those principles, why is it often – contrary to Kant's comments in Part I of *Theory and Practice* – so difficult to see what duty requires? Perhaps the artificially simplified example of embezzling a deposit misleads. In more realistic cases it can be hard to see what duty requires in a given situation. Typically we face a *plurality* of principles of duty, so the task of practical judgement is not just a matter of identifying some way of satisfying a single principle of action, but of finding some way of acting that satisfies a plurality of principles of action. It is often far from simple to find a way of acting that is both honest and kind, or that both respects others' freedom and protects their safety. Practical judgement is demanding because it is a matter of living up not just to a single principle, but to "a sum of rules, even of practical rules".

While the simplified, abstracted example of embezzlement may suggest that judgements of duty are "incomparably simpler, clearer, and, for practical use, more readily grasped and more natural" (*TP* 8:286) than judgements of self-interest, real life examples are often far more difficult. In real situations, practical judgement is often complex in the ways in which 'makers' judgements' are complex. In designing a bicycle an engineer will try to satisfy many considerations: the bicycle must be well-balanced without being too bulky; strong enough without being too heavy; durable without requiring materials that are too expensive; and so on. In acting on principles of duty we must refrain from coercion and from perjury, from fraud and from violence, from cruelty and from manipulation, and so on. Moreover, we typically have also to meet a range of other practical constraints that are not morally required but (for example) prudential or technical. This means that moral judgement is often far more complicated than Kant's account of the person tempted to embezzle suggests.

Kant illustrates the complexities that arise when we have multiple principles of duty in Part II of *Theory and Practice*, by considering duties of domestic justice, where a plurality of principles has to be satisfied. Here too it is tempting to forget that the focus is on enacting theory in practice, and to fall back on examples, thereby assuming that some existing constitution provides a model of justice to be followed. But appeals to experience, or to the status quo, are no more reputable as a basis for a theory of justice than are appeals to experience, custom or examples in a moral theory.

> Nowhere does a practice that ignores pure rational principles deny theory so arrogantly as in the question of what is required for a good constitution of a state. The cause is that a lawful constitution of long standing gradually accustoms people to a rule of appraising its happiness as well as its rights in terms of the condition in which everything up to now has followed its quiet course but not … to evaluate it in terms of the concepts of both provided by reason. (Kant, *TP* 8:305)[11]

Justice, like other parts of morality, is anchored in principles or theory. As Kant sees it, republican justice must be anchored in the three linked principles of freedom, equality and independence. *All three principles* must be enacted if citizens are mutually to respect one another's external freedom. Any one of these principles, taken in isolation, could be satisfied in very many ways. Yet jointly satisfying all three principles constrains just constitutions in quite marked ways. Of course, here too practical judgement will not select a wholly determinate constitutional and legal structure: but attending to more principles – having "more theory" – nevertheless markedly reduces indeterminacy.

---

[11] See also: "These principles are not so many laws given by a state already established as rather principles in accordance with which alone the establishment of a state is possible in conformity with pure rational principles of external human right" (Kant, *TP* 8:290), as well as Kant's acid comments about Britain, "where the people carry on about their constitution as if it were the model for the whole world" (Kant, *TP* 8:303). Justice too is corrupted by trying to derive it from examples.

Matters are less clear when we turn to consider the demands of cosmopolitan justice. We are so far from a just world order that we have difficulty judging even whether it is possible.[12] In Part III of *Theory and Practice* Kant returns to a theme that he takes up in various other writings, including the earlier *Idea of a Universal History from a Cosmopolitan Point of View* and his late works *Conjectures on the Beginnings of Human History* and *Conflict of the Faculties*, and asks whether and under what conditions practice is even possible in this domain. His thought is presumably that if there were *nothing* that we could do to work towards global justice – if we were doomed either to a Sisyphean future of alternating improvement and decline (Kant, *TP* 8:307–8), or to a future of moral decline, terror and horror – then there could be no duty to work towards global justice. A theory of duty could hold for and be enacted at the personal and civic levels, but not globally.

In *Theory and Practice* (as in other writings) Kant does not claim to know the trend of human history. He simply claims that practice does not require any *guarantee* or *knowledge* of success, but does require reason to think that failure is not inevitable. The *possibility* of success or progress is enough at least to open the question of global justice:

> I shall therefore be allowed to assume that ... the human race ... is also to be conceived of as progressing towards what is better with respect to the moral end of its existence, and that this will indeed be *interrupted* from time to time but will never be *broken off*. I do not need to prove this presupposition ... I rest my case on my innate duty, the duty of every member of the series of generations ... so to influence posterity that it becomes always better ... (Kant, *TP* 8:308–9)[13]

A reasonable hope for better times to come is, Kant argues, enough to make questions of global justice into practical questions. So his account of the relation of theory and practice is relevant to questions of global justice. Here too we would make a mistake if we took our actual experience – so often dire and depressing – as the basis for a theory of justice or the practice of politics. On the contrary:

---

[12] On this issue see Howard Williams, *Kant's Critique of Hobbes: Sovereignty and Cosmopolitanism* (Cardiff: University of Wales Press, 2003); Elisabeth Ellis, *Kant's Politics: Provisional Theory for an Uncertain World* (New Haven, CT: Yale University Press 2005).

[13] In many of his essays on history and politics Kant depicts the earlier stages of human history as progressive and the present as open, thereby allowing for the possibility but not the inevitability either of failure and decline or of progress. See 'Historical Trends and Human Futures', in Onora O'Neill, *Constructing Authorities: Reason, Politics and Interpretation in Kant's Philosophy* (Cambridge University Press, 2016), 186–98.

It does not matter how many doubts may be raised against my hopes from history, which, if they were proved, could move me to desist from a task so apparently futile, as long as these doubts cannot be proved. (Kant, *TP* 8:309)

Yet because the possibility of cosmopolitan justice is one of an "immeasurably distant success" (Kant, *TP* 8:310), we can make only the most tentative practical judgements about action that would move us towards the goal. We cannot at this stage know even whether a world state would constitute a move towards global justice, or whether it would be "still more dangerous to freedom … leading to the most fearful despotism" (Kant, *TP* 8:311). Equally, we cannot be certain that global justice is best achieved through a "rightful condition of *federation* in accordance with a commonly agreed upon *right of nations*" (Kant, *TP* 8:311). Great as these uncertainties are, Kant nevertheless concludes that even at the cosmopolitan level what "holds for theory also holds for practice" (Kant, *TP* 8:313).

These comments on the moral and political content of *Theory and Practice* have been highly selective. What I hope that they show is that the key to the essay is its insistence on the priority of theory (in the broad sense) for matters of practice, including the practice of morality and justice. While Kant thinks each one of us capable of grasping principles of duty, he would not view such a grasp as a form of expertise, a term we usually confine to grasp of theory or principles that can be used in the service of some specialised or professional ends, goals or requirements. Yet his initial analogy between technical judgement and judgements of duty is nevertheless apt, since in both cases grasp of principles precedes, guides but does not wholly determine practice. Theory in the broad sense is the only available guide to practice. It can point us towards a more specific view of what we ought to do, although not to a particular act.[14] As with theoretical judgement, the rules will offer incomplete guidance. But provided we take account of a wide enough range of principles of duty, they can specify what ought to be done to a useful degree.

---

[14] Individuating future acts is in any case problematic. We can formulate definite descriptions – 'the walk I shall take this afternoon' – but in doing so we do not point to particulars, however much information we tuck into the act description.

CHAPTER 8

Kant on indeterminacy, judgement and interpretation[1]

Nobody has written more or more illuminatingly on judgement than Immanuel Kant. Yet many of his views on judgement are overlooked, and there is disagreement about others. Here I shall discuss the main distinctions that he draws between types of judging and their links to other types of cognitive action, including practical and theoretical reasoning. I shall leave aside some thoroughly explored aspects of Kant's writing on judgement, including the forms of judgement and the specific roles he sees judgement as playing in epistemology, aesthetics and teleological reasoning.[2]

Indeterminacy of meaning provides the background to Kant's accounts both of theoretical and of practical reasoning, and of judgement. Yet indeterminacy is often seen as a problem for practical reasoning, and in particular for practical judgement. There have, for example, been endless criticisms both of Kant's ethics and of more recent 'Kantian' ethics, which accuse them of 'empty formalism' and of failure to identify determinate, action-guiding demands. Practical judgement supposedly moves from indeterminate principles to particular acts, yet (as Kant sees it) reasoning, understanding and judgement are all of them rule-governed, but all deploy incomplete rules. Consequently the relevant rules cannot tell us just how to judge, and "at some point we have to judge immediately, spontaneously".[3] Is this a problem? Does it matter if we can reach only indeterminate claims about the way things are or (in contexts of action) about what to do?

[1] An earlier version of this chapter was presented as the de Gruyter Lecture at the American Philosophical Association meetings in Chicago in March 2016. I am grateful to Rudolf Makkreel for helpful comments on successive versions.
[2] For an outstanding bibliography see Robert Hanna, *Kant's Theory of Judgment*, Stanford Encyclopedia of Philosophy, revised edn. 2013.
[3] D. A. Bell, 'The Art of Judgement', *Mind*, 96 (1987), 221–44, at 226.

A first thought might be that it is not always necessary to reach highly, let alone wholly, determinate judgements. In answering truth-oriented questions, including empirical questions, indeterminate (generic, approximate, vague, schematic) answers are often enough, and aiming for greater, let alone complete, determinacy may be neither necessary, nor possible, nor useful. Only where we calculate rather than judge should we expect to reach wholly determinate results. But is there parallel comfort to be had if Kant's account of practical reasoning and judgement cannot yield determinate answers? Deliberation aims to guide action, and act-tokens (like other particulars) will be determinate in all respects. Indeterminacy, it seems, cannot be shrugged off in practical matters.

I shall look at some connections between judgement and indeterminacy through the lens of Kant's scattered discussions of judgement and interpretation. I begin with comments on his well-known distinction between *determinant* (alternatively: *determining, subsumptive*) judgement and *reflective* (alternatively: *reflecting*) judgement, concentrating on the sorts of cognitive action they require, and then turn to *practical* judgement and ways in which it differs both from determinant and from reflective judgement.

Incomplete rules for judgement

Kant famously maintained that reason deals with 'universals', that is abstract or indeterminate structures such as concepts, rules, principles and laws, while judgement makes claims about particular cases. But he also insists that there can be no complete rules for judging. To find complete rules for the application of any given rule would require a further rule, and so on into unending regress:

> If the understanding in general is explained as the faculty of rules, then the power of judgement is the faculty of **subsuming** under rules, i.e. of determining whether something stands under a given rule ... or not. ... if it [the understanding] wanted to show generally how one ought to subsume under these rules, i.e. distinguish whether something stands under them or not, this could not happen except once again through a rule. But just because this is a rule, it would demand another instruction for the power of judgement, and so it becomes clear that although the understanding is certainly capable of being instructed and equipped through rules, the power of judgement is a special talent that cannot be taught but only practiced. Thus this is also what is specific to so called mother-wit, the lack of which cannot be made good by

any school; for although such a school can provide a limited understanding with plenty of rules … the faculty for making use of them must belong to the student [*dem Lehrling*e] himself. (Kant, *CPR* A132–3/B171–2; cf. *CJ* 5:169)[4]

The problem afflicts not only 'students', but everyone. As Kant immediately points out:

> A physician therefore, a judge, or a statesman, can have many fine pathological, juridical, or political rules in his head, of which he can even be a thorough teacher, and yet can easily stumble in their application [*Anwendung*], either because he is lacking in natural power of judgement (though not in understanding) … or also because he has not received adequate training. (*CPR* A134/B173)[5]

In this passage Kant emphasises the indeterminacy of all uses of the faculty of judgement, but seemingly mainly has in mind the limitations of *determinant* or *subsumptive* judgement, in which a 'universal' (concept, principle, rule or law) is given, and the aim is to *apply* it to a case that is to hand. He is surely right that anyone (physicians, judges, statesmen and other experts included) may fail in applying concepts, i.e. in subsuming particular cases under them. In applying concepts to cases we have at some point to go beyond the rules, and may be guided by examples, analogies or resemblances, or even by mere whim or hunch. Hence Kant repeatedly describes judgement as 'blind', and suggests that examples provide "the leading-strings [*Gängelwagen*—lit. 'the go-cart'] of judgement" (*CPR* A134/B174).

However, determinant judgement is only one type of judgement, and Kant also writes extensively on reflective and on practical judgement. He distinguishes determinant from reflective judgement as follows:

> The power of judgement in general is the faculty for thinking of the particular as contained under the universal. If the universal (the rule, the principle, the law) is given, then the power of judgement, which subsumes the particular under it … is **determining**. If, however, only the particular is given, for which the universal is to be found, then the power of judgement is merely **reflecting**. (Kant, *CJ* 5:180; cf. *FI* 20:211)

---

[4] Evidently proliferating rules cannot eliminate indeterminacy because "… judgement cannot always be given another rule by which to direct its subsumption, for this would go on to infinity" (Kant, *TP* 8:275).

[5] Cf. Kant's comment on "physicians or jurists who did well during their schooling, but [are] at a loss when they have to give an expert opinion" (*TP* 8:275).

While a particular – e.g. some object, situation, text or action – must be given for both these sorts of judging, in reflective judging no 'universal' (concept, rule, principle, law) is given. Rather reflective judging must *find* a 'universal' by which the particular can (best) be described or interpreted. Reflective judging is *more* open than determinant judging, although (as noted above) determinant judging too is not mechanical, but 'a matter of judgement'. Since most concepts are vague or boundaryless, criteria for their application in determinant judging will be irremediably incomplete; only concepts that are exhaustively defined within some formal system can have definitions that wholly eliminate indeterminacy.[6]

In determinant judging, we start with some concept (or concepts) and seek to *apply* it (or them) to a case that is to hand: we ask 'Is this bird a sparrow?', 'Is this killing a murder?' But in reflective judging we start with less: a case, but no concept or concepts. We then ask what *sort* of case it is: 'What sort of a bird is this?'; 'What sort of a crime – or perhaps what sort of an act – is this?' Reflective judging is needed where cases or situations, actions or texts, must be interpreted, and is fundamental not only to Kant's accounts of aesthetic and of purposive inquiry, but to his numerous discussions of textual, including scriptural, interpretation.[7] Reflective judging *embraces* indeterminacy: its aim is not to resolve or minimise indeterminacy, but to seek (further) indeterminate ways of describing, articulating or interpreting cases. Reflective judging may variously seek ways of interpreting cases that are revealing or interesting, or on the other hand tendentious or partisan.

Practical judging is different again, and is neither determinant nor reflective. Like the other types of judgement, it deploys indeterminate 'universals' (concepts, rules, principles, laws), but here no particular is 'given'. Practical judging must be undertaken *before* the relevant particular exists: we cannot pick out future act-tokens. It can therefore be *neither* a matter of applying concepts (i.e. subsuming particular cases under them) *nor* a matter of finding or devising (what are taken to be) useful, interesting or revealing concepts or descriptions for particular cases. It is *neither*

---

[6] Kant takes a particularly strict view of the possibility of offering definitive analyses of concepts. He claims that "only mathematics has definitions" (*CPR* A729/B757ff.) and that other concepts can have no more than *explanations* or *expositions* that are to varying degrees indeterminate.

[7] See Rudolf A. Makkreel, *Orientation and Judgment in Hermeneutics* (University of Chicago Press, 2015), esp. 63ff. for discussions of Kant's references to various 'orientational contexts' (field, territory, domain and habitat) that reflective judging may use in seeking apt ways of characterising or interpreting cases.

determinant *nor* reflective, neither a matter of application nor a matter of interpretation.[8]

Everyone, experts included, makes judgements of all three sorts. *Determinant* judgement may be needed to answer questions such as 'Is this patient's fever malaria?'; 'Was A's removal of B's possessions theft?'; 'Does this public body have a power to raise additional taxes?' *Reflective* judgement may be needed in order to consider more openly what *sort* of disease a patient's symptoms suggest, what *sort* of crime the available evidence suggests, or which *sort of* legislation could fulfil a manifesto pledge adequately. *Practical* judgements may be needed to decide *which* medicine to prescribe for a particular patient, *what* sentence to impose on a convicted offender or *how* to allocate the revenue brought in by a new tax.

Reflective judgement, interpretation and authority

Kant's claim that in reflective judgement "the universal is to be found" can seem puzzling. How are we to look for, recognise or select one rather than another 'universal' (concept, rule, principle, law) as apposite? In particular, how are we to do so where an appeal to the free play of cognitive capacities could be risky or misleading, and hermeneutic inventiveness downright irresponsible? Given the incompleteness of rules, judging will always be spontaneous to a degree, but Kant often comments disparagingly on uses of reflective judgement that are *merely* spontaneous, and discusses two more disciplined ways of judging reflectively that are spontaneous, but not *merely* spontaneous. One appeals to *authority* and the other to *reason*.

In daily and professional life the assumptions used to guide reflective judgement often appeal to authority. They rely on and appeal to the received views and established norms of accepted practices and institutions. Kant sees appeals to authorities and their requirements as entirely legitimate *in appropriate contexts*. He repeatedly maintains that expert, professional or institutional judgement and interpretation is rightly guided by legislation, precedents, doctrines and authorised versions of texts that

---

[8] A fair amount of ethical writing, often with Wittgensteinian or hermeneutic sympathies, has tried to construe ethical judgement as reflective. This is plausible only for ethical judgement about existing or past cases, where the particular to be judged can be given. It is not possible for practical judgements about what to do, which do not seek to 'appraise' or 'attend to' or 'evaluate' existing situations. Attentiveness to existing situations is *at most* a preliminary for *practical* judgement, and reflective judging cannot bear on the particular acts an agent will have done at some future time. See Onora O'Neill, 'Instituting Principles: Between Duty and Action', in Mark Timmons (ed.), *Kant's Metaphysics of Morals: Interpretative Essays* (Oxford University Press, 2002), 331–47, and above, pp. 87–104.

are taken as authoritative in the relevant professional and institutional contexts.

For example, in *The Conflict of the Faculties* and other late works[9] Kant distinguishes the 'higher' university faculties of theology, law and medicine from the 'lower' faculty of philosophy (roughly humanities), and argues that the former not merely *may* but *must* appeal to authority in interpreting the doctrines, laws, professional practices and canonical texts of their domains. These 'higher' faculties are so-called because they are established by the state for its own purposes, such as training pastors for the established Church, lawyers who master the law of the land, and physicians who can be certified as fit to practice. These experts not merely *may* but *must* defer to the powers that establish their authority and define their competence, and their interpretation of cases and texts rightly draws on authorised versions, received doctrines and established precedents.

Kant goes further and insists that the 'higher' faculties may appeal *only* to authority, and that their members should not reason about the laws, doctrines or interpretations to which they are bound in duty by the authorities they serve:

> So the biblical theologian as a member of a higher faculty draws his teaching not from reason but from the *Bible*; the professor of law [*der Rechtslehrer*] gets his not from natural law, but from the *law of the land* … As soon as one of these faculties presumes to mix with its teaching something it treats as derived from reason, it offends against the authority of the government … (*CF* 7:23; cf. *R* 6:109, *R* 6:115–16)

Biblical theologians must not look beyond ecclesiastical tradition and established doctrine in interpreting canonical religious texts; their counterparts in the faculty of law must not look beyond the law of the land:

> The jurist, as an authority on the text [*der Schriftgelehrte Jurist*], does not look to his reason for the laws that secure Mine and Thine, but to the code of laws that has been publicly promulgated and sanctioned by the highest authority (if, as he should, he acts as a civil servant) … [and must] straightway dismiss as nonsense the further question whether the decrees themselves are right. (*CF* 7:24–5)

However, Kant does not view authorised or doctrinal interpretation as the only adequate approach to reflective judging. The *philosophical theologians* of the 'lower' faculty must meet different standards. They must take

---

practical reason and the moral principles that it can establish as "the highest interpreter of the scriptures" (*CF* 7:41). For them "the moral improvement of men constitutes the real end of all religion of reason, it will comprise the highest principle of all Scriptural exegesis" (*R* 6:102). Similarly in the domain of politics the task of justifying a reasoned approach to public affairs is assigned to the *moral politician* who "takes the principles of political prudence in such a way that they can coexist with morals" (*PP* 8:372).[10] The philosophical theologian and the moral politician *may not* appeal to authority, and *must* bring practical reason and thereby morality to bear on interpreting texts and judging situations. The tasks of the 'lower' faculty are therefore onerous. To interpret texts and to justify policies they must first determine which moral principles practical reason can establish, and then show how those principles can guide interpretation and action. I shall take these tasks in that order.

The very claim that interpretation – whether of texts or situations, objects or action – can be guided by reason may seem implausible. Might not the only alternative to reflective judging that invokes authority be an appeal to untrammelled spontaneity, for example to individual choice or preference, subjectivity or enthusiasm? Kant accepts that this is possible – indeed sometimes popular – but emphatically rejects the idea that spontaneity *alone* offers an adequate approach to reflective judging, or specifically to the interpretation of texts. In *What is Orientation in Thinking?* he writes sarcastically about those who appeal solely to spontaneous or 'lawless' choice or enthusiasm and concludes that doing so leads to cognitive and moral shipwreck:

> the unavoidable consequence of declared lawlessness in thinking (of liberation from the limitations of reason) is that freedom to think will ultimately be forfeited and – because it is not misfortune but arrogance which is to blame for it – will be *trifled away* in the proper sense of the word. (*WOT* 8: 145)[11]

As Kant sees it, the interesting and important choice is therefore not between interpretation that appeals to authority and interpretation that

---

[10] He contrasts the admirable 'moral politician' who subordinates political judgement to practical reason with the self-serving 'political moralist' who subordinates political judgement to self-interest: "… [the] political moralist … frames a morals to suit the statesman's (=politician's) advantage" (*PP* 8: 372) and favours "an immoral doctrine of prudence" (*PP* 8:374–6).

[11] See also "… we cannot derive or convey the recognition of laws, and that they are moral, on the basis of any sort of feeling … if we do not wish to open wide the gates to every kind of enthusiasm. Feeling is private to each individual … thus we cannot extol it as a touchstone for the genuineness of a revelation since it teaches absolutely nothing … and no cognition whatever can be based on this" (*R* 6:114).

relies on mere spontaneity or enthusiasm, but between the former and interpretation that relies on reason. Only appeals to reason can support interpretation that neither appeals to authority, nor is wantonly lawless and risky. But what exactly does reason require and what can principles of reason contribute to the task of interpretation?

Vindicating reason: form and scope

The *Critique of Pure Reason* begins with a dismal account of what generally passes for human reason, which Kant thinks often misleads us. The iterated use of everyday patterns of theoretical reasoning – causal inference, mathematical reasoning – can lead to the metaphysical illusions later discussed in the Transcendental Dialectic. The fundamental categories of experience are simply that: their legitimate use is confined to experience, which is error prone. On the other hand, appeals to 'authorities', whether custom or law, individual preference or shared practice, can yield no more than *conditional* reasons for action and *doctrinal* readings of texts, so cannot reach or convince those who reject or query the authorities invoked. Kant often seems as unconvinced by claims that there are *general* or *unconditional* standards of reason as any sceptic or postmodernist. Yet he aims to offer a critique of reason that does not lead to sceptical or erratic conclusions.

His strategy for vindicating an account of reason is to articulate the *minimum* that would-be reasoners must offer those whom they seek to convince either to believe what they claim or to act as they propose. Anything that is to convince others must, he argues, put forward claims that those others could in principle grasp or follow, or propose principles of action (maxims) that those others could in principle adopt as guides to action. Those who aim to convince others *must* therefore reject claims that their intended audiences *could not* follow in thought, or *could not* adopt for action. And those who want to offer reasons to *all* others must provide *unconditional* considerations that *all* others could follow in thought or could adopt for action, so *must* reject proposals and principles that some (let alone many) others *could not* follow in thought or *could not* adopt for action.

Kant variously calls the universalised formulation of this negative and doubly modal requirement, the principle of *Universalisability*, or the *Categorical Imperative* or '*the supreme principle of (practical) reason*'. The best-known version runs "act only on that maxim through which you can at the same time will that it be a universal law".[12] So the grandly titled 'supreme principle of reason' apparently demands *only* that reasoned acting, speaking and thinking be based on principles that *can* be willed as universal laws. As Kant sees it, this principle is basic to theoretical as well as to practical reasoning: it is the supreme principle of reason *tout court*.[13]

At first thought there seems to be a lot to be said against the idea that this meagre little principle is the supreme principle of reason. It seems to demand too much and to offer too little. It seems to demand too much by requiring fully reasoned thought and action to be in principle followable by *all*. It seems to offer too little because it can be read (or misread) as setting negligible constraints on thought, speech or action. Should not those who aim to offer reasoned proposals do more than make proposals that others *could* understand, or *could* adopt for action? For example, should not reasoned thinking or acting provide a basis for reaching *agreement* (as Habermas and Rawls have suggested)? However, on closer reading the constraints of universalisability may be neither negligible nor excessive, either for practical or for theoretical purposes.

Kant maintains that anything that can count as an unconditional reason that could in principle reach *all* others must satisfy requirements both of *form* and of *scope*. Even reasoning that seeks only a limited audience must have '*the form of law*', that is to say be based on concepts and principles that the relevant audience could in principle follow (in thought or in action, as the case may be). But reasoning that is to reach an unrestricted audience must have not only '*the form of law*' but also universal *scope*, so must not rely on concepts or principles that some others could not in principle follow in thought or adopt in action. This combination of constraints on form and scope can be demanding, and can justify a wide range of principles of action, including ethical duties, principles of justice and epistemic standards.

Incomplete reasoning that invokes 'authorities' of one or another sort can meet the first requirement, but not the second: its conclusions will often be law-like in form, but will not be universal in scope. Appeals to 'authorities' such as actual laws or regulations, actual customs or shared beliefs, do indeed appeal to *law-like* principles that can be relevant to a plurality of cases: but they offer no reasons for those who do not assume or accept the relevant authorities to embrace specific beliefs or to act as proposed.

---

[12] *G* 4:421.   [13] Cf. *CPrR* 5:3.

The *scope* of such reasoning is therefore inevitably conditional or limited. Kant called it *heteronomous reasoning*, or (in a now obsolete sense of the term) *private reasoning*. When applied to the interpretation of texts it can yield *doctrinal* interpretations that take some authority for granted, so lack universal *scope*. When applied to proposals for action it can yield technical, conditional and institutional conclusions, which once again lack universal scope.

Kant contrasts *conditional* reasoning with the *unconditional* reasoning needed to justify universal moral and epistemic norms, including norms of duty and of justice. If we reject principles that *cannot* in principle be adopted *by all*, we must reject principles of destroying or damaging others, of coercing or doing violence to them, and of undermining their capacities for action by deception or manipulation. Action on principles that aim to destroy, damage or subvert capacities for action cannot be thought of as universally available, since they aim to undermine or destroy (at least) some others' capacities to act on like principles.[14] Those who seek to coerce, to deceive, to oppress, to enslave, to do violence or the like therefore *cannot* offer *all* others reasons to act on the principles they espouse.

This line of argument can provide a basis for a plurality of substantive but limited conclusions about human duties. It will not show that there are duties to adopt unqualified principles of non-coercion, non-deception, non-oppression etc., or other unqualified principles forbidding the destruction or subjection of agents or their agency. However, it can show that those who seek to offer others reasons for action that could be adopted by all must *reject* principles of coercion, violence, deception, oppression etc.[15] For if (*per impossibile*) these principles were universally adopted, agency would be destroyed or damaged for some or for many, and so the principles could not be principles for all. Important epistemic norms could, I believe, be given parallel derivations. If (*per impossibile*) norms of deceit, inconsistency or self-contradiction were universally adopted, epistemic capacities would be destroyed or damaged or undermined for some or for many, and so the principles could not be principles for all. These points offer *just* enough to suggest why the doubly modal, negative

---

[14] For present purposes I leave aside the derivation of the basic principles of imperfect duties, which are slightly more complex because the relevant principles of action refer to ends. See Chapter 6, above, and my *Towards Justice and Virtue: A Constructive Account of Practical Reasoning* (Cambridge University Press, 1996).

[15] Duties form a set of mutually *qualifying* requirements: otherwise innumerable conflicts between principles of duty would undermine the practicality of duty. For parallel reasons, human rights are standardly seen as *qualified* rights.

demand that Kant's vindication of reason proposes is not one more appeal to authority and is not empty.[16] For present purposes I leave it open whether this weak conception of reason supports a sufficient range of ethical and epistemic norms in order to return to questions about interpretation of texts and about practical judgement.

Reasoned interpretation and sacred texts

Kant's vindication of reason provides a basis for justifying a *plurality* of moral duties that set constraints on action and are fundamental for practical judgement. But it is far from obvious how morality can contribute to the interpretation of texts.[17] Yet Kant holds that the same principles of duty that can orient action in practical judgement can and should be used to interpret the sacred texts of religious traditions, including Christian Scripture: "... the sacred narrative ... should at all times be taught and expounded in the interest of morality" (*R* 6:132).

It is easy to miss the boldness of this thought. Kant does not claim that reason can extract an intrinsic moral meaning from sacred texts, which can then be expounded to the faithful. That approach to exegesis appeals not to reason but to established authority, is the stock in trade of biblical theologians and has guided millions of sermons. But Kant emphatically rejects the thought that a text *as such* could have unconditional authority. He writes that the Bible is no more than a book that has "fallen into human hands";[18] that traditional faith may be no more than something which "chance ... has dealt to us" based on a "revelation we happen to have".[19] He takes it that there is no intrinsic reason to suppose that contingent cultural documents and traditions are morally admirable, or even morally sound. The task of reasoned interpretation as undertaken by 'philosophical theologians' is therefore *not* to look for a true, inner or 'original' meaning in the Scriptures, but to *impose* a moral, hence reasoned, interpretation on them. Kant accepts that

> This interpretation may often appear to us as forced ... and be often forced in fact; yet, if the text can at all bear it, it must be preferred to a literal interpretation that either contains absolutely nothing for morality, or even works counter to its incentives.[20]

---

[16] For more detailed versions of the line of thought in this section see Part I of my *Constructing Authorities: Kant on Reason, Politics and Interpretation* (Cambridge University Press, 2016).

[17] I shall focus here mainly on Kant's account of the interpretation of religious texts 'within the limits of mere reason', and say very little about his parallel comments on legal reasoning and interpretation.

[18] *R* 6:107.   [19] *R* 6:110.   [20] *R* 6:110.

The same strategy of using reasoned and consequently moral interpretation can be applied to other sacred texts. Kant points out that the classical authors managed to interpret "the coarsest polytheism" as "symbolic representation of the properties of one divine being" (*R* 6:111) which served to bring their meaning closer to "a moral doctrine intelligible to all human beings" (*R* 6:111). He makes parallel comments on interpreting the sacred texts of Judaism, Islam and Hinduism: "for the final purpose of … the reading of these holy books … is to make better human beings".[21]

Of course, other ways of interpreting Scripture and other sacred texts abound. Some appeal to mere spontaneity, feeling or enthusiasm, others to one or another presumed authority. However, only interpretation that is guided by morality, hence by practical reasoning, avoids the arbitrariness of invoking either undisciplined spontaneity or arbitrary authority. Only it can shape interpretation in ways that are neither doctrinaire nor arbitrary. As Kant sees it, the discipline of reasoned interpretation is **negative** (it does not defer to presumed authorities), **law-like** (it embodies principles) and has **universal scope** (these principles could be adopted by all). Reasoned interpretation will deploy the standards of practical reason – hence of the Categorical Imperative – and the principles of duty that it can vindicate, and will aim at interpretation 'in the interests of morality'.

This is strong stuff, and it is hardly surprising that the Prussian censors condemned Kant's late writing on religion. He privileges principles of interpretation over the texts themselves, over the *ipsissima verba*. If we ask "… whether morality must be interpreted in accordance with the Bible, or the Bible … in accordance with morality",[22] he responds uncompromisingly that if literal interpretation does nothing for morality, a forced interpretation that is guided by reason, and so by morality, is to be preferred.

Why practical judgement is different: 'more theory'

The tasks of theologians, of lawyers, of doctors and of other experts go beyond interpretation. They must also put expertise into practice, so must make practical as well as reflective judgements; as must all of us. Practical judgement may be variously instrumental, technical or professional, or

---

[21] *R* 6:111. None of this, Kant insists, gives the 'lower' faculty licence to reject or diminish popular religion, or to undermine the work of the biblical theologians and scriptural scholars of the 'higher' faculty.

[22] *R* 6:110n.

moral, prudential and political, but it is neither determinant nor reflective since it is used to enact principles rather than to describe or interpret cases.

How much can an account of practical judgement show about moving from indeterminate principles to determinate acts that instantiate those principles? Kant comments in the *Critique of Practical Reason* that this can be difficult, but does not suggest how it is to be done:

> judgement *under laws of* pure practical reason seems therefore to be subject to special difficulties having their source in this: that a law of freedom is to be applied to actions as events that take place in the sensible world and belong to nature (*CPrR* 5:68)[23]

However, in this passage he then states that the rule of judgement [*sic*] under laws of pure practical reason is "ask yourself whether, if the action you were to propose were to take place by a laws of nature of which you were yourself a part, could you indeed regard it as possible through your own will" (*CPrR* 5:69). This rule states how *practical reason* is to identify principles of duty, but does not offer an account of how *practical judgement* is to select one rather than another way of enacting principles of duty. An adequate account of practical judgement should surely offer more. It should show how agents can make judgements when the 'universal' (rule, concept, principle, law) is justified *but the particular is not given*.

The task of practical judgement is articulated more clearly in *Theory and Practice*, where Kant makes it explicit that it is not *applied to the world*, but rather is used to *shape the world* (in small part). In practical judgement we start with principles, which we then seek to enact, instantiate or realise. Practical judgement is quite different from reflective judgement, which can be used to evaluate existing or past states of affairs or situations, but not to guide action. In some cases practical judgement is institutional or technical, and in others it is moral. In both cases the task of judgement is not the application (*Anwendung*) of principles to existing acts, but their enactment or instantiation (*Ausübung*) in an actual situation.[24] Practical judgement guides acts not yet performed rather than evaluating those already performed.

---

[23] Cf. earlier on the same page: "it seems absurd to want to find in the sensible world a case which though, as such it stands under the law of nature, yet admits of the application to it of a law of freedom and to which there could be applied the supersensible idea of the morally good, which is to be exhibited in it in concreto".

[24] Cf. "Man nennt einen Inbegriff selbst von praktischen Regeln alsdann Theorie, wenn diese Regeln als Prinzipien in einer gewissen Allgemeinheit gedacht werden, und dabei von einer Menge Bedingungen abstrahiert wird, die doch auf ihre Ausübing notwendig Einfluß haben" (*TP* 8:275).

In *Theory and Practice* Kant first sets out an extended example of the use of practical judgement in enacting technical principles or rules. Technical practice is a matter of "effecting an end which is thought as the observance [*Befolgung*] of certain principles of procedure [*des Verfahrens*: of the activity] represented in their generality", that is to say as a matter of living up to (*observing, conforming to, enacting, instantiating*) certain principles or standards. Here, he writes "The worth of practice rests entirely on its conformity with the theory underlying it" (*TP* 8:277).[25] Practical judgement is complex, because it is guided by "a sum of rules, even of practical rules [which is] called a theory" (*TP* 8:275).[26] It is not a matter of seeking to enact practical principles one-by-one. Kant concludes that having *more* rules, or '*more theory*', is often helpful for practical judgement.

As I read these passages, the relation of principle to practice in practical judging is therefore quite different from that of principle to particulars in either determinant or reflective judging. Practical judgement is neither a matter of *subsuming* an available particular under a 'universal', nor a matter of *finding* some appropriate 'universal' for describing or interpreting an available case. Practical judgement is in the first place a matter of *living up to* principles, of *enacting* or *crafting* action to fit a principle: it aims to shape rather than to fit the world.

But why is having *more rules* or '*more theory*' helpful for practical judgement? In *Theory and Practice* Kant illustrates this question for *two* types of practical judgement: technical judgements and moral judgements. He illustrates putting *technical* expertise into practice with the case of an artilleryman who knows the relevant scientific theories (mechanics, ballistics), but finds that their relation to practice is imprecise. He may fail in practice because he lacks enough theory, so needs '*more theory*', such as theories of friction and air resistance. *More theory* would enable him to understand and so to control the trajectory of projectiles more accurately. Kant concludes that

---

[25] The sense in which practical rules are called 'theory' in these passages is evidently that they are *abstract* or *indeterminate*, and not that they are *theoretical* as opposed to *practical*: their intended use is to change rather than to fit the world.

[26] The German reads "Man nennt einen Inbegriff selbst von praktischen Regeln alsdann Theorie, wenn diese Regeln als Prinzipien in einer gewissen Allgemeinheit gedacht werden, und dabei von einer Menge Bedingungen abstrahiert wird, die doch auf ihre Ausübung notwendig Einfluß haben" (*TP* 8:275). Kant makes it plain that he is focused on *theory guiding action*, rather than *applying to action* by using the word *Ausübung* (*enactment, instantiation*) rather than *Anwendung* (*application*). Practical rules are called 'theory' in these passages only because they are *abstract* or *indeterminate*, and not because they are *theoretical* in a sense that contrasts with *practical*: their intended use is to change rather than to fit the world.

> in such cases it was not the fault of theory if it was of little use in practice, but rather of there having been *not enough* theory … Thus nobody can pretend to be practically proficient in a science and yet scorn theory without declaring that he is an ignoramus in his field … (*TP* 8:275–6)

A parallel demand for *more theory* can also support moral judgement, which is also a matter of working out how to respect a *plurality* of constraints, including not only empirical, technical or institutional constraints, but the demands of duty. Practical judgement that respects "a theory based on the *concept of duty*" (*TP* 8:276) needs to respect the multiple constraints that are specified by a *plurality* of principles of duty: here too "the worth of practice rests entirely on its conformity with the theory underlying it" (*TP* 8:276).

Moral judgement too is not a matter of living up to one-duty-at-a-time. If we were to address principles of duty one-at-a-time, we would be less able to judge how best to enact them in actual situations than we are if we consider the plurality of duties that make legitimate claims.

With commitment to a plurality of duties, unclarity reduces. For the task is then to identify ways of acting that reject principles of violence or coercion, of deception or dishonesty, and other principles that damage or victimise, while also exemplifying a range of imperfect duties as well as taking account of relevant non-moral constraints. 'More theory' is helpful for moral judgement, which must fasten on action that satisfies a plurality of constraints.

However, commitment to a plurality of principles of duty will unavoidably still leave action underdetermined. Kant made this explicit for the case of imperfect duties, when he wrote in *Metaphysics of Morals*:

> if the law can prescribe only the maxim of actions, not actions themselves, this is a sign that it leaves playroom (*latitudo*) for free choice in following (complying with) the law, that is, that the law cannot specify precisely in what way one is to act and how much one is to do by the action for an end that is also a duty. (*MM* 6:390)[27]

This also holds for maxims of action on perfect duties: indeterminacy cannot be eliminated, and practical judgement is never mechanical.

Principles of duty that can be justified by appeal to the Categorical Imperative   make   serious   demands,   but   each   leaves   action

---

[27] Kant makes various more specific versions of this claim: "there is no law of reason [for cultivating one's own perfection] for action but only a law for maxims of actions" (*MM* 6:392); "The law [of beneficence] holds only for maxims, not for determinate actions" (*MM* 6:393); "ethical obligation to ends … involves only a law for *maxims* of actions" (*MM* 6:395).

underdetermined, and so does their conjunction. This indeterminacy may be reduced but cannot be wholly eliminated by taking account of technical, legal and institutional constraints.[28] Taking account of a *plurality* of ethical and epistemic principles augments the extent to which principles can guide action, but does not yield algorithms for action, or for morally acceptable action. Yet if indeterminacy is ineliminable, may this not create unmanageable problems for practical and in particular for moral judgement? Will it leave agents trembling indecisively like Buridan's ass each time they make a practical judgement? Can we say more about practical judging?

Picking, choosing and practical judging

One way of understanding what practical judging demands is to view *any* action that violates no duty as morally adequate, and to accept that judgement can do no more. Why should we have to offer reasons for *picking* one rather than another act that satisfies the demands of duty? On some views, choice and reasoning need not select particular acts, or even exhaustively specified act types, from others that are morally and functionally equivalent: practical judgement cannot and need not resolve indeterminacy 'all the way down'. In 'picking' a tin of soup from a display where nothing except location distinguishes it from adjacent tins, there may be *no reason* to choose one rather than another tin.[29] Why need practical judgement reach further?

However, mere picking may not be adequate where differences between available acts matter. Good practical judgement often needs careful discrimination, including discrimination between closely similar acts. Most practical judging is *not* at all like picking a tin of soup from a display, where the chosen tin sits on a shelf in its magnificent but barely discernible individuality (next to the unchosen tins). It is better exemplified by fluent speakers whose well-judged conversation simultaneously observes complex standards for truth-telling, for speaking grammatically, for confidentiality and for courtesy; or by accomplished dancers whose movements respect the music and traditions of a dance, and embody spontaneity while also communicating complex narratives and emotions; or by skilful drivers who

---

[28] Similarly basic epistemic norms, such as 'do not argue from inconsistent premises' or 'do not disregard evidence', will leave belief and knowledge underdetermined, and here too indeterminacy can be reduced but not eliminated by augmenting evidence and refining arguments.

[29] A distinction explored in E. Ullmann-Margalit and S. Morgenbesser, 'Picking and Choosing', *Social Research*, 44 (1977), 757–67.

not merely respect moral and legal requirements (safety, speed limits) but drive with anticipation, fluency and steadiness.

Good practical judgement is both spontaneous and well judged: it is intelligently spontaneous. Good moral judgement is intelligently spontaneous and respects a plurality of principles of duty. In moral judgement too having *more theory* is productive and formative for practical judgement. Moral judgement aims at action that is simultaneously reasoned, spontaneous and well judged. It may, for example, be both honest and kind, both helpful and protective of others' self-respect, while also meeting numerous conventional and technical requirements.

Kant rejects the arbitrary judgements of enthusiasts not because they exemplify spontaneity, but because their choosing manifests *only* spontaneity and ignores both reason and authority, so overlooking both morally and institutionally significant matters. Enthusiasts who make what he called 'a lawless use of freedom' are likely to make capricious and morally inadequate practical judgements. However, spontaneity need not be lawless: disciplined spontaneity may attend either to the claims of authority, or to those of reason, and in the latter case to the claims of duty and epistemic claims as well as to the realities of situations and the permissible desires and aims of the agent and of others.

An account of good practical judgement needs to be anchored in attentiveness to a plurality of requirements and considerations. An account of good moral judgement needs to be anchored in attentiveness to the moral requirements as well as other requirements and considerations for which reasons can be given. When Kant remarked that "the power of judgement is a special talent that cannot be taught but only practiced" (*CPR* A132/B171) he indicates that judgement of all sorts is underdetermined by rules or theory, but can nevertheless be shaped by a plurality of rules that, taken together, provide enough context and structure for judgement of all sorts. In particular, a plurality of rules can provide *enough* 'theory' for good practical, and (where relevant) good moral, judgement. Like determinant and reflective judgement, practical judgement is underdetermined by reason or by rules: but like them it is "capable of being instructed and equipped through rules" and can be intelligently responsive to and shaped by a plurality of rules, among them by moral rules with reasoned justification.

PART III

Means, ends and demands

CHAPTER 9

Reason and the resolution of disputes[1]

Can reasoned argument help end disputes and conflicts? A colleague of mine once remarked that where he came from – Long Island, as it happens – arguments were something parents had on Saturday nights. Others have a more benign view of the matter: they hold, or at least hope, that reason, which trades in arguments, is at least a desirable and sometimes an effective way of settling differences.

This disagreement is in part little more than a concern with different matters. My colleague was pointing out that many people equate arguments with uses of argument, and in particular with aggressive and intemperate uses of argument, hence with fights, rather than with the coherent structures prized by those who admire reason. Anyone who thinks arguments can embody reason, rather than mere antagonism and forensics, might still hope there will be fewer fights if we become better at introducing the calming influence of logical form and right reason into our arguments and so into our disputes: they will agree that arguing as such has little to commend it, but will pin some hope on reasoned arguing.

My aim here is to discuss what reason *can* and *cannot* offer towards the resolution of disputes, and to consider whether it provides what its admirers claim. Even if it offers much, negotiating the acceptance of this offer – that is bringing disputants to use reason rather than to fight – will often be formidably difficult. I shall say nothing of the ways in which disputants could be got to use reason rather than to rely on other tactics. This is not because there is nothing to be said: proposals for changing the ways in which disputes are conducted have been much discussed and undertaken not only by mediators, bargainers and negotiators, but also (perhaps impurely) by politicians, lawyers, counsellors and many other experts. I will not trespass on their territories, which I am not even

---

[1] Onora O'Neill, 'Reason and the Resolution of Disputes', *Notre Dame Law Review*, 67 (1992), 1365–77. Available at: scholarship.law.nd.edu/ndlr/vol67/iss5/4.

competent to chart. All that I hope to contribute is some reflections on the question whether, *if* reasoning could be introduced into disputes, this could help resolve them. This is not, however, a pointless task, for there would be little point in labouring to conform our own or others' activities to standards of reason if these are in any case illusory standards, or if their adoption could not help resolve disputes.

In the last century many have been ready to insist that the alleged contrast between reason and other ways of settling disputes is illusory. The unmasking of reason's supposedly usurped authority has at times become a major cultural industry: deconstructionists and other postmodernists entered in the vanguard in the late twentieth century, but close behind them there were the rather more numerous ranks of communitarians and committed greens. The communitarians demoted reason to the accepted standards of wider, but not universal, scope: they denounced what they termed 'the Enlightenment project', and its political wing, which they identified with liberalism. Many greens discern a malign alliance between reason and the attempts to dominate nature, which may lead us to global disaster.

In the face of this onslaught the defenders of reason seem strangely silent and ineffective. I think it is not hard to see what makes them hesitate. Their problem is surely that it is not clear how they should defend reason: to provide a reasoned defence of reason looks as if it must backfire, since it will be circular, and avoiding circular arguments is thought to be part of what it is to reason. On the other hand, an unreasoned defence of reason appears to concede the case against reason by allowing that something other than reason is fundamental.

A direct answer to this challenge is, I believe, possible; I have articulated it elsewhere.[2] However, here I want to take the low road rather than the high road, and look at particular aspects of reasoning that have been called to task by various sceptics about reason. Instead of trying to show how a vindication of reason is in principle possible, I shall start by considering some of the standard claims that are made for and against particular conceptions of what it would be to rely on reason in practical affairs. I shall say nothing about those processes of sorting and sifting, of comparing and articulating, which are presumed to be common to theoretical and

---

[2] For fuller discussion of this view of the authority of reason see the papers in the first section of my *Constructing Authorities: Reason, Politics and Interpretation in Kant's Philosophy* (Cambridge University Press, 2016).

practical uses of reason, and nothing about any modes of reasoning that may be distinctive to theory.[3]

Instrumental reasoning

The most admired and the most denounced form of practical reasoning is instrumental reasoning, but this is in large part because there have been many excessive claims about its capacities and its competence. Bentham and his followers think that it can be articulated in models of rational choice, and that it can be put to use in handling all of life's disputes, since it will guide us in working out the utility of available options and choosing between options on the basis of well-defined, usually maximising, decision procedures. On the other hand, opponents of 'the Enlightenment project' denounce instrumental reason for cloaking arbitrariness with illusory authority. Who is right here?

The critics of instrumental reasoning trace its supposed arbitrariness to the arbitrariness of the ends whose efficient and effective pursuit it demands. If these ends are equated with whatever happens to be preferred, then indeed the recommendations that emerge from instrumental reasoning can never be less arbitrary than those preferences. If we do not think of preferences and desires as intrinsically oriented to the real and the good, as Plato did, then their efficient pursuit may not be either intrinsically reasoned or intrinsically good.

All of this is robust and convincing. But it hardly amounts to a refutation of instrumental reasoning. What it attacks, after all, is the practice of hitching instrumental reasoning to subjective desires or preferences, which happen to arise in particular individuals at particular times, and treating this as all there is to reasoning practically. What is attacked is a specifically modern conception of the locus of instrumental reasoning, that assimilates it to utilitarian or economic reasoning, by which we are supposed to identify *optimal* acts, rather than the more commonplace and more strictly instrumental aspects of practical reason, by which we routinely identify *feasible* means and *foreseeable* results, without necessarily referring to preferences or to maximising strategies. Utilitarians, economists and their allies have no monopoly of these supposedly more modest uses of instrumental reasoning, and instrumental reasoning is not called into question because it has been put to exorbitant uses by these optimisers.

---

[3] However, I take it that there is a great deal to be said and that both procedures of sifting and sorting etc. and the specifically theoretical use of *reason* also require vindication.

Indeed, it is hard to see what it would be to reject the practice of reasoning instrumentally, if this is construed simply as the requirement of seeking some means to those goals one is committed to, avoiding acts which obstruct those goals and exercising foresight over the likely results of action. No agent in fact evades these constraints, and those whose action conforms to them imperfectly suffer at best failure and inefficiency, and at worst madness or disaster.

What is objectionable is not instrumental reasoning, but a *merely* instrumental conception of practical reason. Moreover, it is objectionable not only because it assigns unjustified weight to whatever desires and preferences agents happen to have, but because it makes false assumptions about the coherent structure of those desires and preferences. In order for instrumental reasoning *alone* to monopolise the tasks of practical reasoning, the preferences of agents have to be massaged so that they look connected and transitively ordered, and then regimented by imposing a metric by which trade-offs between different preferences can be computed. If we want to talk about the rationality of social as well as individual choice, we also have to assume that this massaging and regimenting will squeeze the preferences of all agents into one uniform metric. Economic and utilitarian rationalities, I suggest, are suspect not because they are instrumental, but because of their fictitious account of the formal structure of subjective ends, and because they do not show why we should take all and only subjective ends seriously.

However, unhitching instrumental rationality from those intrinsically arbitrary ends does not seem in itself to tell us much about the use of reason in resolving disputes. For instrumental reasoning alone does not get us very far. It leaves us only with conditional recommendations: *if* you are committed to some end, seek some effective means; *if* you undertake some act, take account of the likely results. Where there is conflict, agreement about effective means to given ends or about the likely results of given acts is not enough to resolve disputes. The polemic against instrumental rationality has in fact been misnamed, since it is really a polemic against weighing subjective ends so heavily and against fictitious accounts of their formal structure. Yet the polemic is not pointless if it leads us to a clearer awareness of the limited claims on behalf of instrumental reasoning that can be justified. What is left will include a limited conception of means–ends rationality, to which neither communitarians nor greens nor anyone else should object. However, the cost of cutting instrumental reasoning down to size may seem to be that reason will offer indispensable, but inadequate, patterns for structuring the resolution of serious disputes.

Social norms and real options

One way forward might be to point out that instrumental reasoning *as we actually know it* is typically oriented by actual social norms. This is true even of utilitarian calculations, which have to *begin* by identifying certain possible lines of action or *options*. Only then can the reckoning of consequences and their evaluation in terms of preferences be undertaken. This is also true of processes of reason that do not aspire to utilitarian completeness, but use instrumental reasoning in more modest attempts to identify relations between means and ends.[4]

However, sets of options are not just 'given' to those who seek to reason: they are lists of act-types which particular agents think feasible or desirable or both. It would be impossible, in principle as well as in practice, to list *all* the options available in any situation. So we always take shortcuts; in particular, we cut the agenda down to a shortlist of options. As everyone knows, controlling the agenda is often the crucial move for controlling the outcome. But when we control the agenda of options, for which feasible means and likely outcomes are to be 'worked out', we in fact allow various socially entrenched norms and standards to form and limit the process of reasoning. To borrow a well-known example from Sartre: a son who is considering whether to leave home to try to join the Free French, or whether to care for his mother in a difficult situation, has picked out two socially sanctioned and feasible act-types, and conceives of his problem as that of choosing between them. He does not spend any time evaluating options deemed undesirable, such as fleeing to Switzerland, betraying the resistance to the Nazis or entering a monastery, let alone the myriad possible ways of filling – or wasting – time that might in principle be possible for him. Least of all does he waste time on the countless imaginable options that he assumes are not feasible in the situation.[5] Real life calculation either of optimal or of feasible action is necessarily framed by assumptions about which actions are worth serious consideration. It is common, but inaccurate, to speak of these actions as 'available'. They are presumably thought to be available – if they were not, who would be concerned to choose among them? – but they are also specifically taken to

---

4 See Jon Elster, *The Cement of Society: A Study of Social Order* (Cambridge University Press, 1989), for reasons why explanations that appeal to maximising calculations cannot avoid presupposing social norms.

5 Cf. Geoffrey Hawthorn, *Plausible Worlds: Possibility and Understanding in History and the Social Sciences* (Cambridge University Press, 1991). Agents do not survey all possible options, but a much more limited set of plausible options. Moreover, their conceptions of what is plausible embody not only a view of which acts are feasible, but a grid of social and other norms.

be part of a privileged group of 'real' options, in that they are thought to have a certain moral or practical claim. Because instrumental reasoners cannot genuinely consider *all* options, their reasoning is always framed by a grid of conventional standards and concerns, which pick out some options as worth considering and exclude others.

The supporters of instrumental rationality do not, it appears, discard or bracket ordinary social norms, but rather work within them and emphasise *one* set of constraints on choosing between the options defined by those norms. Instrumental reasoning, as it is actually done, is framed by specific grids of categories and norms. The most serious shortcoming of an instrumental account of practical reasoning may be less that it subordinates all of life to a single calculus of preference or of self-interest, than that, whether or not it is conceived of as hitched to agents' actual preferences, it uncritically accepts established categories and norms.

This shortcoming also raises a serious practical problem. Can reason help resolve disputes when different parties start with differing grids of categories, or see different lists of possible actions as constituting the 'real' options? The fantasy that disputes can be solved by instrumental reasoning alone evaporates fast when we note that in seriously disputed matters the antagonists nearly always have different views of the 'real' options. Here, it seems, instrumental reasoning will be quite helpless because categories, norms and options are disputed, and there will be no way in which to reach a common understanding of 'the options'.

Many who have realised that practical reason is hostage to established categories and practices in this way have concluded that it is illusory to think that there are ways of reasoning that will work for parties who do not share a common background. They hold that reasoning can and must take place within a framework of shared, socially entrenched assumptions. Attempts to reason without a shared framework of assumptions lead not to the resolution of disputes, but to loss of comprehension. The scope of practical reason runs no wider than the boundaries of 'our' form of life or tradition or community, reaching only those who share 'our' categories and norms.

This line of thought leads quite readily to a communitarian conception of practical reason, where reason is seen as ensconced within, indeed defined by, the discourse or ways of thought of some community or some tradition. Within that community and tradition, reasoning both about means, and in other terms sanctioned by the tradition, can be practised, but reasoning cannot cross the boundaries of traditions. All that reason can offer to the resolution of disputes is what it can offer to those who already agree on much. Reasoning is in place among those who share the same grid of categories, the same social norms, not to mention the same conception of reason. On this account, reason itself must be relativised to the actual norms and practices of each community of reasoners.

Evidently this conception of reason will disappoint many who think of reason as useful to the resolution of disputes. Disputes are often between those who do not share or who do not wholly share either categories or norms; and if reason is incompetent here, it will seem that it has nothing to offer to the resolution of the deepest and most dangerous conflicts, in which the very terms of debate, the very articulation of the dispute, is itself a source of fierce dispute. And yet the presumption that disputants who are to use forms of reasoning to work towards a resolution must share their terms of discourse seems to be one that nobody could reject. Unless disputants can understand one another's terms, they cannot be said to agree or to disagree about anything at all, hence cannot seek, let alone agree to, any resolution of their dispute.

Communitarianism, conservatism and ethnocentrism

At this point in reflecting on the role of reason in the resolution of disputes we seem to have reached a dilemma. Where disputants share an understanding of categories and norms, in short a culture, they can use the norms of that culture (which will no doubt include standards of instrumental rationality) to arbitrate their disputes. The resolutions they reach might appear arbitrary from some absolute standpoint outside that culture, but nothing establishes that there is such a standpoint. Alternatively, where disputants do not share the categories and norms of a common culture they cannot resolve disputes by reason. One way of reading the challenge communitarian writers raised to liberal political philosophy is that they insisted that reasoning about justice and politics must always be internal to the boundaries of community, because the very basis of reasoning requires that categories and norms be shared.

If the possibilities for reasoning about practice and politics are read in this way, the implications seem initially to be profoundly *conservative* and *ethnocentric.* The boundaries of actual communities and practices at any given time will be held to be the boundaries of possible discourse. In a sense, there can then be no disputes with outsiders, for outsiders will be incomprehensible. To come to understand the categories and norms of other cultures or communities would require, not reason, but 'conversion' to a quite distinct form of life. This picture of the obstacles to reasoned articulation of disputes can be found in writings on ethics and action by Wittgensteinians as well as in some communitarian writing. It points towards a deep form of ethical and even of conceptual relativism, which unnervingly makes the most radical disputes we actually face not merely irresolvable by reason, but incapable of articulation in ways that are intelligible to rival parties. On this view, it is unsurprising that what looks like reasoning so often becomes a fight: disputes between liberals and religious fundamentalists, between nationalists and cosmopolitans, between the advocates of justice and the friends of the virtues, between ideals of public and of private life can then be avoided by silence or confronted with violence, but since the disputants cannot comprehend or communicate with one another, they cannot be resolved by reason.

However, most communitarian writers do not take so narrow a view of the categories and norms which define a community. In particular, many of them have an answer at least to the charge of conservatism. They do not suppose that reasoners are imprisoned within the terms of discourse which they now have, and so are able to communicate only with those who share their present prison. They note that any developed community questions, debates, interprets and reviews its own terms of discourse.[6] Communitarians who acknowledge the historical transformation of categories and of norms need not be conservatives. They can make sense of the self-transformation of communities, who use their current grids of categories and norms of rational debate to develop different categories and different norms. Further, these transformations can be judged in terms of existing norms as more or less useful, rational and acceptable. Such communitarians not only can allow for historical change, but for improvements. They may, for example, judge a certain revision of existing practices an 'improvement' because it not merely grows out of existing practices, but renders them more intelligible and systematic. They can preserve an understanding of the past of their own community, and can glimpse possible futures which surpass their present.

Reasoning that is based on social norms can overcome conservatism by this strategy, but ethnocentrism is harder to leave behind. Historicised conceptions of normative rationality lack a ready way of explaining how the reasoning of outsiders can be or become accessible to them, or their own reasoning accessible to outsiders. Whether the boundaries of

---

[6] This point has been fundamental for communitarian claims, beginning with Alasdair MacIntyre, *After Virtue* (London: Duckworth, 1981), and Charles Taylor, *Philosophical Papers: Volume 2, Philosophy and the Human Sciences* (Cambridge University Press, 1985) and *Sources of the Self: The Making of Modern Identity* (Cambridge, MA: Harvard University Press, 1989).

community are conceived of as narrow and exclusive, or more broadly as great cultural traditions with many separate strands, there seems to be no account of reasoning as presupposing social norms which does not see it as the exclusive preserve of insiders. A historicist turn does not lead away from relativism, and does not offer a framework which can make sense of reasoning with outsiders.

Yet this conclusion seems to be deeply at odds with our actual experience, including our experience of dealing with outsiders. Whether we define our community in terms of shared religion, citizenship, nationality, ethnicity or clan, or narrowly in terms of some specific intersection of all of these, still it seems that as a matter of common fact we do understand much of what outsiders are saying. It is, after all, because we more or less understand them that we often reject their categories and norms, resent their lack of respect for our tradition, and seek to convince them that ours is admirable and their own defective. This suggests that there is some hope for reasoning which links not merely 'our' present to 'our' future, but 'our' present to 'others'' present. We are, so to speak, conceptually multilingual, and among the languages we usually understand are those our enemies use. Thus, Christians and liberals may have fundamentally divergent conceptions of human beings, yet many of them are familiar with both conceptions. If this sort of multilingualism is widespread, then why should the plurality of communities, each with their distinctive categories and norms, prevent the resolution of disputes by reason?

However, this appeal to our cultural 'multilingualism' may seem too fast. If disputes are to be resolved by reason we surely have not merely to *understand* what the other party is saying, but to *agree* with them on at least some matters. Without points of agreement there are no shared premises from which any process of reasoning can work. Understanding others' terms of discourse surely does not require us to agree or accept those terms of discourse, let alone the views of those who use them. On the contrary, it seems that, often enough, understanding others' beliefs is the basis for fierce resistance to their very categories of thought. Have not 'heretics' been identified and persecuted, whether by the Inquisition, by the KGB or by their successors, on the basis of a considerable understanding of the views they are propounding and without any agreement?

This conception of understanding in the absence of any agreement may be illusory. Even persecution, opposition and lesser forms of resistance are predicated not on understanding alone, but inevitably on some range of agreement. In the first place, there must be enough agreement for an understanding of others' terms and categories to be possible. Inquiry and interrogation, through which disagreement comes to light, must both be framed by some agreement. Any community, whose boundaries were so impervious that those whom the boundary separates could not communicate with one another, would have boundaries which obstructed not merely agreement, but disagreement. Perhaps such radically alien communities are imaginable. If they exist, no reasoning will contribute to resolving disputes with them – indeed, hostilities with such 'aliens' are perhaps not to be thought of as disputes. However, the actual situation of human communities is not like this: disputes abound, and with them some footholds for their rational resolution.

Constructing points of agreement

But footholds may not be enough. We do not doubt, for example, that the Israelis and Palestinians understand one another's positions very well, and that there must therefore be much on which they agree. However, we have good reason to doubt whether this measure of agreement can provide a basis for reasoned resolution of the matters which they dispute. The insufficiency of reason of this sort is not, in fact, confined to cases where communities differ deeply in religion, language, culture and tradition. We all know cases of feuding relatives who understand one another all too well, who agree on all too much, but whose dispute still cannot be resolved by reason. This suggests that the real limitation to reasoned resolution of disputes is not that categories and norms are not shared, or that there are no points of agreement, but simply that in many cases there are not enough points of agreement, or not the right points of agreement. Disputes may be intractable because, despite agreement on many points, these offer very little prospect of reasoned resolution of the particular matters most fiercely disputed.

Hence, if we are interested in the reasoned resolution of disputes, we need to take account not only of instrumental rationality (cut down to size) and of actually available points of agreement between particular disputants, but of the *construction* of further points of agreement that may be more useful in reasoning towards agreement on the matters in dispute. Yet, in formulating this thought, have we not reached the limit of the distinctive role that reasoning can play in the resolution of disputes? For is not the construction of new points of agreement a matter of pressure or conversion, of re-education or indoctrination, of arm-twisting and manipulation, rather than of reason? Have we not accepted, at this point, that reason can only get to work in sifting and sorting, in comparing and making coherent the matters to which disputants are already committed?

There is one further reasoned strategy which may be used to construct points of agreement between disputants who find that they still lack sufficient points of agreement to negotiate or bargain, or more generally to reason, about the matters at issue between them. This further strategy can best be explicated by reflecting on a quite minimal demand on anything that can count as reasoning between two parties who disagree on some matters. The only moves that will count as giving *reasons* will be ones both parties *can* follow. Insofar as we seek to resolve disputes by reasoning, the underlying principles on which we rely must therefore be sharable principles. For example, because the principle of instrumental rationality cannot be successfully rejected by any agent, it has a wholly general authority for the conduct of life, and so counts as a principle of practical reason.

However, the rejection of unsharable principles demands more than acceptance of instrumental rationality. It sets further substantive demands on how we should communicate and act; some of them are usually considered moral demands. Here I shall say nothing about the moral status of those demands, but will try to articulate why they are demands of reason. Put intuitively, if the kernel of practical reasoning is a matter of basing action and communication on principles that others too can follow, then those who seek to reason must reject strategies that destroy, disable or undermine others' capacities to follow principles. Some of the principles practical reasoners must therefore reject can be readily identified. For example, principles of destroying or injuring others' capacities for action are *in principle unsharable with those who are to be victims of acting on these principles*: we cannot expect those whom we destroy, injure or make into victims to act on the principles on which we would act in destroying or injuring them. Destruction and injury take many forms: violence destroys and injures bodies; coercion destroys and undermines the will; deception destroys and undermines understanding. Each of these has unending variety. Those who make principles of violence, of coercion or of deception fundamental to their conduct of disputes cannot claim to be seeking reasoned resolution to those disputes. Rather they are resorting to methods of settling disputes which will, in principle, bypass the agency and the reasoning of those with whom they are in dispute. If reasoning has to avoid relying on principles that others *cannot* share or follow, then it cannot be simply a matter of acting and communicating in ways that respect certain formal structures, or that respect instrumental rationality. Rather reasoned action has to be based on principles of helping to respect and to secure, rather than to damage and destroy, the capacities for action and understanding of those with whom one seeks to reason.

This argument does not show that those who are committed to reason may never use violence, coercion or deception, or that they may never injure in other ways. Actual human disputes often cannot be resolved without some injury to some parties. For example, the standard systems of dispute resolution within states with a constitutional and legal order, including fair administrative and legal procedures, work against a background of limited and controlled uses of violence and coercion by the police and by penal institutions. Perhaps we can devise no way of organising our public life that is less injuring. If so, a commitment to reason in these domains of life will be a commitment, not to an unattainable total elimination of all forms of injury, but to building and maintaining both institutions and characters in ways that will minimise destruction and injury of agents and of their capacities, so minimising reliance on intrinsically unreasoned procedures.

In many domains of dispute, we do not do as well in minimising reliance on intrinsically unreasoned procedures as we do in the public sphere of well-ordered states. Transnational disputes, disputes in states where constitutional and legal order are absent or fragile, and disputes in aspects of life where legal and even social order do not penetrate, all are open to methods of dispute resolution which do not reject destruction and injury—for example, war, crime and domestic violence. In these domains the sign that disputes are being increasingly settled by reason would not be that disputants increasingly align their action or discourse with certain formal procedures, but that they seek and respect transformations of institutional setting and individual character which secure the undamaged and unthreatened agency of all parties to any dispute. Only those who are committed to effectively institutionalising this objective can claim to be committed to reasoned resolution of disputes. Those who are not so committed accept and may inflict avoidable injury on other reasoners: in doing so they too fail to reason.

CHAPTER 10

Consequences for non-consequentialists

Both consequentialist and non-consequentialist ethical reasoning have difficulties in accounting for the value of consequences. Taken neat, consequentialism is too fierce in its emphasis on success and disregard of luck and failure, while non-consequentialism seemingly overvalues inner states and undervalues actual results.

In *Uneasy Virtue*[1] Julia Driver proposed a form of objective consequentialism which claims that characters are good if they typically (but not invariably) produce good results. This position addresses the problems moral luck raises for consequentialism, but requires some form of realism about traits of character. However, if our knowledge of mental states is ascriptive, this form of objective consequentialism may make excessive demands. Non-consequentialists may gain insofar as the theories of action to which they are typically committed are less demanding, and are built to take account of the *typical* or *systematic* connections between states of character and results of action.

Characters and consequences

Consequentialists claim a special relationship with consequences. They build their accounts of moral value and ethical requirements on an account of valuable (or at least valued) consequences, and their accounts of practical reasoning on instrumental reasoning deployed in pursuit of valuable (or at least valued) consequences.[2] They sometimes accuse non-consequentialists of ignoring consequences, alleging that they value acts for their underlying motives or intentions, or for some other internal feature of agents, regardless of results. Non-consequentialists are aware of this criticism. They

---

[1] Julia Driver, *Uneasy Virtue* (Cambridge University Press, 2001). Page references will be given parenthetically in the text.
[2] For some comments on distinguishing valuable from valued consequences see Chapter 3, above.

know that, as Barbara Herman has put it, they stand accused of thinking "that, because states of affairs are not possible bearers of value in Kantian ethics, what actually happens seems to be outside the purview of morality".[3]

Consequentialists have not, I think, commented sufficiently on non-consequentialist ways of taking account of consequences. It seems to me that they often assume that they gain by making consequences central to ethical reasoning, and that non-consequentialists lose out, yet they do not show that this is the case. I believe that it would be useful – both for consequentialists and for non-consequentialists – to set out clearly the ways in which consequences can be and should be taken into account (or disregarded) in differing ethical theories. Julia Driver's discussion of types of link between *good character* and *good consequences* contributes usefully to this aim, in the first place by proposing a grid of possibilities in the initial chapters and second by the careful attention she pays to the part that luck plays in ethical assessment when acts attempted and results achieved drift apart.

She begins by distinguishing *evaluational internalism* from *evaluational externalism*. *Evaluational internalists* hold that characters are good in virtue of 'internal' features of agents. When an agent acts with the appropriate internal feature, but does not produce good consequences (or any consequences), evaluational internalists will think that this need not tell against goodness of character (*xv*). They accept that luck may disconnect good character from good consequences, and for that matter bad character from bad consequences. One can have and even act with a morally desirable internal state to no good effect, or even to bad effect.

Some forms of evaluational internalism are consequentialist: for example, subjective utilitarians judge character on the basis of *agents' expectations* of the results of their action. Others are non-consequentialist. Julia Driver offers as an example Kant's view that a good will, *even if frustrated in its effects*, is still morally worthy (68–9). There are indeed well-known passages that make this claim, such as one early in the *Groundwork* where Kant says that a good will that fails to achieve its expected effects would "like a jewel … still shine by itself, as something that has its full worth in itself" (*G* 4:394). Some consequentialists are pleased to reject this resonant thought. Others are more bothered: they are reluctant to think that the virtues of prisoners or the powerless, or the generosity of widows who give mites, are

---

[3] Barbara Herman, 'What Happens to the Consequences?', in her *The Practice of Moral Judgement* (Cambridge, MA: Harvard University Press, 1993), 94–115. Cf. also Driver, *Uneasy Virtue*, 79–80.

not *really* virtues because they lack much in the way of effects. They may be even less willing to praise action that expresses malign intentions or motives but happens to have good effects.

As Driver sees it, evaluational internalists make some good points. They detach moral evaluation of character from excessive demands for success in action. Their ethics does not make unrealistic demands on agents. But she thinks that evaluational internalisms also have fundamental defects. Evaluational internalists are required to count traits that may be either useless or counterproductive as virtues, just because they (supposedly) have intrinsically valuable properties.

Evaluational externalists, by contrast, hold that character is good in virtue of factors external to agency. Julia Driver distinguishes several forms of evaluational externalism, including Aristotelian positions. *Aristotelians* ascribe good character to those who deploy their knowledge of human flourishing to judge situations accurately, and then act effectively to produce good results. For Aristotelians, failure in acting defeats the ascription of good character. As Driver sees it, however, Aristotelian evaluational externalists link evaluation *too closely* to knowledge of what is actually good and to success in achieving good results. So they see no moral merit in action where ignorance rather than knowledge plays a decisive part (modesty is her favoured example), or in action whose success is frustrated by ill luck.

Driver calls her own form of evaluational externalism *objective consequentialism*. It defines good character as possession of traits or virtues that produce good results. So it can take seriously those virtues in which ignorance rather than knowledge is important. However, unmodified objective consequentialism is, she thinks, too fierce in its emphasis on success and disregard of luck. Taken neat, it would take *no* account of good and ill luck: if everything hinges on *actual* results, we cannot claim that an agent was really virtuous when action that might have had good results in other (perhaps more likely) circumstances actually has bad results in a given case (*xix*). In this simple form, objective consequentialists judge acts by their *actual* results, so have to view 'unlucky' agents as less than virtuous, even as vicious.

Driver modifies objective consequentialism to limit its indifference to questions of luck, and reformulates it as the claim that "a virtue is a character trait that systematically produces a preponderance of good" (xvii).[4] She explicates the notion of *systematically producing good* as

---

[4] See also: "a virtue is a character trait that leads to good consequence systematically" (*Uneasy Virtue*, xviii); "a virtue is a character trait (a disposition or cluster of dispositions) that, generally speaking,

producing good in *normal* or *typical* conditions, but not necessarily in every *actual* condition. With this modification, objective consequentialists can take account of (ill) luck in judging action. Only *systematic* failure to produce good consequences will show that a trait is not a virtue at all, or that it is a vice.

Objective consequentialism and the revaluation of values

So the objective consequentialist claims that when traits cause valuable feelings and action, we judge them virtuous; when they do not, we judge them not virtuous, or even vicious. Character traits are internal states of agents at or through some time that lack intrinsic *value*, but have *derived* value if they have valuable consequences. Objective consequentialism "places no intrinsic value on states of mind, or on factors that are internal to agency" (68). Objective consequentialism seems to me a coherent and interesting position. One of its interesting features is that taken seriously it is likely to reject many widely accepted views about which traits count as virtues or as vices. This contrasts with much consequentialist writing, which has often been morally tame and anxious to show that solid consequentialist reasons can generally be given for conventionally good behaviour and conventional virtues. Similarly consequentialists have been defensive about charges that consequentialists are cavalier about rights, and have pointed to evidence that undermines this claim. By contrast, many earlier consequentialists took more unconventional moral views, as have rather fewer contemporary consequentialists.[5]

Objective consequentialism has at least some, and probably many, startling implications. Take, for example, the eighteenth-century trope that private vices may be public virtues, and in particular that greed and competitiveness are vices in individuals, but nevertheless have systematically beneficial social effects. On Julia Driver's view, if these causal claims are true, then greed and competitiveness are *really* virtues of individuals. Ayn Rand was right! It is just *bien pensant* conformity to suggest that all conventional virtues will count as virtues for objective consequentialists. Perhaps lots of conventional virtues are not virtues at all, and are wrongly respected. Perhaps many are the remnant of the virtues of earlier

---

produces good consequences for others" (60); and "a virtue is a character trait that produces more good (in the actual world) than not systematically" (82).

[5] An example of the latter would be Peter Singer's work on animal liberation and effective altruism across many decades.

ages, for example of periods when monkish or martial traits had better consequences than they are now taken to have.

Objective consequentialists will count as virtues all traits with systematically good consequences, even if they are not usually thought virtues. Even 'non-moral' characteristics such as dexterity or charm seem to qualify as virtues. Julia Driver restricts the claim that just *any* trait with beneficial effects is a virtue to some degree, by proposing that what counts is not just producing good, but specifically producing good *for others*, or preventing harms *to others*. (I am unsure whether this means that charm is not a virtue after all; cf. *Uneasy Virtue* 106.) She also proposes that we limit the traits that are to count as virtues to those that produce *intentional* action, suggesting in her final formulation that "a character trait is a moral virtue iff it is a disposition to produce (i.e. it tends to produce) *intentional* action that is systematically productive of the good" (107). (I am not sure where this leaves modesty and other virtues of ignorance.) These two reformulations are likely to leave us with a remarkably transformed tally of virtues and vices.

I raise a smallish question at this point: if objective consequentialism is likely to lead to radical transvaluations of accepted values, can discussions of the position coherently appeal to examples and cases that rely heavily on conventional moral assumptions for their interpretation and acceptance?

Traits, dispositions and consequences

However, to my mind the most difficult feature of objective consequentialism is not that it gives us reasons to reject or revise well-entrenched substantive moral views, including many conventional classifications of virtues and vices. The harder questions are raised by the robust, and in my view implausible, claims that objective consequentialists make about internal traits.

For objective consequentialists, traits are internal states that are not intrinsically valuable. Objective consequentialists retain internalism *in the theory of action* (*theory of mind?*) but reject it *in ethics* since they do not "make an appeal to special internal states as definitive of virtue" (*Uneasy Virtue* 60). Internal states have only *indirect* value, derived from their systematic or typical consequences. Julia Driver notes that others have suggested that, since she accepts that there are internal states and only denies their intrinsic value, she might be said to reject *antecedentism* rather than *internalism* (69). She accepts internalism about inner states, in taking it that we can know what traits agents have; she denies internalism in ethics – alternatively denies 'antecedentism' – in favour of consequentialism.

The claim that character traits are knowable internal states of agents at or through certain times requires robust metaphysical and epistemological backing. If internal states are to cause expressions of feeling, attitudes and action they must be knowable independently of their results. The consequentialist way of taking consequences seriously sees earlier events or states as deriving value from their typical consequences. Consequentialisms of the standard sort claim that *acts* are valuable because of their (expected) consequences. Virtue consequentialisms claim that *traits* are valuable because of their (typical) consequences.

Consequentialism works as a way of evaluating acts because they can be identified independently of their consequences. In jumping into a pond I cause ripples to spread across its whole surface, disturb the tadpoles, lower my body temperature and startle the passers-by. Here causal claims are in order because the act – my jumping into the pond – is identifiable independently of its effects. Had circumstances been different, my jumping into the pond might have caused other effects: the pond is covered with ice, so no ripples; it is the wrong season, so no tadpoles; the water is warm, so I am not cooled; there are no passers-by, so none are startled. My jumping is distinct from the effects of my jumping, and causal reasoning can connect them.

If consequentialism is to be applied to the evaluation of character traits they too must be knowable independently of their consequences. Objective consequentialists need to show that traits can be identified independently of the expressions of feeling and attitude, acts and further consequences that they bring about. That is why they need to accept some form of psychological internalism or (we might say) some form of *realism about traits of character*.

Some passages in *Uneasy Virtue* leave me unsure whether Julia Driver is wholly committed to this robust view of internal states, including virtues or vices, which objective consequentialism requires. In these passages she speaks not of *internal states* but of *dispositions* to feel and act in certain ways. On the surface, a disposition claim simply reports a tendency for certain types or patterns of events to occur: in this case for certain types of expression of feelings or attitudes, or certain types of action, to occur. In ascribing dispositions we need not claim that there is any unitary underlying cause that explains each disposition claim. Where a disposition claim is linked to causal claims, something *additional* is said or assumed. For example, it may be that a disposition is *explained* by some state of affairs, or by some mechanism or event. My car's tendency to be sluggish on cold mornings is, for example, a dispositional claim for which I believe that there may be one or more underlying causes (I may be unsure what they are). In ascribing the disposition to the car, I make *no specific claim about the cause or causes* of the sluggishness. Ascribing traits of character need be no different. In judging that a colleague lacks discretion on the basis of aspects of his action, and the attitudes and feelings he expresses, I make no claim about the causes of his action or attitudes, and need not assume that there is a unitary cause for all his indiscretions.

The thought that virtues are dispositions is epistemologically minimalist. If we view character traits *just* as dispositions to act in certain ways we claim that an agent manifests certain tendencies or patterns. We do not claim that those tendencies and patterns are the causes of acts, expressions of attitudes or feelings, nor therefore can we claim that dispositions can or should be classified as virtues or vices on the basis of their supposed consequences. Those who see character traits minimally as dispositions cannot adopt objective consequentialist accounts of the virtues. To see traits as *causes* of feelings, attitudes or acts one needs to view them, and so also virtues and vices, more robustly as (real, internal) states of agents.

An epistemologically *minimalist* view of traits as dispositions or tendencies is, in my view, more convincing than a more robust internalist view that they are individuable, knowable states of agents. It is certainly metaphysically and epistemologically less demanding. But I think that if I were a virtue consequentialist of the sort that Julia Driver seeks to be, I would be constrained to adopt the more robust view of traits, since it is required if we are to think of *traits as causes*, of *virtues as traits that systematically or typically cause good consequences* and of *vices as traits that systematically or typically cause bad consequences.* Only a metaphysically and epistemologically robust account of traits allows room for the thought that the value of their consequences determines the value of traits.

The reason why a minimalist view of traits is convincing is that the only evidence we have for traits consists of patterns of action and expressions of feeling and these always underdetermine the ascription of traits. But to claim that a trait is a cause of expressions of feeling, or attitudes, or acts we have to view it as knowable and identifiable. We are not only short of evidence that specific traits cause certain sorts of action; we are short of the conceptual framework within which we can pick out traits in the required way. So we are short of the conceptual framework within which an objective consequentialist account of virtues makes sense. We often cannot tell how many internal states (or events), or which sorts of internal states (or events), cause a given pattern of expression of feelings and attitudes and of action. Does a pattern of behaviour that includes vacant looks and inaction indicate depression, boredom, inattention – or several, or all, or none of these? Do hyperactivity, a constant grin and wild chatter indicate cheerfulness or mania, or displacement activity that masks insecurity, or several, or all, or none of these?

If we take a more minimal, ascriptive view of traits, we will not seek evidence for internal states beyond the pattern of action and expression that robust internalists – in my view mistakenly – regard as effects of internal states. The task of pattern recognition is well illustrated by the stock Kantian example of the accurate shopkeeper who gives the right change to everyone, including children. Kant observes that we cannot tell whether his maxim – here taken to articulate a trait – is one of *honesty* or of *concern for reputation*. Indeed, for all we know, the shopkeeper's action might reflect fear of the police or of divine retribution, blind conformity, lack of arithmetic confidence and many other traits.

However, Julia Driver claims, "there is great textual evidence for regarding Kant as an evaluational internalist" (71). If so, his shopkeeper example wrong-foots him. My own reading is that Kant was not an evaluative internalist; indeed that he denies that we can have determinate knowledge of our own or of others' traits. A robust view of internal states and of our knowledge of them would be hard to reconcile with his repeated claim that we are not transparent to ourselves, or with his insistence that our evidence for ascribing traits or principles either to ourselves or to others greatly underdetermines those ascriptions. The shopkeeper example illustrates rather than undermines Kant's view, as do the asides on which the so-called 'grim' reading of Kant is based, in which he asks "whether any true virtue is to be found in the world" and considers whether "up to now there may never have been a sincere friend" (Kant, *G* 4:407–8).[6] (I will come back to the good will that shines like a jewel.)

A minimal, ascriptive account of traits, including virtues and vices, may be the most we can reach: but it comes at a cost. If traits are inferred from expressions of feeling, from attitudes and from action, they cannot be causes of action. Claims that traits *cause* the range of evidence on whose basis they are ascribed are misplaced. Inferences to tendencies do not provide sufficient material for causal explanations, except of the *virtus*

---

[6] See also Marcia W. Baron, *Kantian Ethics Almost without Apology* (Ithaca, NY: Cornell University Press, 1995); Barbara Herman, *The Practice of Moral Judgement* (Cambridge, MA: Harvard University Press, 1993); Onora O'Neill, 'Kant's Virtues', in Roger Crisp (ed.), *How Should One Live? Essays on the Virtues* (Oxford University Press, 1996), 77–97.

dormitiva sort where the 'cause' is simply a redescription of a range of effects: an F pattern of action and expression is 'caused' by an F trait. Ascriptivism about traits is incompatible with objectively consequentialist views of virtues, which have to see traits as independently knowable internal states.

In taking an *interpretive* or *ascriptive* view of character traits, we view the problem of judging character as more like pattern recognition than like hunting for internal entities with causal powers. Classifying patterns of expression and action as expressing certain traits allows us to remain quite neutral about the nature and number of the states of affairs that cause particular expressions of attitude or action. The causes of expressions of feeling, or of acts, might include motives, volitions, passions, beliefs and other mental events and states, brain events and states, bodily events and states, or mixes of all of these. There is no guarantee that the causes of action and expression will be intelligibly linked to our folk classification of patterns of action.

Non-consequentialism and the consequences of action

How do non-consequentialist positions deal with these difficulties? On Julia Driver's account, here matters are even worse. Non-consequentialists – at least those of them who offer accounts of virtue – appear in her grid of possibilities to claim *both* that virtues are internal states that can be independently known *and* that their value is intrinsic, rather than due to their systematic consequences. It seems they get the worst of both worlds. They are still saddled with the metaphysical and epistemological problems of explaining how we can tell *which* internal states agents have and *how* they are known, *but* they cannot appeal to the value of consequences to determine whether any given trait is a virtue or a vice. So they are left having to find some way of discerning the intrinsic moral properties of epistemologically and metaphysically problematic internal states. Objective consequentialists, on her account, believe that Kantians and other evaluative internalists are forced into this acutely uncomfortable position (71).

However, as I see it, not being a consequentialist about virtues does not lead to this position, and may have advantages. It allows one to take the view that the relation between *dispositions* on the one hand and *expressions of feeling and attitude and acts that express them* on the other is not causal. I can, for example, take an ascriptive view of virtues, ascribing traits to agents on the basis of evidence provided by their expressions of feeling, attitudes and action. For example, I may simply note that the accurate shopkeeper provides a good deal of evidence for ascribing a range of distinct traits, note that I lack enough evidence to ascribe any single trait to the exclusion of others, and note also that certain tests might reduce the indeterminacy and allow me to be more confident about one or another – or a third – ascription of traits.

But what happens to the consequences if we take an ascriptive view of traits? Is not the great advantage of consequentialism that it grips the central and salient fact that action bears on and alters the world, that it articulates the causal and the moral links between traits and action? This picture fits consequentialism used to evaluate acts. As we have noted, consequentialists have no problem in individuating acts that are then to be assessed in terms of the value of their *actual* (or *likely* or *systematic*) consequences. Ordinary consequentialists focus on causal relationships holding not between *internal states* and their *consequences*, but between *acts* and their *consequences*. They can identify acts and consider their consequences. If they can assemble the necessary theory and metric of value, and the necessary causal knowledge, they can then infer the value of acts from that of their effects. An ordinary consequentialist can try to work out the results of the accurate shopkeeper's action – he gains a good reputation; he goes bankrupt; he feels self-respect; children flock to buy because they trust him – to calculate the value of his accuracy. Having got so far, the ordinary consequentialist can take either a robust or a minimalist view of traits, and (if the latter) can still evaluate ascribed dispositions on the basis of an assessment of the likely value of action and expressions of feeling that would *typically* express that disposition. However, this move does not yield any evaluation of an agent's *actual* traits, which cannot be independently known.

The objective consequentialist about virtue cannot follow this pattern of reasoning, unless the internal state to be assessed can be independently known. If no internal state can be independently known it will be impossible in principle to pick out the set of consequences whose value is to determine that of the internal state. So if we cannot know internal states independently, objective consequentialist thinking fails as an account of the virtues.

It may seem that the non-consequentialist is in just as bad a fix as the objective consequentialist. If our evidence consists of patterns of action, expressions of feeling and attitude, any ascription of traits will invariably be incomplete and contestable. Reading characters may be more reliable than reading tea leaves, but does not yield a way of identifying the causes of action or attitudes. Yet the non-consequentialist need not worry much, for two reasons.

The first is that reading characters, while important, is not the central task of the moral life. In concentrating on retrospective, third-party judgement of others' traits, including perhaps retrospective judgement of one's own traits, we should not lose sight of the point that the core questions in ethics are practical questions about what we should do or attempt. Practical questions are not addressed by working out what traits we would ascribe to agents if they were to act in certain ways, but by working out how to act. If we systematically set ourselves to get the action right, we will (if luck is not against us) create patterns of evidence for the third-party or retrospective task of ascribing traits, and perhaps virtues.

Second, non-consequentialists who take an ascriptive view of character can take account not only of expressions of attitudes and of action, but also of their consequences. Some consequences are taken into account in the very process of describing and classifying action. Act descriptions may be revised – corrected, enriched or extended – by taking into account more of what are seen as consequences of action minimally described. King Alfred *bakes a cake*, but since he lets it burn to cinders he may be described as *absent-mindedly burning the cake he is baking*; a TV celebrity chef *bakes a cake*, but since what he displays is a previously baked cake, we may describe him as leaving *the cake he was seen to mix in an oven until after the programme is made*. In describing action we make complex and numerous decisions about *how much* of the consequences to build into the description of a given act. The choice of act description is governed by many complex purposes and may even occasionally be prescribed by law, as when a prisoner on remand for causing grievous bodily harm is charged with murder if the victim dies of the injuries within a year.

In describing acts, non-consequentialists often incorporate some information about consequences, but not about the full range of 'further' consequences that are supposedly of interest to consequentialists. For example, in describing the purchasing habits of ordinary consumers, no account is taken of the myriad further effects of market behaviour that a consequentialist would need to take seriously. It is an interesting question how good various forms of non-consequentialism are at taking account of these 'further' consequences, which consequentialists (at least officially) do take into account. A full exploration of the differences in this area would need some discussion of the handling of consequences in arguments about rights, of the doctrine of double effect, of indirect responsibility and of unintended consequences.

But I do not want to finish without a comment on the good will that 'shines like a jewel' even when it fails to produce right action and good effects. For this is a core passage which lies behind Julia Driver's reading of Kant as the paradigm non-consequentialist evaluational internalist. The context of Kant's comment on the good will is a sentence in which – as in many other passages – he emphasises the distinction between *willing* and mere *wishing*. He is considering the case in which "only the good will [is] left (not of course as a mere wish but as the summoning of all means insofar as they are in our control)" (Kant, *G* 4:394). Kant ascribes good will to agents only when there is evidence that they are striving with all their powers to act in certain ways. The agent with good will acts in ways that will be *systematically*, but not *invariably*, expressed in right action. Normally good willing is not frustrated; normally it is expressed in right action: we ascribe good will on the basis of evidence of commitment, but not of invariable success in action. In some cases, as Kant sees it, "the special disfavour of fortune or the niggardly provision of a stepmotherly nature" (*G* 4:394) robs the agent with good will of success, and good will of its normal expression. This suggests that Kant's reflections on the cases where good willing is frustrated by special circumstances are quite close to the considerations that lead objective consequentialists to value traits that *systematically* have good consequences despite the cases where they do not *actually* have good consequences.

CHAPTER 11

Demandingness and rules[1]

Rebelling against rules

Approaches to ethics can be demanding in several ways. They can be *theoretically demanding* if they can be justified only by arguments that need (implausibly) demanding premises. They can be *motivationally demanding* if living up to them would routinely require exceptionally demanding motivation, such as levels of self-denial, impartiality or altruism that are hard to achieve. They can be *practically demanding* if they require more, or more specific, types of action than are likely to be feasible for those who are to live up to them, even when inadequate motivation is not an issue. Here I shall discuss ways in which ethical theories can be practically demanding, and in particular consider whether some of the most widely discussed approaches to ethics demand more than is feasible even for well-motivated agents.[2]

Excessive practical demands are often attributed to excessive reliance on rules, and in particular on rules that specify too many or too detailed requirements. These charges have often been made both against Utilitarian and other consequentialist positions, and against Kantian and contractualist positions. Positions of all these types have been criticised in particular for making excessively demanding claims about duties. Utilitarians and other consequentialists are said to demand that an 'overload' of obligations be met; Kantians are said to have a rigouristic and inflexible view of the requirements of duty; contemporary liberals, including contractualists, are also said to make too much of requirements, and specifically of duties and rights, at the expense of other matters that are morally important.

[1] This chapter appeared previously in Timothy Chappell (ed.), *The Problem of Moral Demandingness: New Philosophical Essays* (Basingstoke: Palgrave Macmillan, 2009), ch. 3.
[2] There are likely to be links between these different sorts of demandingness: heavy practical demands may make heavy motivational demands, and may need demanding theoretical backing. However, I shall not discuss these connections.

A more general sense that a wide range of European conceptions of morality have insisted on excessive, even stultifying, practical demands spreads far beyond the criticisms levelled against these specific positions. It pervades Nietzsche's writings and constantly reappears in a wide range of more philosophical writing that claims variously to be Aristotelian, or Wittgensteinian, or more vaguely 'virtue ethical'. Most of these swathes of writing do not follow Nietzsche in making sceptical or nihilistic claims about ethics. They are sceptical or critical not about ethics in general, but only about those ethical positions that make much of rules and duty, and (it is assumed) demand a lot of those who are to live by them. Their most common range of complaints is that those who propose demanding views of ethics accept and promote a view of ethical life that is inadequate, even corrupt, in that it undermines or constricts other aspects of the good life, such as the practice of virtue, commitment to 'personal projects', the cultivation of attachments and relationships, and sensitivity to the specificities of cases. Many twentieth-century philosophical critics of ethical rules and duty, from J.-P. Sartre to Bernard Williams to Alasdair MacIntyre, think that ethics is important, but that it should shun appeals to duty or obligation, and give up the view that rules or requirements are ethically important.

Criticisms of ethical demands, and specifically of the demands of duty, are not confined to philosophical writing on ethics. They also pervade a wider range of non-philosophical twentieth-century writing that expresses, even urges, rebellion against the claims of duty. In Britain this rebellion became most widely known through the writings of early twentieth-century novelists from E. M. Forster and D. H. Lawrence across the further reaches of Bloomsbury, and the poets of the First World War. Opposition to the demands of duty was manifest in widespread unease about the traditional demands of duty and discipline, king and country, Church and family. Parallel positions were widespread throughout European cultures.

However, a century of philosophical and popular rebellion against the ethics of duty has not led to general acceptance of this position. On the contrary, contemporary philosophical writing on ethics is full of arguments to show that certain ethical requirements can be justified and that ethical claims not merely are but should be practically demanding – *at least up to a point*. And while public discourse now tends to avoid the words *duty* and *obligation*, it does not shy away from claims about requirements. The change is that requirements are commonly articulated from the perspective of those to whom they are owed, that is, from the perspective of recipients of *rights*, who are entitled to action or forbearance that respects and protects their rights. Clearly there can be no claim-rights unless others have duties to respect or secure them. So the ethics of duty is not wholly dead or moribund. Parts of it flourish under another name, finding a popular contemporary form in widespread advocacy of human rights. The term *duty* may have become unfashionable, but the view that ethics demands action that respects and realises rights claims is very widely accepted.

Ethics without demands?

The debates between those who see ethics as rightly making strong practical demands and those who think that some forms of demandingness are unacceptable are evidently not closed. If we are to assess these disputes it is worth asking what we might be left with if we were to reject all moral rules, all conceptions of obligation or duty, and with them all claims about rights (other than positive legal rights). One alternative would be to embrace some form of nihilism or anti-morality, another to look for an approach to morality that does not – or ostensibly does not – rest on any view of rules for action, such as (supposedly) some forms of virtue ethics: an approach that allows for good but not for required action, hence not for duties or their counterpart rights.

Another less radical approach would be to allow notions of duty at most a subordinate role by setting them in either a consequentialist or a contractualist framework. On some views, theories that see duty as a derivative matter differ from more Kantian positions that centre on rules or duties, in that the fundamental moral category for consequentialists is some conception of the good (objectively or subjectively conceived) and for contractualists some notion of consent, agreement or reasoned agreement. Such approaches offer a way of supporting a range of ethical demands without treating duty as fundamental to ethics. But it is far from clear whether either consequentialist or contractualist positions could escape the accusation – or the compliment? – that even if they do not think duty fundamental to ethics, they are nevertheless too demanding.

An overload of obligations?

The consequentialist version of domesticating obligations encounters trouble because it appears to demand *too much* – perhaps, indeed, more than is demanded by positions that ostensibly place more weight on rules, duties and rights. The objection was first widely discussed after Peter Singer argued that Utilitarian versions of consequentialism were and should be practically very demanding, and more specifically that those who lead comfortable lives owe hugely more to those in poverty than had widely been assumed. Utilitarian starting points, he claimed, require the better off to make radical changes in the way they live in order to secure (to borrow a phrase from elsewhere) a positive option for the poor which (he argued) was what maximising consequentialism (even in a weak form) demanded.[3]

Singer's view of the demanding character of Utilitarian obligations was extensively criticised by James Fishkin in his book *The Limits of Obligation*, which pointed out that consequentialism (in its standard maximising forms) is not merely relentlessly but implausibly demanding.[4] No sooner is one duty fulfilled than the next one looms. The point seems entirely correct as an account of a structural feature of maximising forms of consequentialist, but how one takes it is another matter. On some views, this shows that maximising consequentialism is a non-starter as a basis for ethics, or at least that maximising consequentialism *about acts* is a non-starter as a basis for ethics, because it leaves no room for freedom, virtue, 'personal projects' or other valuable matters. On another view, this relentless demandingness just shows what a truly admirable ethical position maximising consequentialism provides. It is not clear to me how this disagreement of perceptions is to be resolved, and it is intriguing to see how strongly people experience or argue for one or the other reaction.

Many of these debates still centre on Singer's central example of duties to the distant poor, and opinion is still widely divided. On the one hand we have writers who follow Bernard Williams in arguing that maximising consequentialism is intolerable because it leaves no room for 'personal projects', and commits its adherents to acting with relentless impartiality and without concern for personal relationships as they work towards good consequences. On the other hand, many contemporary political philosophers and theorists, in particular those who write on global justice, argue that this is just how we ought to live, and see personal projects as sheer selfishness genteelly redescribed.

---

[3] Peter Singer, 'Famine, Affluence, and Morality', *Philosophy & Public Affairs*, 1 (1972), 229–43. He initially argued for large transfers of resources to the poor by individuals, but later for institutional change to achieve such transfers; the underlying ethical point is the same. His 1972 article remains a focus and an inspiration for a large literature on international justice, including by many who do not share his Utilitarian starting point. See for example Garrett Cullity, *The Moral Demands of Affluence* (Oxford: Clarendon Press, 2006).

[4] James S. Fishkin, *The Limits of Obligation* (New Haven, CT: Yale University Press, 1982).

Algorithms and other sorts of rules

Some years ago I came to the conclusion that, regardless of how attractive or unattractive we find it, the structural claims of maximising consequentialism – as so far developed – fail not because they are too demanding, but because they are too undemanding. They cannot guide action, so do not provide any basis for a convincing ethical position with practical implications.[5] The failure, put in terms often used to criticise Kantian ethics, is not rigourism but empty formalism: maximising consequentialism does not establish an overload of obligations because it is practically indeterminate, so establishes nothing about obligations. Utilitarianism appears practical only if we help ourselves to rather large 'simplifying' assumptions such as disregarding most of the available options, then assuming rather than establishing the likely consequences of the few we consider, and adopting morally conventional views of their expected value. It is therefore a waste of time and breath to dispute just *how* demanding classical Utilitarianism, or other forms of maximising consequentialism, really are.

Maximising consequentialism advocates a four-step rule to guide action. Agents are to identify the available options for action; they must then reckon the expected consequences of each option; they must then evaluate the expected consequences of choosing each option; finally they are to choose the option that maximises expected good consequences. The first three steps are not feasible. There is no way of listing all available options exhaustively.[6] We are unable to calculate all the expected consequences of the options we can list with confidence or precision.[7] Moreover, even if we could calculate those expected consequences, we lack a robust metric for evaluating them. Of course, *if* we could carry out these three steps, the maximising would be a simple matter. But as we cannot, it is not. Consequentialism in practice at best approximates these moves, making genteel rather than deeply argued claims about which acts are optimific. This may bring relief from the overload of obligations problem, but at the cost of invoking non-utilitarian considerations.

If we overlook these problems we may imagine that maximising consequentialism provides an algorithm for action, or even for ethics. We may think that its great merit is that it tells us how act. This might or might not be desirable – that depends on how we view ethical demandingness – but it

---

[5] I first argued for this position in Onora O'Neill, *Faces of Hunger: An Essay on Poverty, Development and Justice* (London: George Allen & Unwin, 1986).
[6] See Timothy Chappell, 'Option Ranges', *Journal of Applied Philosophy*, 18 (2001), 107–18.
[7] See James Lenman, 'Consequentialism and Cluelessness', *Philosophy & Public Affairs*, 29 (2000), 342–70.

is not in the least plausible. An algorithm provides wholly definite instructions for each context:

> An algorithm is a finite procedure, written in a fixed symbolic vocabulary, governed by precise instructions, moving in discrete steps … whose execution requires no insight, cleverness, intuition, intelligence or perspicuity, and that sooner or later comes to an end.[8]

Strictly speaking algorithms are therefore possible only within formal systems, within which contexts and moves can be exhaustively specified: a system of arithmetic will provide an algorithm for multiplication; a statement of the rules for playing noughts and crosses will allow us to work out (although it won't state) an algorithm for avoiding defeat even when the other player has the first move. But even when we multiply or play noughts and crosses in real life we will need more than algorithms: multiplication can be done 'in one's head' or aloud, or in writing, and the order of the multiplicands can be varied. Even noughts and crosses can be played on paper, on a blackboard or on the sand; it can be done using varied marks, and various implements to make them, and so on. There are no true algorithms for action. Still less are there algorithms for acting well.

However, the fact that there are no algorithms for action does not show that there can be no rules for action. Most rules are not algorithms, and no rules for action are algorithms. Rather practical rules *constrain* action in some way, ruling out certain types of action without providing full instructions for their own enactment.[9] Whether we are talking about legal or social, ethical or technical rules they do no more than constrain action. Many constraints are minimal and vague; others are local and fairly specific. Rules such as 'Don't overload the car' or 'Check your fuel gauge before you drive onto the motorway' are relatively specific, but even they leave open a great variety of ways of doing as they require or advise. Since action-guiding rules or principles are practical propositions, they are invariably indeterminate and can be enacted in a variety of ways.

Once we think of rules as constraints, we can see that while they can be *more* or *less* demanding, they are not invariably *relentlessly* demanding. Typically they make practical demands that are fully compatible with a great variety of ways of acting and living, although they do not leave

---

[8] David Berlinski, *The Advent of the Algorithm: The 300 Year Journey from an Idea to the Computer* (New York: Harcourt, 2000), p. xviii, facing.

[9] The impossibility of providing full instructions for the implementation of rules is about as uncontroversial as anything of philosophical importance. Both Kant and Wittgenstein, who have rather different things to say about rules, discussed and endorsed it.

everything open. The quickest way to see this is perhaps to note that we constantly manage to comply with a wide range of different rules: at this moment you are (in all probability!) neither perjuring yourself, nor injuring anybody, nor creating a fire hazard. However, this is not a matter for much congratulation, since it is not particularly difficult. We can comply with many different constraints simultaneously, and constantly do so.

I think that this point is enough to suggest that an ethics of rules and duties, far from making relentless practical demands, can leave considerable scope for different ways of living and acting. A set of practical rules is not structurally demanding, in the way that maximising consequentialism would be – if it could be enacted. This is because practical, non-algorithmic rules contain act descriptions that are always indeterminate, so capable of enactment in a range of ways. This is not, perhaps, enough to show that an ethics of rules or duties can be relaxing rather than demanding, but it is enough to show that an ethics of rules or duties *need not* create an overload of obligations. Still, any ethics of rules is likely to have problems of its own, including those that arise when excessive demands are made, and I shall comment on two that have historically been much discussed.

Two problems with rule-based ethics

a.   Can rules tell us what to do?

A common objection to ethical views that endorse rules and duties is that they are not enough to guide action. This complaint objects to ethical rules not because they are too demanding, but because they are not demanding enough. The nub of the objection is that since practical rules are *not* relentlessly demanding they are useless: they do not tell us what to do (in sufficient detail). This criticism insists that ethical positions in which rules, duties or rights have a central place suffer, like maximising consequentialism, not from rigourism but from formalism, indeed from empty formalism. The complaint is that rules are practically useless unless they can guide us to one rather than another of their possible enactments.

It is true enough that ethics of rules – whether they see duties or rights as fundamental to ethics – do not tell us exactly what to do. But if we insist on being guided to a very specific, let alone a particular, enactment of a rule, then it seems to me that we are insisting that ethical rules should be relentlessly demanding, even that they should be algorithms. If we insisted (*per impossibile*) that all ethical requirements must be governed by algorithmic rules we would indeed be demanding extreme demandingness.

It is true enough that when we seek to live up to any rule, what we do is always a determinate type of act, indeed a particular act. But it does not follow that rules can – let alone should – determine their own application. Often it is said or assumed that making the move from rule or principle to any particular act is a matter of practical judgement. But all too often very little is said about how practical judging works. The sense that ethical rules are useless because they are non-algorithmic suggests a fear that nothing can be said about the practical judgement by which we move from a principle or rule to some enactment of that principle or rule. But a certain amount can be said.

Practical judgement is at least a matter of finding some enactment of the rule or duty in question. There are various types of case to consider. In one type of case there may be nothing to choose between two (or more) available instantiations of a rule. In such cases the rule that agents seek to live up to will indeed offer no guidance on choosing between the two enactments. Anyone as obtuse as Buridan's ass will then have a problem: faced with two equidistant and equally enticing bales of hay, his rule did not tell him which to eat, and he perished. But the point of the story is that there is indeed nothing to choose between the two options, so it is a matter of indifference which is chosen. Only an ass would consider this a problem.

The more interesting and more typical case for practical judgement is where a rule has a number of available instantiations that differ in various ways. Can practical judging guide agents to one rather than another instantiation? How does it do this? What does it take to judge well how to live up to a principle in specific circumstances?

If we imagine living our lives as seeking to live up to a single rule or principle, then it may seem impossible to provide any useful account of practical judgement. *Ex hypothesi* any adequate enactment of a rule must, it seems, be as good as any other. But it is absurd to imagine that anybody would live their lives trying to conform to a single rule. Typically we find ourselves trying to live up to a largish number of rules, principles or standards, some of them of ethical significance, and many of them practi-cally significant in other ways. We may try to earn an adequate living without being dishonest, but also without over-exertion. We may try to help our friends without spending too much, being corrupt, or adopting a principle of universalised benevolence. And so on.

As soon as we acknowledge that *many* rules or principles make their claims in any given situation, we can also see where to look in deciding which of the numerous ways in which a principle could be enacted should command our attention. In general terms, practical judgement is a matter of looking for ways of acting that satisfy all of the rules or standards that we take to be relevant. The aim of practical judgement is the joint satisfaction of these rules or standards.

Practical judgement can therefore be likened to the 'makers' judgements' that are needed in designing or making a product. In building a house numerous constraints must be met. The house must be built of available and affordable materials; it must provide shelter and insulation for the climate and for the needs of those who will live in it; energy consumption and other running costs must be affordable; local planning requirements must be met; the building must be completed within budget. These design, environmental and financial criteria constitute a set of rules, constraints and standards, which cannot all be met perfectly, but that also cannot always, or perhaps generally, be traded off against one another: a house that is poorly insulated or leaks is a bad bargain even if very affordable. A house that costs too much for any purchaser will be a poor product even if it is very magnificent and meets every planning and environmental requirement. Good practical judgement is manifested in selecting acts that satisfy a range of important rules or standards.

b.   When rules conflict

However, the fact that we always or virtually always act on a plurality of rules may be thought to reveal a problem more severe than the one that it resolves. Rules may conflict, and if so having more than one of them looks more likely to exacerbate than to resolve difficulties.

Here it is helpful to distinguish two cases. The first case, which would indeed lead to intractable problems, would arise if agents attempted to live up to two or more rules that can *never* be jointly instantiated. For example, somebody who makes it a principle to be both reclusive and open in all his dealings is doomed to dithering since there is no way in which both demands can be met, in any situation. (Of course, it may be possible to get some distance by being reclusive in private matters and open in public matters, or the like; but then the example is no longer one of attempting to live by intrinsically conflicting rules or principles.)

The second case would be that of seeking to live by a plurality of rules that may but need not come into conflict. This, it seems to me, is a common situation. We may seek to be honest, careful and financially prudent, but there may in some circumstances be no way of meeting all three standards. Particularly in dire circumstances, there may be no act by which we can meet two or more rules or standards that matter to us. It is

said that during the siege of Leningrad those who did not hoard food were
likely to die – and those who did hoard risked execution, so were likely to
die. It is not clear how those committed both to fairness and to securing the
survival of their family should act in such dire circumstances. Indeed, it is
not clear how those committed to the principle of securing the survival of
their family should act. In the darkest times every way of acting on a rule
may seem to risk failure to live up to its demands, or to the demands of
other rules.

These two cases suggest that those who are committed to acting on rules
must at least try to adopt rules that are not intrinsically incompatible, but
must also recognise that intrinsically compatible rules may contingently
come into conflict. They may try to ensure that such contingencies do not
arise, or arise rarely, for example, by prudence and time management, and
by taking care about the commitments they make and the company they
keep – but they cannot guarantee that no contingent conflicts will arise.

What should an agent do who, despite strenuous efforts, finds that in a
particular situation there is no way of living up to all of the principles that
matter to him? Here I think that the only way of dealing with the problem
is to acknowledge that some duties will remain unmet, although they are
not intrinsically incompatible with other important rules and standards,
and then to think about the claims of these contingently unmeetable
duties. Many examples are so familiar that we hardly think of them as
conflicts of obligation: a person may be detained by some emergency in
which she is needed, so cannot keep some promise to a friend – for
example, cannot meet him at the station – but makes amends by telephon-
ing ahead, by efforts to make substitute arrangements, and by apologising.

Such responses by agents who face contingently unmeetable obligations
are often described in philosophical writing as a matter of dealing with
remainders. The term is apt: the unmet obligation in these cases is something left over, that has to be dealt with rather than dismissed with an airy
'*Ought* implies *can*, I can't meet this (supposed) obligation, so it is not case
that I ought to have met it, so it was not really an obligation'. However,
many discussions of remainders focus mainly on 'left over' *attitudes*, such as
an agent's self-directed regret, remorse or guilt, or other-directed blame by
(supposed) victims.

This seems to me too narrow a perspective on unmet, including contingently unmeetable, obligations. There is more to be thought about
when an agent seeks to deal appropriately with the shortcomings of her
own action in circumstances where it proved contingently impossible to
live up to all of a range of rules, including ethical duties. A wider view of the

same issues would consider the *action*, and not only the *attitudes*, that may be appropriate when a duty is unmet. In such an account, active responses and remedies, such as restitution, apology, the repair of relationships, forgiveness or punishment can also be seen as part of the repertoire for dealing with unmet obligations.

A limited conclusion

I have suggested that opposition to ethical positions that see requirements (hence duties and rights) as important cannot be plausibly based on general arguments against demandingness. Maximising consequentialisms are not inevitably 'too demanding': indeed, far from generating an overload of obligations, their proposed decision procedure for ethics cannot be followed in practice, so generates no determinate requirements at all. Rule-based ethical theories, such as Kantian and contractualist positions, are not inevitably 'too demanding' since they do not propose moral algorithms, but set constraints that cannot provide fully determinate guidance.

The practical question is not whether certain *types* of ethical theories and positions are invariably too demanding. It is whether *specific* ethical positions, that prescribe *specific* requirements, can provide a basis for action, allowing for the fact that any position in which duties or rights have a place will contingently generate practical conflicts, and that practical judgement will be needed to manage those conflicts.[10]

---

[10] See the chapters in Part II, above.

PART IV

'Applied' ethics and practical judgement

CHAPTER 12

Applied ethics: naturalism, normativity and public policy

Normative argument is supposed to guide ways in which we might change the world, rather than to fit the world as it is. This poses certain difficulties for the notion of applied ethics. Taken literally the phrase *applied ethics* suggests that principles or standards with substantial philosophical justification, in particular ethical and political principles with such justification, are applied to particular cases and guide action. However, the 'cases' which applied ethics discusses are themselves indeterminate, and the relation of principles to these 'cases' differs from the relation of principles to cases in naturalistic, truth-oriented inquiry. Writing in 'applied ethics', I shall argue, does not need elaborate case histories or scenarios, since the testing points for normative principles are other normative principles rather than particular cases. Normative principles and contexts to which they are applicable are indeed needed for any reasoning that is practical, but they are not sufficient. Practical ethics needs principles that can not only be *applied in certain cases or situations*, but *enacted in certain ways*, and requires an account of practical judgement and of the public policies that support that judgement.

Instruction and edification

The term 'applied philosophy', as we all know, is relatively new, as is the term 'applied ethics'. What preceded them? Is the change only one of terminology? Have we moved on in some definitive way beyond long traditions of didactic and instructive writing? If so, just what has changed and how valuable is the change? I begin with a brief reminder of some ways in which some of the tasks now taken to be important for 'applied ethics' were previously addressed.

Literature – in the broadest sense of term – has traditionally been seen as a proper way in which to explore ethical and other practical issues with the aim of shaping action and practice. Some sorts of literature are overtly instructive or didactic, but often not particularly reflective: we may think of sermons and homilies, advice manuals and casuistical work. Other literary works are reflective, but not overtly didactic. Works of imaginative literature, in particular novels, have often had high practical and moral ambitions. They are taken to offer both a reflective moral education and a critique of major social and political issues: think of Dickens's *Hard Times*, or Fontane's *Effie Briest* or E. M. Forster's *A Passage to India*. Such writing can shape action indirectly by forming character, outlook and cognitive capacity, so has normative implications. Some sorts of non-fictional writing have also traditionally been seen as having strong normative implications: the study of history was traditionally seen as instructive, as training the judgement and teaching statecraft, the study of rhetoric as improving capacities to persuade and take part in civic affairs.

However, applied ethics does not continue this tradition. Like other contemporary writing in the humanities and social sciences, and indeed like much contemporary fiction, it does not purport to edify or instruct, and is reticent about claims to form character, outlook or cognitive capacity. Overtly instructive writing flourishes, of course, in myriad books of practical advice and instruction: but this is no longer how we seek to do ethics. Attempts to provide ethical instruction or edification, or to shape readers' character, outlook or cognitive capacities, are likely to be seen as old-fashioned, even naïve, and as making normative assumptions for which no adequate reasons are given, of seeking (at best) to persuade and not to reason. Applied ethics has hoped to do more, and to reach wider audiences.

Non-naturalism: description and internal critique

Applied ethics is both more ambitious and more academic than these traditional approaches to ethics. Yet it differs radically from most other current writing in the humanities and social sciences. It is, I think, worth considering just where the difference lies. Applied ethics clearly differs from the truth-oriented inquiries of the natural sciences. More surprisingly it also differs from most of the supposedly non-naturalistic work to be found in the humanities and in so-called 'qualitative' social inquiry. The natural sciences seek to explain natural events and their causes, as does some work in the humanities. Other work in the humanities and qualitative social inquiry aims at description (above all at *thick description*), at an understanding of *meaning* or (as it is often rather oddly put) of *meanings*, but eschews normative claims. It seeks to discover, articulate or analyse how the world has been *represented* in one or another *text, image, discourse, mentalité, practice* or *culture*, or what is now called *identity* (and used, less confusedly, be spoken of as a *sense of identity*). It therefore sees normative claims as legitimate, indeed important, *objects* of study, but not as its proper *aim*.

This conception of the proper task and method of writing in the humanities and 'qualitative' social inquiry allows for criticism of normative claims, but only if that criticism is *internal* or *immanent*. Such criticism can reveal internal tensions and incoherencies in the representations that are articulated or analysed, but will not offer reasons for normative claims to those who do not accept the modes of thought and representations described and dissected.

This point is quite often overlooked. In particular, if is often assumed that certain approaches to social inquiry, such as public opinion polls, public consultations and 'deliberative' exercises, can have normative implications for public policy. But when such work is taken to have practical importance (whether for policy formation, or for social or personal life), this assumption is invited to take too much weight. Knowing how matters are sometimes or often represented does not automatically lead to or support normative conclusions, other than normative conclusions that are relativised to these representations. The findings of public opinion polls and exercises in public engagement or deliberation therefore cannot settle ethical or policy questions, and can make at best a limited contribution to public policy formation.[1] Finding out what some people think or feel, or even what a lot of people think or feel, about some domain of issues – or even what they think and feel after being informed, discussing and deliberating – however interesting, does not *by itself* lead to *any* normative (let alone specifically ethical) conclusions. A consensus can be iniquitous, impractical or irrelevant. Rather, any transition from claims about representations to claims about what ought to be done, whether for reasons of self-interest or prudence, or for ethical or political reasons, needs additional premises and arguments if it is not to be an instance of the naturalistic fallacy, of an argument from the dubious authority of consensus or majority opinion – or, indeed, of no argument at all.

---

[1] Those who think they can make a larger contribution may do so because they assume that the (supposedly) democratic approaches of pollsters have unquestionable moral and political weight. This thought has two limitations. First, most forms of polling and deliberation have at best indirect democratic credentials. Second, the moral claims of democratic processes fade if normative conditions are not met. Most obviously, arguments from democracy carry little weight unless the rule of law and a range of rights of the person are in place.

At best, then, internal critique of the representations accepted by some individual or group may have normative implications for those who already accept that way of representing matters. If they have failed to take on board the full implications of the representations to which they are committed, internal critique may offer them reasons to revise their positions. I have found internal critique quite a useful approach in discussing socially entrenched or received views of ethical requirements, such as some contemporary conceptions of press freedom as simply a form of freedom of expression, and some views of informed consent requirements currently taken in clinical and research practice.[2] However, where there is no dominant ideology or practice to be dissected and queried, internal critique is not likely to be normatively fertile.

If this sketch is approximately true – and it is, of course highly simplified – then it must fall to other approaches to make and defend normative claims. Applied ethics is an obvious, indeed assertively eager, applicant for this work.

Methodological and epistemic non-naturalism

These claims about the normative limitations of much writing in the humanities and the 'qualitative' parts of social inquiry may seem surprising. Those working in these areas often see their work as *non-naturalistic*, and contrast it with work in the natural sciences and in other, often more quantitative, work in the social sciences. The characteristic methods for studying and understanding the representations that constitute social, cultural and human worlds indeed differ from those used to study events in the natural world. Work in the humanities and 'qualitative' work in social inquiry aims at *Verstehen* rather than *Erklärung*, at a grasp of the *formal* causes (structure, meaning, articulation) of the representations that constitute social, cultural and human worlds, rather than at a grasp of the *efficient* causes of events that make up the natural world. So these interpretive approaches are certainly non-naturalistic, even anti-naturalistic, and if they are non-naturalistic, should they not be apt for grounding normative claims?

This hope cannot, I believe, be sustained because non-naturalism comes in various kinds, and writing in the humanities and social inquiry is not non-naturalistic in the way that normative work requires. The *methodological non-naturalism* that is common in some writing in the humanities and

---

[2] Onora O'Neill, *Rethinking Freedom of the Press* (Dublin: Royal Irish Academy, 2004); Neil C. Manson and Onora O'Neill, *Rethinking Informed Consent in Bioethics* (Cambridge University Press, 2007).

'qualitative' work in social inquiry is often combined with a more fundamental form of naturalism. Work that inquires into the *nature* of representations is naturalistic in a broad, epistemic sense of the term. It aims to be true of the way aspects of the world – namely certain representations – are or have been, rather than to show that aspects of the world should be changed to fit certain standards. The direction of fit of such work is the same as the direction of fit of work in the natural sciences: it is empirical, not normative in its aims, and is non-naturalistic only in its focus on representations rather than on natural objects and events. Work in the humanities and social sciences that aims to be true of human and social life may be *methodologically non-naturalistic* in its focus on representations and meaning rather than on events and causes, but is nevertheless *epistemically naturalistic*.

The evidence that most work in the humanities and in social inquiry is epistemically naturalistic is, I think, ubiquitous and commonplace. It is now seems uncontroversial that historical writing should aim for truth in the sense of fidelity to evidence, rather than at patriotism or propaganda at the expense of fidelity to evidence; that the academic study of grammar is a descriptive, not a normative discipline; that social anthropology should aim at accurate articulation of the self-understanding of the societies studied rather than at satisfying a dubious appetite for the exotic; that the study of rhetoric is not an upmarket training in winning friends and influencing people, but a way of reaching a deeper and more perceptive understanding and appreciation of texts. Of course, these aims may be betrayed in practice, and there is no doubt plenty of unreasoned or unselfconscious persuasion and propaganda in work that purports to study representations: like the natural sciences, the humanities and social inquiry have their wishful thinkers, and no doubt some charlatans.

So the normative ambitions of applied ethics are at odds with the epistemically naturalistic approaches of most academic work in the humanities and in 'qualitative' social inquiry. Here we have a genre of academic writing that seeks to identify and vindicate normative, action-guiding claims, and then relate them to the facts of situations or cases (including, of course, facts about the representations accepted by the relevant agents). So applied ethics aspires to meet the demands *both* of normative *and* of truth-oriented, epistemically naturalistic inquiry. Taken together these are heavy demands.

The more obvious reasons why these are heavy demands are that the principles that are needed for 'applied' ethics are normative principles; and that some of them must be ethical principles. Hence applied ethics cannot be indifferent to the underlying rigours of metaethics. Here, as we all know, there are uncomfortably few options – or perhaps we should say a few uncomfortable options. Consequentialists must advance with a convincing account of the good, whether objective or subjective, before they can hope to articulate instrumental claims that shadow causal reasoning and pick out normative principles that can serve for applied ethics. Contractualists can justify normative demands only by showing why one or another account of hypothetical reasoned agreement binds agents to principles to which they have not in fact agreed. Relativists may hope – in my view without realistic expectations – to wring normative principles from claims about how things are understood or represented. Particularists may hope to traverse from thick descriptions of situations directly to normative judgements of those situations. Nobody would underestimate the demands faced by any of these ways of securing ethically significant normative claims. The only alternatives that I can see are also strenuous: they seek to make the most of the rather meagre constraints of consistency and coherence, augmented perhaps by Kantian requirements to eschew principles that cannot be principles for all.

Given these towering difficulties, one might expect those who seek to do applied ethics to falter at an early stage when they reflect on the difficulties the lie behind any justification of normative principles. I think that it is worth wondering why many do not, and indeed are quite optimistic about finding convincing normative principles. I think that this is usually because the demands of metaethics are explicitly bracketed rather than ignored, often with the optimistic thought that all plausible ethical theories will endorse a common range of central ethical principles, whose implications can then be explored. In other cases optimism is sustained more economically by explicitly framing examples and problems in terms of established norms that are neither justified nor challenged. A fair amount of work in 'applied' ethics takes for granted established legal frameworks, the norms of established professional cultures or human rights claims. For example, it is not unknown for philosophical discussion of press freedom in the USA to invoke the First Amendment to the US Constitution, presumably assuming that its juridical status guarantees ethical authority; it is not unknown for human rights claims to be accorded ethical authority on the basis of their ratification by the states party to the relevant conventions, without offering any argument to show how ratification can ground ethical norms.[3]

---

[3] Even its capacity to ground juridical norms is suspect, given that many of the states party ratified cynically, without either will or capacity to assign or enforce the obligations needed to establish justiciable rights.

The defect of such moves is evident. Each relies at one or more points on some version of an argument from authority. But this must be a dispiriting move for an enterprise that sets out to provide ethical reasoning that lays claim to attention beyond the circles that already accept a particular authority. As long as we uncritically presuppose a certain theory, theology, ideology, institutional framework or professional outlook, any normative implications derived from it will, it seems, be conditional on accepting the assumptions embedded in the outlook, views or representations from which the argument begins – so on some version of an argument from authority or from consensus. Reliance on such arguments defeats the wider normative ambitions of applied ethics by unargued acceptance of the preferred theory, theology, ideology, institutions or practices.

In the end, I suspect, writing in applied ethics is mainly confident that the normative principles it invokes can be justified because it assumes that somebody else will provide the metaethical arguments needed if reasons for normative claims are to reach beyond the like-minded. However, even if we assume such a division of labour, and accept that 'applied' ethics borrows rather than establishes ethical norms, a less obvious difficulty cuts deeper. This second difficulty is that it is not easy to see what it means to *apply* a practical principle, hence not easy to see how normative principles – even if they can be justified – can guide action. I now turn to this second difficulty.

Normativity: application or enactment?

The distinctive feature of normative work is that its direction of fit is unashamedly the converse of that of empirical or descriptive work that aims at truth-claims. Its theories are neither explanatory nor interpretive, its aims are neither *Erklärung* nor *Verstehen*. Rather than arguing that aspects of the world, among them representations, satisfy certain descriptions and principles, it argues that aspects of the world should be changed to fit certain descriptions and principles. That is what it is for work to be normative or prescriptive rather than empirical or descriptive. I do not think there is much disagreement on this point. But I think there is far less agreement about what it is to 'apply' normative principles, and how they are to guide action.

The term 'applied ethics' suggests that normative principles are *applied* to particular cases, just as concepts or theories are applied to particular cases in truth-oriented inquiry. However, this is a misleading analogy. Writing in applied ethics depicts normative principles as applying to specific *types of case or situation*, rather than to particular cases. A focus on *types* of case seems both acceptable and unavoidable because the aim, after all, is not to take over the activities of practitioners in one or another domain of life by dealing with actual cases, but to suggest how certain sorts of activities might generally be well undertaken. So writing in 'applied' ethics has to abstract from the details of actual cases, in favour of discussing schematically presented *types* of situation or case. Even discussions illustrated by reference to one or another well-documented example of a particular past case will see this case through the lens of specific descriptions – hence as a *type* of case. When 'cases' are discussed in applied ethics, they are seen as *types of context or situation* that may fall under a principle.

Parenthetically, this means that the elaboration of examples, which is taken very seriously in some work in applied ethics, has little point. I do not mean just that there is little point in devising examples in which protagonists who formerly made their way under the aliases A, B and C are suddenly renamed Alison, Buddy and Carla, with studiously gender-neutral or balanced social implausibility. I mean that the general presumption that more detail will be better is unconvincing. Better for what, we might ask? What advantage does additional detail supply? Certain additional details *can* indeed be used to reveal the implications of rigid application of simple principles: but for that purpose an illustrative example with a single feature that illuminates the principle under discussion will be enough. I may come to rethink my commitment to the death penalty when I grasp the tension between this principle and a principle of protecting the innocent from punishment, especially irrevocable punishment. I do not need to consider actual miscarriages of justice, or actual criminal trials: I merely need to know that miscarriages of justice happen. I may rethink my acceptance of the use of torture of supposed criminals when I see that it is likely to corrupt testimony and undermine prosecutions. Again I do not need to consider actual cases where torture has elicited unreliable confessions: I merely need to know that this happens. These might not be the best or the only reasons for rethinking commitment to these principles, but they may all the same be weighty and sufficient considerations, and show that we do not need to think about narrowly or vividly specified types of case, let alone particular cases, when thinking about the implications of a normative principle – ethical or other.

The more fundamental problem is that speaking of the 'application' of principles to 'cases', as is standard in some writing in applied ethics, suggests a misleading analogy with the application of empirical or theoretical principles to cases in epistemically naturalistic inquiries, where principles stand in need of reformulation, refinement, revision or rejection if they do not fit actual cases. By contrast in normative, including ethical, discussion agents who are committed both to *specific principles* and to *specific accounts of cases or situations to which those principles apply*, will have no reason to reformulate, refine, revise or reject a principle if a case or situation fails to fit the principle. The fact that the way things are often flouts normative principles that we take seriously is a reason for seeking to change the world (in small part) so that it lives up to those principles, not a reason for dropping or changing the principle.

In empirical, truth-oriented reasoning the relation of principle to particular cases is correctly termed *application*, and principles must fit the cases to which they are applied, or be put in question. However, in normative reasoning reference to cases merely indicates a *type of context or situation* in which a principle might be deployed (and even this point may have to be qualified). Empirical and theoretical principles are put in question by counterexamples that do not satisfy them; normative principles are not. Application of theoretical and empirical principles is essential to reasoning about the world, and can determine what should (provisionally) be believed. 'Application' of normative principles is only a matter of identifying *a context for use*, and since principles are indeterminate does not determine what should be done. Normative, including ethical, principles are not *deployed* merely by identifying types of context for their use, but rather by *enacting* them. Normative reasoning aims to be action-guiding. Its aim is to *enact* rather than to *apply* principles, and this cannot be done merely by specifying the types of context or situation for which a principle may be relevant.

Once we distinguish the *application* of principles from their *enactment*, additional questions come into focus. Given that principles, like the types of situations and cases to which they relevant, are indeterminate, they can have many possible enactments. Normative principles cannot determine just which of many differing enactments should be aimed for in a given situation. Indeed, given that multiple normative principles are relevant in most situations, it may be difficult to enact all of them, and hard to assign priority among them. Do the indeterminacy and multiplicity of principles shackle their capacity to guide action?

On one view, any worry about indeterminacy may seem trivial. Only if we imagine implausibly that principles are to provide algorithms for action, it might be said, will it seem problematic that they underdetermine their enactments. To enact a principle is simply to take *some* course of action that satisfies it; to meet an obligation is to act in *some* way that satisfies that obligation; to respect a prohibition is to act in *some* way that does not contravene that prohibition. Equally, to enact a multiplicity of principles is simply to take *some* course of action that satisfies them.

Yet, on reflection, this account of acting on normative principles says too little. It represents all ways of enacting a principle as on a par: but surely there are better and worse ways enacting any principle, or plurality of principles. Yet to say more about why some enactments are better than others we seem to need some additional point of reference. We need, it seems, not merely to justify certain principles, and to identify types of situation or context – 'cases' – for which they are relevant, but also some account of *practical judgement that indicates how they should be enacted.* Yet this has proved notoriously elusive.

These points might be taken – quite often *are* taken – as reasons to turn one's back on any ethical position that centres on principles, and to look to some account of intuition or judgement of cases or situations, to carry the entire burden of practical, including ethical, decisions. I do not think this a promising route, although I shall say little about it on this occasion.

Defeasibility and practical judgement[4]

I think there are broadly two ways to approach the problem that indeterminate principles do not show agents how to select among their possible enactments. One way would be to try to eliminate, or perhaps manage, the problem by formulating more specific principles. The other would be to offer an account of *practical judgement* that can go at least some way towards guiding the move from indeterminate principles to particular enactments.

Any thought that problems that arise from the indeterminacy of principles can be eliminated or even managed by formulating more determinate principles seems to me implausible. Setting out more elaborated or specific principles does not eliminate indeterminacy. Normativity *requires* indeterminacy because it requires relevance to situations that are still open and unresolved. There is no way of building so much into principles that indeterminacy is eliminated – and going in that direction by incorporating unending distinctions, restrictions and exceptions, thereby formulating more and more specific principles, is likely to have diminishing practical point. Any account of practical judgement needs to accept that normative principles are ineliminably indeterminate.

---

[4] See the chapters in Part II above.

But if this is the case, applied ethics may falter for further reasons. Practical principles, including ethical principles, are not deployed one-by-one. The types of cases that provide contexts for their use invariably fall under multiple normative principles, including multiple ethical principles. The fact that we are *typically* committed to numerous normative principles, including numerous ethical principles, that demand *joint* satisfaction can generate tension and conflict – even irresolvable conflict, so seemingly threatens to undermine the prospects for any principle-based approach to practical let alone ethical reasoning. I think that this thought is too hasty, and that commitment to a plurality of indeterminate principles does not automatically lead to irresolvable problems.

Agents who are committed to a plurality of principles often find that this creates no great difficulty. Nearly all of the time most agents manage to meet the demands of many well-entrenched ethical principles: we constantly and simultaneously refrain from perjury and injury, from theft and slander – and it is not too difficult! Indeed, nearly all of the time agents live up to all of these principles and a plethora of other practical principles which we might variously think of as legal, professional or social rather than specifically ethical. Needless to say, these ordinary achievements are hardly a reason for self-congratulation.

Yet in some cases the joint satisfaction of a plurality of practical principles creates problems. For example, given a principle of respect for marriage a whole slew of thoughts about what each party owes the other and about what others owe them as a couple slides into place – whether to be accepted and enacted or to be challenged or modified. However, if we add to the specification of the type of case that a marriage is bigamous or forced, many of those assumptions may falter. At this point respect for the personal liberty and well-being of the person who has been deceived or forced is in tension with a principle of respect for marriage. While we can 'save' the principle of respecting marriage by arguing that here there is no real marriage, or only a 'form' of marriage that should not be respected, this move merely cloaks the real problem, which is that there are strong reasons for thinking that normative principles, including ethical principles, are not only *indeterminate*, but *defeasible*. There is no plausible way of establishing a hierarchy of practical principles to show which should be relegated when joint satisfaction is impossible. If so, how are agents to work out *which* of many normative principles should take priority in a specific situation? Once we acknowledge that we do not enact normative, including ethical, principles one-by-one, we must accept that where it is not possible to enact all relevant principles jointly, some will have to be accorded priority and others relegated.

But, if normative principles cannot be enacted one-by-one and without further consideration in each situation in which they can be deployed, it seems that their vindication cannot settle what should be done when a case of a given type arises. We may claim that a normative principle shows what must be done, as we say, *ceteris paribus*: but this comforting tag obscures the reality that normative principles do *not* show what must be done, since the very cases that are most problematic will be complicated ones where *ceteris non paribus*.

Viewing normative principles as *defeasible* appears unavoidable, yet will it not blunt the edge of any normative claim and leave the ambitions of applied ethics stranded? When we apply empirical principles, contrary cases constitute *prima facie* counterexamples and demand some refinement, reformulation, restriction or rejection of the principle applied. When we enact normative principles, it is unclear on what basis we view certain possible enactments as unacceptable or inadequate, as grounds for thinking that the (type of) case is 'an exception', or that the principle is defeated by some other principle. It looks as if viewing normative principles as defeasible ends up endorsing at least a partial retreat from seeing them as genuinely normative.

Practical judgement and effective policies

However, on another view, which I shall sketch, the defeasibility of normative principles is a strength, not a weakness, because it provides the basis for an account of practical judgement. By this I do not mean simply that it opens a way to escape from unwelcome aspects of rigid reliance on principles, as maintained by those who think principles irrelevant to ethical conduct. Those who doubt the importance of principles in practical reasoning do not see them as *defeasible*, but as *dispensable*; they cast doubt on the very need for normative principles, and throw the burden of justification onto responses to cases.[5] Those who see principles as defeasible still take them to be important, and insist that even where justified principles cannot be enacted, they must be taken seriously. What they need to show is how agents who are committed to multiple normative principles are to deploy them. How is the move from a plurality

---

[5] Cf. the references to particularisms, note 2 to the Introduction, above.

of defeasible principles to one or another particular enactment of those principles to be made? How does practical judgement work?

Reflective Equilibrium is often seen as offering part of an answer to this question. It is a popular half-way house for those who find themselves uncomfortable both with the thought that there are indefeasible normative principles and with claims that principles are dispensable. By adopting a coherentist method that takes into account not only principles but 'considered judgements', it suggests that we can find a way both to adjust principles in the light of 'cases', and to shape enactments by principles. However, it seems to me that Reflective Equilibrium is really a way of seeking coherence among a set of principles of greater and lesser generality. 'Considered judgements' are *not* responses to particular cases (which can be pretty unconsidered). Rather they are normative judgements of *types* of cases – that is to say, they are themselves (more and less specific) practical principles. Reflective Equilibrium in the end is a way of 'equilibrating' – seeking coherence – among a plurality of principles of greater and lesser generality.

However, an appeal to coherence among principles does not show enough about practical judgement. Often there are many ways of accommodating a plurality of principles coherently to one another, and some coherent accommodations may surely be better than others. Practical judgement should presumably offer some way of distinguishing better from worse enactments of principles. Reflective Equilibrium does not provide a way of doing this.

Nevertheless, Reflective Equilibrium offers a useful clue to the process of practical judgement. By drawing attention to the claims and the problems of living by a *plurality* of principles, it pinpoints the right starting point for an account of the enactment of practical principles. The task of practical judgement is to select among possible ways of *jointly* enacting the various principles to which an agent is committed. We never find ourselves confronted with the task of conforming to a single normative requirement (if we did the task of practical judgement would be considerably simpler![6]).

The practical ambitions of 'applied' ethics are, I suggest, secured rather than undermined by the fact that we approach any situation with a *plurality* of defeasible normative requirements in mind. This is just as true of practical reasoning in which ethical issues are marginal, as it is of practical reasoning in which they are centre stage. Practical judgement is as

---

[6] Or alternatively complicated, for example if the single principle cannot be deployed without demanding metrics such as those which Utilitarianism requires. Cf. Chapter 11, above.

much needed in bringing a building project in on time, on budget and to the specified design as it is in working out how to keep all promises made without unkindness. It is needed as much in working out how to respect standards of courtesy while conforming to the norms of contemporary business practice as it is in working out how to care for patients while respecting their individual 'autonomy'. These and countless other situations require judgement – practical judgement – about ways in which and the extent to which a range of ethical and other requirements can be jointly enacted.

This may seem surprising. I think this is because a large tranche of writing in applied ethics focuses on distinctive types of case where joint satisfaction of normative principles, and specifically of ethical principles, is contingently impossible, as in the literatures on moral dilemmas and dirty hands.[7] This focus is readily taken as suggesting that commitment to a plurality of principles leads only to conflict, even to tragedy. It may, however, be a mistake to focus too narrowly on these cases, although understandably tempting (especially for those eager to show the difficulty or even the incoherence of relying on principles). Of course, something will have to be said about the distinctive cases where joint satisfaction of principles is impossible and some of the normative principles to which an agent is committed – ethical or other – cannot be jointly enacted.[8]

However, the more instructive issues arise when a plurality of principles *can* be jointly enacted in a number of ways, but the matter is not straightforward. These, I believe, are the types of cases that reveal most about the task of practical judgement. They are very common and do not need any elaborate stage setting. A short list of principles that quite often come into some tension with one another might include: looking after family interests while avoiding nepotism; protecting public security while respecting the civil liberties of dissidents; respecting both freedom of expression and individual privacy; providing important public goods (water and air

---

[7] I take it that the case of principles that are intrinsically not jointly satisfiable is not of *practical* importance: those who commit themselves to two or more such principles (e.g. to principles of being wholly open and wholly secretive in all matters) need to reconsider the justifications of the principles to which they are ostensibly committed.

[8] In such cases, where the claims of some principles to which an agent is committed cannot be jointly enacted, they can nevertheless be acknowledged. Such acknowledgement will require attention to the ways in which remainders arise in the wake of unmet or contingently unmeetable requirements, in and beyond ethical reasoning. It would, I believe, be possible to make the literature on remainders richer and more convincing by concentrating rather less on emotional and attitudinal responses to unmet obligations – remorse, regret, guilt – and rather more on practical responses such as making amends, reparations, renegotiation, compensation, apology and many others.

quality, road and product safety) while respecting individual liberty; protecting public health while respecting individual freedom to take certain risks; protecting children without over-protecting them; protecting employees' rights without undermining management. The list could go on and on.

Just as these tensions are recurrent, so too are the approaches that can be used to avert and manage potential conflicts and tensions between principles. Principles are most readily enacted when the means and space for their enactment is institutionally and culturally secured. So a large part of the task of practical judgement is a matter of developing and maintaining an institutional and cultural framework that will make the joint satisfaction of important principles, including important ethical principles, more feasible in more contexts. We rely on public institutions and cultural practices to avert, limit, routinise and resolve tensions in the enactment of principles that would *otherwise* frequently lead to tension or conflict. Practical judgement in the face of plural and contingently conflicting demands is often most effectively achieved not by focusing on the resolution of dilemmas, however exquisitely characterised, but by public policies that routinely avert and reduce conflicts and tensions, and provide recognised routes for their accommodation.

If we think of applied ethics merely as discussing principles and the types of situations in which they might be applied, we say too little about the practical task of working out how principles are to be enacted in those situations, and how conflicts and potential conflicts between them are best handled or averted. Nor do we learn much about this practical task merely by labelling it *practical judgement*. We could, however, learn a good deal about this task by considering the institutional and cultural means by which joint enactment of a plurality of potentially conflicting principles might be eased, even routinised.

Much discussion of ways in which conflicts between principles can be managed or averted – or exacerbated – is to be found in empirical studies of institutional structures and public policy, rather than in normative writing. Writing on 'applied' ethics needs to discuss institutional remedies for likely conflicts between principles ranging from time management to dealing with principal-agent problems, from the regulation of conflicts of interest and limitation of role conflict to the avoidance of perverse incentives and moral hazard. And it needs to pay attention to the ethical difficulties and tensions that dysfunctional or hyper-complex institutions and practices create. Yet there is no reason why a wider and more practical approach to ethics should not take these matters seriously.

So practical ethics can go beyond the consideration of principles and the types of situations in which they could or should be applied by saying more about the institutional structures and cultural support needed if respect for significant ethical and other principles is to be adequately achieved in public, professional and private life. It could, for example, focus more on ways in which systems of accountability could be structured to support rather than undermine the intelligent placing and refusal of trust or on shaping institutional structures that can secure and allocate the obligations needed if human rights are to be taken seriously. It could say more about ways in which supposed rights to freedom of expression can – or cannot – be reconciled with intellectual property regimes. It could say more about the relevance – or inadequacy – of demands for transparency in improving communication and public policy. It could say more about better and worse ways of constructing regulatory regimes to secure and support compliance with ethical principles. These are rich pastures, and those of us who take normative reasoning seriously need to take the details seriously.

To do *practical* ethics we need not only to think hard about the justification of ethical principles, and the specification of types of or context for which they are relevant. We need to think less about 'application', and address the implications of the fact that agents are always committed to a *plurality* of *indeterminate* and *defeasible* normative principles, so that conflict and tension between enactments of principles may arise. In short, we need to move from discussions of principles relevant to specifiable situations and contexts, to discussions of policies and institutions that support processes of practical judgement by making it easier to achieve adequate enactments of those principles in a wide variety of demanding situations.

Commitment to a plurality of normative principles, I have suggested, does not undermine, but rather provides a basis for practical judgement. Practical judgement is exercised both in identifying ways in which normative principles can be jointly enacted – when they can – and otherwise in building and maintaining structures and policies that help to avert, limit or resolve tension and conflicts between enactments of normative principles, and in dealing with remainders where joint enactment is impossible or not achieved. Normative, including ethical, principles are not adequately deployed simply by identifying *types of situation or cases* which fall under them, in which (not *to which*!) they could be *applied*. Their full deployment is a matter of constructing, supporting and working within structures and policies, institutions and cultures that buttress the feasibility of the joint enactment of the principles to which agents are committed.

CHAPTER 13

Practical principles and practical judgement in bioethics[1]

In bioethics, and in the philosophical debates that form part of its background, there has been a long-running dispute about ethical principles. The advocates of principles think that they are central to ethical reasoning or decision-making, and have proposed and defended various influential ethical principles. The best-known approach to bioethical reasoning that appeals to principles remains that of Beauchamp and Childress,[2] who suggested that bioethical reasoning should centre on four principles, those of beneficence, non-maleficence, autonomy and justice. In some of the literature the ugly neologism 'principilism' has been used to label this well-known approach and similar approaches.

A lot could be and has been written about the merits and the shortcomings of each of these specific principles, and about alternative ways in which each might be interpreted. A lot could and has also be said about other principles that have been advocated in bioethics – the principle of utility, various principles of justice, and many specific principles such as those indicated by phrases such as 'reproductive autonomy' or 'the precautionary principle'. However I shall leave discussions of specific principles that may be important for bioethics, or more generally for ethics, on one side in order to consider the more basic question whether (as some suspect) principles are intrinsically inadequate or morally suspect, or (as others think) they are an essential component of ethical reasoning and deliberation.

Opponents of 'principilism' allege that a focus on principles is formally inadequate, ethically defective, or both. Ethical reasoning and decision-making should, they think, focus on or be responsive to cases, case studies,

---

[1] Published previously as 'Practical Principles and Practical Judgement', *Hastings Center Report*, 31 (2001), 15–23. I have amended the title to indicate the specific focus, which could be taken for granted in the *Hastings Center Report*.

[2] Tom L. Beauchamp and James F. Childress [1979], *Principles of Biomedical Ethics*, 4th edn. (Oxford University Press, 1994).

or to specific situations, relationships or practices, and in any case centre on something less abstract than principles. They may claim that practical principles (let alone rules) are corrupting, stifling or even illusory, *a fortiori* that they are ethically disastrous. Some propose that ethical concern should focus on virtues and community, on care and commitment, and on other distinctive excellences, and assert that none of these can be adequately specified or captured by principles or rules.[3]

Those who see a formal deficiency in principles, and in ethical positions that appeal to them, may point in either of two directions. As they see the matter, principles will either be so abstract and indeterminate that they fail to guide action, or if they are not indeterminate but rather offer an effective procedure or algorithm[4] for guiding action, will prescribe with relentless uniformity and ethical insensitivity for cases that may differ in deep and ethically significant ways. This double-barrelled criticism has a long history in ethics: it is essential a repetition of the claim that Kantian ethics – evidently principle-based – suffers either from excessive *formalism* or from excessive *rigourism*. Occasionally and fascinatingly both of these incompatible criticisms of ethical principles have been made simultaneously: but evidently a principle that is too empty to guide action will not be determinate enough to regiment it into total uniformity – and vice versa. At best the two criticisms can be made consecutively: like those who fall from the frying-pan into the fire, advocates of principles are then seen as escaping one catastrophe only to suffer another.

Those who see ethical deficiencies in principles usually attribute them to these supposed formal difficulties. They suggest either that principles (being indeterminate) cannot really help us in deciding what to do, or alternatively that principles (being algorithms) could help us decide what to do, but at the cost of demanding a leaden and ethically dubious uniformity of response across differing cases. In place of principles, they suggest, we should focus on the specificities of actual situations, on case studies, on particular examples and exemplars, on the situation to hand in

---

[3] The opponents of principles and rules are more heterogeneous than this may suggest. Some, including communitarians and those interested in ethical pluralism, object only to 'abstract' and 'universal' principles and rules, and base their own accounts of ethics on the more determinate norms of communities, that is on socially embodied principles. Others have more radical objections, and hold that ethical judgement must be wholly particularist, dealing with each case as it arises. See the chapters in Part II, and the third and fourth sections in this chapter, below.

[4] "An algorithm is a finite procedure, written in a fixed symbolic vocabulary, governed by precise instructions, moving in discrete steps ... whose execution requires no insight, cleverness, intuition, intelligence or perspicuity, and that sooner or later comes to an end", David Berlinski, *The Advent of the Algorithm: The Idea that Rules the World* (New York: Harcourt, 2000), p. xviii, facing.

its rich complexity. There is no single label that fits all opponents of principle-based ethics equally well: their positions range from those who think of themselves as particularists and insist that ethical judgements are a matter of *perceiving*, *intuiting* or *appraising* the salient aspects of particular cases or 'concrete situations', to those who may think of themselves as drawing on the thick concepts of specific cultural traditions. This thought lies behind another ugly (if less recent) neologism, which has been adopted from time to time by some of those who oppose principles, who speak of themselves as 'situationists'. 'Situationism', as I understand the term, prizes the particularity or the specificity of cases, the thick and culturally significant descriptions by which we pick out their salient ethical features, or even insists that ethical judgement is directed solely at particular cases.[5] Only a focus on what is *specific* to cases or (it is often said, as if the terms were synonyms) on the *particular*, which principles invariably overlook, can secure ethical responsiveness to significant differences.

Varieties of practical principle

To fix ideas it is useful to pick out very broadly the types of principles that have been variously thought essential and destructive in bioethics. Bioethics is evidently not directly concerned with principles of logic, with mathematical principles, or with principles of pharmacology: neither formal nor theoretical principles are its concern. We may say very broadly that it is thought by some to be concerned with *practical principles*, that is with principles that could at least sometimes be used in working out how to live our lives, or some parts or aspects of our lives. Practical principles are for agents.

Practical principles come in many different kinds, and not all of them are of ethical importance. Books on the principles of midwifery or of corporate finance or of engine maintenance are books about the use of practical principles, and may be of considerable use in relevant contexts. So much more has to be said if we are to pick out what makes a practical principle an ethical principle. I do not intend to say any of it here, because I aim to approach ethical principles by way of taking seriously the fact that they are (thought of as) practical principles, so must be fit to carry the tasks that practical principles of various sorts routinely carry. Working from an

---

[5] This picture of ethics has a long history, especially in Christian thought. A well-known statement reiterating the position is Joseph Fletcher, *Situation Ethics* (Philadelphia, PA: Westminster Press, 1966). Parallel secular views of ethical reasoning have often been proposed by Wittgensteinian and feminist writers, and are strongly represented in attacks on moral theory and moral principles.

account of the tasks of practical principles in general can, I believe, put us in quite a good position for assessing whether 'principilism' is essential to or destructive of bioethics.

Practical principles of all sorts have three features. First, all practical principles contain *act descriptions*, taking this idea in a very broad sense that includes descriptions of emotional responses and attitudes. These act descriptions may vary from the very specific to the very abstract. Practical principles that contain very specific act descriptions include: *keep smiling*; *make sure that the drug cupboard is locked before you leave the room*; and *record the newborn's AGPAR score*. Practical principles that contain very abstract act descriptions include *injure nobody*; *pay attention to the bottom line*; *look before you leap* (in its non-literal interpretation!); and *keep your head when all around are losing theirs*.

Secondly, practical principles do more than *state* act descriptions. They also take up a *position* or *stance* with respect to the action falling under the description they contain. Many practical principles prescribe or forbid, in effect setting certain requirements; many others recommend or warn but do not set requirements. Principles that formulate *requirements* (prohibitions, obligations, permissions, exceptions, etc.) can quite naturally be thought of as *rules*; those that formulate *recommendations* (including warnings, suggestions for good tactics or good practice) cannot. Both rules and recommendations may be variously classifiable as ethical or legal, prudential or social, technical or professional, and no doubt in many other ways. Practical principles with ethical content will therefore *prima facie* be as relevant to recommending virtues and excellences, and to warning against vices and failures, as they are to prescribing constraints and demands, obligations and freedoms. (So there is no fundamental reason for thinking that ethical principles must be concerned only with obligation to the exclusion of virtue – or vice versa.)

Thirdly, practical principles usually specify or assume some *domain of agents* for whom they are to be regarded as relevant. Some practical principles are formulated as principles of universal scope, relevant for all agents. Others are formulated for and addressed to restricted ranges of agents, for example for physicians or for pharmacists, for parents or for patients. Frequently the domain of agents for whom a principle is proposed is left rather vague. Familiar principles such as *exercise due care and attention*; *do not use excessive force*; *love your neighbour*; and *do everything in moderation* do not make it explicit that they are intended for all agents. By contrast, other practical principles incorporate explicit *agent descriptions*: *parents are responsible for their children's safety at the swimming pool*;

travellers in SE Asia are recommended to take anti-malarial drugs; *nursing staff may not leave suicidal patients unattended.*

Practical principles that state requirements – rules – have (a degree of) deontic structure that links them to one another. This may not be obvious on the surface. Some rules use explicit deontic terms ('ought', 'may', 'should'); others use imperatives to convey the notion of requirement: *thou shalt not kill*; *first in, last out*; *treat the worst injured first*. Rules may be systematically linked to one another in two ways. First, the rights and obligations, permissions and prohibitions pertaining to one individual are systematically linked: for example, an agent who is required to do some act (whether ethically, legally, socially, prudentially etc.) will also be allowed to do it, and forbidden to omit it. Secondly, the rights and obligations, permissions and prohibitions of two or more agents may be systematically linked: A can be entitled to B's action or forbearance only if B is obliged so to do or to forbear.

Practical principles that state recommendations are not linked in so systematic a way. They may warn or advise, point out what it would be good or bad, effective or risky, excellent or dubious to do or to be in some area of life. Both relatively specific recommendations to *take regular exercise* and specific warnings that *smoking can harm your health*, as well as less specific recommendations to *keep your cool* or *support your collea-gues* and warnings to *avoid gossip* and *not to push your luck* are stated in open form, as advice or warning to the world at large. Other recommen-dations and warnings may be directed to specified ranges of agents. But in neither case are recommendations and warnings linked to one another by the systematic deontic relations that link principles that formulate requirements.

Abstraction, algorithms and sensitivity to differences

When we consider the full range of practical principles one recurrent objection to 'principilism', and thereby to ethical principles, simply falls away. Practical principles, including ethical principles cannot, hence do not, require uniform action; more specifically practical rules, including ethical rules cannot, hence do not, require uniform action. Because the act descriptions incorporated in practical principles are invariably indetermi-nate they must underdetermine the action of those who conform to them. Even if principles or rules are elaborated to incorporate many details and exceptions, indeterminacy is ineliminable and invariably limits the speci-ficity of prescription.

Simple examples make this quite plain. Even rather specific principles such as *take two pills before meals* or *nothing by mouth* constrain but do not regiment. Nothing is prescribed about where the pills are to be taken, or what the meal is to consist of; nothing is said about the activities or other treatment of the patient who is to have nothing by mouth. The fears that practical principles, and especially rules, must regiment those who conform to them are simply misplaced. The only sorts of rules that could regiment would have to be *algorithms* that prescribe the precise detail of action without regard to situation. Yet the image of the relentless algorithm, of the rule that allows no discretion, is misplaced. Such quasi-algorithms as we can find in human affairs usually apply only to very minor aspects of life. For example a postal service may require a precise minimum value of stamps on letters of a certain weight and with a given destination. Evidently postal rules constrain the preparation of envelopes, but they do not regiment the way that stamps are stuck on, let alone how letters are posted, let alone what they contain, let alone how we are to live.[6]

Ethical principles of the sorts that have usually been advocated are in any case not even remotely like postal regulations; they are not even quasi-algorithms. On the contrary, the ethical principles that have received most attention are highly indeterminate rather than quasi-algorithmic; they may constrain but do not regiment action; they are more likely to recommend types of action, policy and attitude than to offer detailed instructions for living. Suggestions of principles that require a great a degree of uniformity are constantly criticised – and not just in recent years. Aristotle noted in introducing the principle that virtue lies in the mean that this is not be understood arithmetically, or as we might say algorithmically, so that in determining the right amount of food there is no quantity that is right for all persons without variation: what is right for Milo the wrestler would be too much for another person.[7] Practical principles of all sorts are subject to analogous criticisms: prescribed drugs must be appropriate to the disease and body weight of the patient; financial plans must be adjusted to the life circumstances and income of the saver; criminal sanctions must be scaled to the offence for which the criminal is convicted. The degree of uniformity or differentiation to be prescribed in particular aspects of life is a matter for substantive practical reasoning, and (where relevant) for ethical

---

[6] Strictly speaking even postal regulations are never more than quasi-algorithms: even in this well-regulated domain we may lick and stick in various ways. True algorithms belong in formal systems that abstract from everything that they do not determine.

[7] Aristotle, *Nicomachean Ethics*, Roger Crisp (tr. and ed.), revised edn. (Cambridge University Press, 2014), 1106b.

reasoning. There is no basis for a general objection that practical principles, or rules, leave too little discretion, although there may sometimes be good reasons for thinking that one or another principle or rule would do so.

The thought that principles, including rules, might provide complete, regimenting guidance has been a recurrent worry in ethics and in bioethics during the last twenty-five years, and a common enough worry at earlier times. I have argued that it is a misplaced worry, and believe that it is also a worry that a slight attention to well-known philosophical discussions of concepts, rules and indeterminacy could have averted. It has long been known that concepts, and hence also principles and rules that use concepts, are indeterminate, and that it is fruitless to seek to complete them by looking for rules for the application of rules, which can lead only to an infinite regress. On this point both Kant and Wittgenstein endorse Aristotle's point, although many later writers have ignored Kant's discussions of concepts, rules and principles and of indeterminacy and assumed that Kant embraces some form of ethical rigourism.[8]

Varieties of judgement

Even if practical principles (including rules) never provide complete guidance, there may still be a major deficiency in all forms of 'principilism'. The deficiency may lie not in the excessive determinacy of practical principles and rules, and their consequent lack of sensitivity to differences, but on the contrary in their excessive abstraction or indeterminacy and consequent failure to guide action. The short and classical answer to this objection is that it is quite evident that (being invariably indeterminate) principles and rules cannot fully guide action, and that it is well known that they must be complemented by judgement. This 'admission' that practical principles are not by themselves sufficient for guidance will be welcome to the opponents of 'principilism', but many of them will go on to point out that it simply shows that principles are pointless, because judgement not merely *supplements* but can *supplant* principles.

Those who make this claim are in effect suggesting that judgement alone can, does and presumably must underpin ethical reasoning. The burden of proof for this strong claim lies with the proponents of varieties of 'situationism'. In general it is not hard to understand why, *if* they think that

---

[8] A *locus classicus* is Immanuel Kant, *CPR* A133/B172, where he argues that there cannot be complete rules for the application of rules. For a contrary reading of Kant, see Charles Larmore, 'Moral Judgment', *Review of Metaphysics*, 35 (1981), 275–96, at 278. For more extensive discussion see the chapters in Part II, above.

judgement can guide action without appeal to principles, they object to 'principilism'. But it is quite hard to find clear accounts of judgement by which to assess the claim that it can carry the entire task of ethical deliberation.

Since it is common ground between the advocates of 'principilism' and 'situationism', let us accept that there will always be a gap between a (necessarily indeterminate) practical principle, that can at most require or recommend some act *type*, and the particular act that is done and may (or may not) conform to that requirement or recommendation. Disagreement begins with the attempt to understand what might be meant by the claim that this gap must be 'filled by judgement'. How can judgement engage with (or reach towards) the particular? What is the process of judgement? How do we do it? In ethics, and in bioethics, the sort of judgement that we need to understand is *practical judgement*, i.e. judgement that guides action (at least to some degree). Yet, surprisingly, a great deal of writing on ethical judgement by the opponents of 'principilism' is not about practical judgement at all. It is about the ways in which we assess and judge the situations in which action will be done: is about judging situations that are already there to hand rather than future action.

There are two types of judgement that can be directed towards situations or acts that are already to hand, and neither is a form of practical judgement. In the first sort of non-practical judging we ask ourselves whether a particular case falls under some given concept, principle or rule: Was this a case of professional negligence? Was that a case of child abuse? Was the consent given to this or that medical intervention freely given? The adjudicating flavour of the examples is no accident. For in these cases we are assuming both that a situation – an action and its context – is already there to be judged and that there are accepted standards against which it should be judged. Judgement used to determine whether a case at hand falls under given description may be called by either of the Kantian terms *subsumptive judgement* or *determinant judgement*.[9]

A second sort of non-practical judgement is also directed towards situations or acts that are already to hand, but with the difference that it does not assume that the relevant concepts or standards (rules, principles) are already given. Kant discussed this sort of open-ended judgement of cases that are to hand, and labelled it *reflective judgement*. In reflective

---

[9] Kant draws a sharp distinction between two types of theoretical judgement: "If the universal (the rule, principle or law) is given, then the judgement which subsumes the particular is *determinant* . . . If, however, only the particular is given and the universal has to be found for it, then the judgement is simply *reflective*." See Kant, *CJ* 5:179. See chapters in Part II, above.

judging we may ask, for example, 'What sort of treatment of a patient was taking place in this case?', 'How should we describe the attitude of medical researchers who approach their subjects in this or that way?' or 'How should we characterise the mental state of this patient?' Reflective judging of situations – of actions and their context – has played a large part in case-centred, 'situationist' writing in bioethics and beyond, under various labels.

However, neither determinant nor reflective judgement is a form of practical judgement. Both assume that the case to be judged is *ready to hand*, whereas practical judgement by definition is directed at action that has yet to be performed. Practical judgement cannot therefore be directed at particulars: the point after all is to work out what to do. It is undertaken *on the way* to acting, not in order to grasp and judge a particular act that has already been done. Practical judgement is therefore neither subsumptive (determinant) nor reflective. It strives towards *specificity*, with a view to shaping action; it does not and evidently cannot grasp not-yet-existing particulars.[10]

Yet many 'situationists' have viewed ethical judgement as a version of reflective judging. Two quite different versions of this position are common. Some writers – many are ethical particularists – take a more or less *perceptual* or *intuitionist* view of ethical judgement, which they see as at least somewhat analogous to Kant's conception of reflective judging (the particular is given, and the task is to find the appropriate description). They characterise this task variously as a matter of intuiting, perceiving, appreciating or appraising the salient characteristics, including any salient ethical characteristics, of particular situations that have arisen.[11]

The thought that ethical judgement is a capacity to judge particular cases is puzzling in two ways. First, particularists depict capacities to judge as quasi-perceptual, yet there are many disanalogies between ethical and perceptual judgement, particularly when it comes to resolution of

---

[10] The exception may seem to be the case of retrospective ethical judgement of action already performed. However, such cases begin with subsumptive or reflective judgements, and may then move on to a practical judgement of an appropriate response to what has been done. A judge begins with a retrospective, non-practical judgement of the crime committed, and then makes a practical judgement about the sentence to be imposed. Only the latter is a practical judgement.

[11] For versions of ethical particularism see David Wiggins, 'Deliberation and Practical Reason', in his *Needs, Values and Truth: Essays on the Philosophy of Value* (Oxford: Blackwell, 1987), 215–37; Jonathan Dancy, 'Ethical Particularism and Morally Relevant Properties', *Mind*, 92 (1983), 530–47; John McDowell, 'Deliberation and Moral Development', in Stephen Engstrom and Jennifer Whiting (eds.), *Aristotle, Kant and the Stoics* (Cambridge University Press, 1996), 19–35. For discussion of reflective judging in earlier Wittgensteinian writing see Onora O'Neill, 'The Power of Example', in *Constructions of Reason* (Cambridge University Press, 1989), 165–86.

disagreement. Secondly, and more perplexingly, the assimilation of practical to perceptual judgement seemingly overlooks the fact that practical judgement is directed at shaping a further or emerging act or attitude rather than at responding to an act or attitude that is already to hand. It is as if the central feature of ethical judgement had dropped out of the picture in favour of a concern with 'seeing' or 'reading' the situation that precedes action. Important as it is to perceive or read the context in which one acts, doing so cannot disclose what should be done. Moral connoisseurship is not enough to guide action.

A second way of conceiving of capacities to judge cases without relying on principles appeals not to ideas of perception or intuition, but to ideas such as cultural norms, or traditions, or exemplary figures. Judgement is then seen as modelled on the precedents of those who judge well within a given area of life or tradition. Just as legal decisions are thought of as appealing to the precedents set by good judges, and just as technical judgements are to match those of skilled technicians, or professional judgements those of highly competent professionals, so ethical judgements are to match those of saints and heroes, or the teachings of ethical exemplars such as Jesus or the Buddha. Many communitarians and virtue ethicists have favoured this account of ethical judgement.[12]

Undoubtedly the deeds and words of exemplary traditional figures can be influential and important in shaping ethical judgements. But these examples work only because we can discern the principles that inform them. Appeals to cases that are known through religious, traditional or literary sources, or from personal experience will be mute unless we can discern their guiding principle. For pointing to the past – or present – judgements or deeds of saints and heroes is never enough: since cases differ, mere imitation will not be enough. Rather the principle and spirit of the past deed has to be known or shown to be relevant to some present case – which inevitably differs in various respects. Once again it helps to consider practical judgement outside ethics: we may be able to see fairly readily that a sportsman or a technician, a judge or a physician, judges situations well, yet still need to make some effort to grasp just which considerations have guided action and how the example could guide our own action. In generalising from one known case to another and differing case, deliberators have to take it that certain aspects of the past case are the important

---

[12] The single most influential account of ethical judgement along these lines is probably still that given in Alasdair MacIntyre, *After Virtue* (London: Duckworth, 1981), but such views are widespread among hermeneutic and communitarian writers.

ones that should (if possible) be realised in the present case: in short they have to act on the principles embedded in the past cases. If we try, for example, to use the parable of the Good Samaritan to guide action we have to grasp some answer to the very question which the parable addresses: 'Who is my neighbour?' Mere imitation may go in the wrong direction: when we think about care or help for others today it is not, for example, very often useful to construe one-to-one encounters on a lonely road through a desert as paradigmatic.

Those 'situationists' who view ethical judgement as analogous to perception, or as a form of intuition, take a spectator view of ethics and overlook the need for practical judgement that shapes action. Those 'situationists' who view ethical judgement as embedded in social and cultural contexts may or may not be correct, but misrepresent their approach if they claim to dispense with principles. They merely think that morally important principles use or should use the act descriptions and norms of a certain society or culture, and so that while ethical reasoning begins with indeterminate prescriptions, still they are *less* indeterminate than the principles some others prefer. These social norms or rules and norms may or may not differ from those that are commonly argued for in ethical theories, or specifically in bioethics: they are principles none the less. Whether they are superior or more authoritative principles than the less socially determinate principles proposed by Beauchamp and Childress, or by other writers on bioethics, is not here to the point. What is to the point is that those who appeal to social and culturally determinate principles or 'values' *nevertheless* have to find an account of judgement that will work in tandem with principles.

From principles to practical judgement

It seems then that there is no way of dispensing with principles, unless it is possible to establish a quite radical form of ethical particularism, a task of the greatest epistemological difficulty. Most would-be opponents of principles are in a position that is remarkably close to that of 'principilists'. They accept that ethical deliberation will use some (not-too-abstract) principles, whose act and agent descriptions are invariably indeterminate (although they may disagree about how indeterminate they must be) and they will also have to show how the move from principle to act is to be made. Practical judgement cannot however be a matter of inference from principle, or from principles combined with (determinant and reflective) judgements about the context and situation to hand in which action is performed, or attitudes are adopted. The indeterminacy of principles ensures that there is no inference from a principle to a particular act.

And yet practical judgement must shape action. In doing so the fact that certain principles form the starting point for judgement is crucial. A physician who adopts the principle of doing nothing to patients without their informed consent will find that this principle rules out many possible ways of acting and thereby *to some extent* shapes her action. A patient who is committed to following a prescribed course of treatment will equally find that *some* ways of life are ruled out, and that the commitment shapes his life *to some extent*. If for a moment we imagine an agent who is committed to a single principle and faces a single decision then the task of practical judgement is limited but not particularly hard: any act that does not violate that single principle is acceptable. Practical judgement is just a matter of ensuring that action does not violate the relevant principle.

Difficulties arise because practical judgement is never just a matter of making a decision that conforms to a single principle. Agents must always shape their action in the light of commitments to multiple principles, of which only a small minority are likely to be ethical principles. The greatest threat to an ethic of principles arises not from the fact that principles are 'too abstract' or 'too rigid', but from the fact that life is full of cases of (potential) conflicts between principles, including in many cases conflicts between ethical principles. There are countless well-known of instances of conflict among ethical principles: *to save a friend from murder, a lie must be told* (Kant's example); *to save a life, a doctor must be kidnapped* (Mill's example); *to feed the hungry, the Sabbath must be breached* (Christ's example). There are also innumerable instances of conflict between ethical and other practical principles: conflicts between medical needs and hospital budgets; between civil liberties and public health requirements; between quality of life for patients and for their carers; between professional responsibilities and personal projects.

In fact conflicts can even arise from the multiple implications of a *single* practical requirement, which can, it seems, require two incompatible acts. In so-called Buridan moral dilemmas agents are depicted as faced with two indiscernibly differing ethical requirements, such as 'rescuing one of two drowning twins', when rescuing both is impossible.[13] Seemingly, if 'ought' implies 'can', two rescues cannot be managed, and nothing differentiates the two cases, it cannot be the case that both rescues are obligatory: but

---

[13] See in particular Ruth Barcan Marcus, 'Moral Dilemmas and Consistency', *Journal of Philosophy*, 77 (1980), 121–36, esp. her discussion of requirements for ethical consistency at 125.

since (by hypothesis) they are indiscernible and not compossible, neither can be obligatory. Others, notably Bernard Williams, have discussed examples of conflicts between obligations which are not quite Buridan cases, since the two incompatible actions are discernibly different, although they appear to fall under a single principle, for example the dilemma posed by a choice between 'rescuing one's drowning wife' and 'rescuing a drowning stranger', where two rescues are impossible. Williams concluded that any ethics centred on principles and obligations is flawed: it commits agents to a relentless impartiality, and so to neglect of personal attachments and life projects, and appears to disallow rescuing one's wife rather than the stranger.[14]

These examples are not of cases where two (or more) principles are *intrinsically* not jointly satisfiable, because the types of action, policy or life that they prescribe are always incompatible. We can imagine such cases, and all that we can conclude is that it would be incoherent to accept both (or all) of a group of principles that are intrinsically incompatible. Nobody can take themselves to have obligations both to give away all worldly goods and to make a fortune; nobody can view it as obligatory to be open and to be secretive with all; nobody can commit his life both to fundamental medical research and to being a member of a closed religious order. Nobody can be committed to two or more principles or rules whose enactment is *intrinsically* incompatible.

The practically significant and recurrent instances of conflict between principles arise not when they are *intrinsically incompatible* but when they are *contingently incompatible in a specific situation*. This is the sort of dilemma that forms the background to enormous amounts of writing in bioethics. For example, at a roadside accident in the USA a prudent person who is committed to helping others who have been injured may find that prudence and commitments to help conflict, because intervening may expose her to legal claims. This one example must serve here for innumerable other cases of conflict, many of which cannot be resolved by mere time management (doing A, then doing B). Does the evident and pervasive possibility of contingent conflicts between principles tell against the coherence or the usefulness of practical principles, and in particular of ethical principles? Contingent conflicts between practical principles certainly make practical judgement a demanding task.[15] But I do not think that

---

[14] Bernard Williams, 'Persons, Character and Morality', in his *Moral Luck* (Cambridge University Press, 1981), 1–19, at 17–18.

[15] See Barbara Herman, 'Obligation and Performance', in her *The Practice of Moral Judgement* (Cambridge, MA: Harvard University Press, 1993), 159–83, for a reasoned view of deliberation as a task.

contingent conflict shows that the very idea of commitment to practical principles is incoherent.

Practical judgement on multiple principles

Agents *usually* bring multiple commitments and principles, and multiple goals, to any deliberative task. The first part of their task is to judge whether there are ways of acting that satisfy the claims of all significant principles (and do not obstruct other goals), so avoiding both (moral) conflict and (moral) failure. While many of these incipient conflicts might be resolved either by time management or by giving up activities or projects that are permissible but not required, others cannot be. In particular, conflicts between ethical and other principles that set requirements may be very hard to resolve.

Yet something must be said about how the task is achieved, or the process of practical judgement will remain a mystery. Clearly we cannot expect to find a complete account of the moves to be made: that could be given only if there were complete rules for judging providing a practical algorithm. In the absence of a practical algorithm, practical judging simply seeks to identify *some* act or pattern of action that adequately meets the several requirements of the case. In many cases commitment to a plurality of principles that set requirements sets a problem that can be resolved. The task has considerable analogies with solving a design problem. In building a hospital numerous constraints must be met. The hospital must be built of available and affordable materials; it must afford adequate shelter and insulation for the climate and for the needs of vulnerable patients; energy consumption and other running costs must be affordable; technical services must be adequate; local planning requirements must be met; the project must be completed within budget. These design and financial criteria constitute a set of constraints and standards which cannot all be met perfectly, and that also cannot always, or perhaps generally, be traded off against one another: a hospital that is poorly insulated or leaks will be inadequate even if it is very affordable. Nevertheless, it is possible to build hospitals in ways that meet all these demands.

Practical judgement too is a matter of finding some act, or pattern of action, or policy that meets a plurality of requirements and recommendations of varying sorts. It is not best thought of as a matter of 'balancing' different principles or different obligations (whatever that might mean). Often great success in living up to one requirement goes no way to compensate for failure to meet another. Great success in seeking patients' informed consent to their treatment does not compensate for providing them with substandard care. High rates of successful surgery do not compensate for failure to obtain patients' consent. The difficulty of practical judgement is that it has to satisfy a plurality of requirements, yet conflict is not resolvable by fantasising that there is some metric for balancing and trading off different sorts of requirement. Practical judgement is a matter of living up to rather than dismissing multiple requirements. Although there is no algorithm for practical judgement, it can be done better or worse, and may improve or deteriorate. Agents who fail to respect requirements, or who fail to identify obvious lines of action that respect all requirements do not show good practical judgement.

Judgement, conflicts and remainders

Practical judgement is clearly always difficult and often not wholly successful. However, there is more than might at first sight seem likely that can be done in the face of intractable conflict that brings two (or more) principles of obligation into contingent conflict. I shall comment very briefly on two strategies for dealing with recalcitrant conflict between ethical and other requirements.

The first strategy is one of forward planning and evasion. We have a lot of knowledge about circumstances that are likely to create conflicting requirements. A medical practice that regularly overbooks appointments; a patient who covertly places herself under two physicians; a medical researcher who does not handle conflicts between patient care and research interests properly, are all heading into situations in which they are likely to find themselves committed to principles that cannot both be respected, and so to find themselves facing difficulties of practical judgement. Foresight, care and proper institutional structures can do a lot to avert many of these problems. Creating, reforming and adjusting institutions, practices, ways of life and traits of character can reduce and avert contingent conflicts between principles and make practical judgement feasible.[16]

Needless to say, foresight and reform have their limitations. Often we find ourselves in situations in which there is no way of acting that can satisfy all requirements, and indeed in which nothing that the relevant agents could have foreseen or done would have averted the potential for conflict. The most extreme situations, which often give rise to 'dirty hands'

---

[16] See Barcan Marcus, 'Moral Dilemmas and Consistency', 121: "we ought to conduct our lives and arrange our institutions so as to minimize predicaments of moral conflict".

problems, are those in which institutions and practices themselves are based on unacceptable principles, institutions and action of various sorts. Even where nothing is deeply awry, we act against the background of determinate configurations of institutions and practices, of habits and customs, of virtues and failings, of skills and incompetence, of capabilities and vulnerabilities, all of which may variously help or hinder attempts to live up to multiple principles. In daily reasoning about action it will often be pointless or misleading to assume these away. Often agents may think that had institutions been better, or had they themselves made better decisions in the past, no contingent conflict would have arisen. But they will realise that, in the world as it is, they cannot avoid a degree of moral failure.

Where existing realities force hard choices it may be impossible to meet all of the various requirements – ethical and legal, prudential and social, technical and professional – that agents take seriously. The most that they can then do is to recognise the claims of unmet, indeed contingently unmeetable, requirements and recommendations. The fact that a requirement – and on occasion this might be an important ethical obligation or a central professional commitment – has proved contingently unmeetable does not exempt an agent from its claims. The unmeetable requirement may have 'remainders', and remainders are often viewed as calling for expressions and attitudes such as regret or remorse. There are also other, more active and practical approaches to failure, to meet requirements, and these may be more important that the attitudinal responses that have been so much emphasised in discussions of 'remainders'. More active responses might include expressions of apology, commitment to reform, the provision of compensation, forms of restitution, making good and the like.[17]

The importance of foresight and institution building, and of an active approach to remainders, in dealing with practical conflict, does not show that principles are dispensable. It shows that living up to practical principles is hard and demanding. Taking principles seriously is not – as one eminent particularist has suggested – a matter of finding "a system of rules by which to spare themselves some of the agony of thinking and all the torment of feeling that is actually involved in reasoned deliberation".[18] It is a matter of working to make practical judgements that do not violate requirements, and of actively acknowledging and seeking to make good any remaining failure to meet important requirements.

[17] See Herman, 'Obligation and Performance'.
[18] Wiggins, 'Deliberation and Practical Reason', 237.

CHAPTER 14

Enactable and enforceable: Kant's criteria for right and virtue[1]

Kant's distinction between duties of right and of virtue remains controversial, for a number of reasons. A close look at the distinctions he draws and the claims that he makes suggests that a distinction between enforceable duties of right and unenforceable duties of virtue is neither exclusive nor exhaustive. It is not exclusive because it is possible to fulfil duties of right as a matter of principle, in which case what is done is both right and virtuous. It is not exhaustive because certain duties, among them the duty to enter a civil condition and duties of equity, are not in principle enforceable: yet are duties of right. And yet the distinction is central to Kant's practical philosophy.

These demarcations contrast sharply with those found in large swathes of contemporary political philosophy that are self-consciously distanced from ethical questions other than those about justice, and have nothing to say about social or personal virtues. There is nothing new in the thought that justice and virtue are distinct domains of practical philosophy, but an assumption that they are radically separate has been widely accepted only in the last few decades. In part this is because many accept the view, championed by John Rawls in *Political Liberalism*,[2] that no reasoned agreement on wider ethical questions can be secured in ethically plural societies. In part it reflects widespread assumptions that human rights claims provide a sufficient ethical framework for public life and that we should prefer maximal interpretations of each right, which shrinks the space other ethical claims can inhabit. Individual political liberals often have plenty to say about virtue and character, but they now do so (as it were) in a private capacity. Correspondingly, a good deal of contemporary writing on ethics discusses various virtues of personal and social life, but is silent about institutional and public life, and about the claims of justice.

---

[1] This chapter was first published in *Kant-Studien*, 107.1 (2016), 111–125.
[2] John Rawls, *Political Liberalism* (New York: Columbia University Press, 1993).

The supposed gulf between justice and the virtues seems deeper and more fundamental than it used to seem.

A distinction between the domains of justice and of virtue is, of course, nothing new. However, many writers have thought that there is some underlying unity – for example, that both could be derived from a common account of the good, or that they formed two coordinate domains of duty. The distinctions and the links which they drew between justice and virtue can, I believe, still prove instructive. Here I shall consider Kant's distinction between duties of right (including duties of justice) and of virtue, and whether it is clear and convincing. I shall concentrate solely on his *criteria* for classifying duties into those of right and of virtue, and say nothing about his classifications of duties as *perfect* and *imperfect, narrow* (or *strict*) and *wide*.

Kant's fundamental criteria for distinguishing types of duties in the *Metaphysik der Sitten* are *modal*, in keeping with the modal criterion for duty provided by the Categorical Imperative, but introducing more substantive considerations. In particular he claims that all duties must be (in principle) *enactable*; that duties of right (among them those of justice) must (in principle) be *enforceable by others*; and that *duties of virtue* are (in principle) *not enforceable by others*.[3] It is not obvious that this provides either an exclusive or an exhaustive, or indeed a perspicuous, classification or demarcation of different types of duty.

Enactability and enforceability are distinct matters, and I shall take them in turn. The idea that duties – whether of right or of virtue – must be enactable may seem unproblematic. For it does not mean that principles of duty could be enacted by all agents, or on all occasions, or in all situations, but merely that the relevant principles are practical, in that they specify what is to count as an (adequate) enactment or instantiation. In many cases practical principles cannot in practice be enacted, whether because agents lack capacities or opportunities, or simply because the situation is not relevant.

And yet a requirement that practical principles be enactable is not a simple matter. Principles are invariably indeterminate, but their enactments must be particular and determinate, and it is not immediately obvious how practical judgement is to make a transition from an indeterminate principle to a particular and determinate enactment. However, for

---

[3] In addition he allows for the slightly anomalous 'ethical duties of omission', which are duties to act in certain ways rather than to adopt ends, that are not enforceable by others because they require distinctively 'internal' restraint.

present purposes I shall simply assume that this is feasible.[4] My aim here is to understand the criteria by which Kant hopes to distinguish different types of duty.

Doing right virtuously

I find it hard to escape a sense that there is something awry in the classification of duties in Kant's *Metaphysics of Morals*. I have wrestled with this problem repeatedly, and with some misgivings I return to it. The difficulty, as I now see it, lies not with the classification of some duties as duties of right (including duties of justice), and others as duties of virtue, but with a certain vacillation about the *criteria* for counting as a duty of right or of virtue. Does Kant think that every duty that is not a duty of right is a duty of virtue? Is the classification exclusive? Does he think that every duty must be either a duty of right or a duty of virtue? Is the classification exhaustive? Might – or must – there be duties that are neither?

Kant shows some uncertainty about his terminology for classifying duties in a historical comment at the start of the *Doctrine of Virtue*, when he remarks on a contemporary narrowing of the understanding of the term *ethics*:

> In ancient times 'ethics' signified the *doctrine of morals* (*philosophia moralis*) in general, which was also called the *doctrine of duties*. Later on it seemed better to reserve the name 'ethics' for one part of moral philosophy, namely the doctrine of those duties that do not come under external laws (it was thought appropriate to call this, in German, the *doctrine of virtue*). Accordingly, the system of the doctrine of duties in general is now divided into the system of the *doctrine of right* (*ius*), which deals with duties that can be given by external laws, and the system of the *doctrine of virtue* (*Ethica*), which treats of duties that cannot be so given; and this division may stand.[5] (*MM* 6:379)

Here it looks as if we are dealing with a straightforward dichotomy: duties either *can* be 'fit for' external law-giving (i.e. their enactment can in principle be secured by constraints that others can impose) and are duties

---

[4] See Chapters 5, 8 and 12, above, for discussions of practical judgement.
[5] "Ethik bedeutete in den alten Zeiten die Sittenlehre (*philosophia moralis*) überhaupt, welche man auch die Lehre von den Pflichten benannte. In der Folge hat man es rathsam gefunden, diesen Namen auf einen Theil der Sittenlehre, nämlich auf die Lehre von den Pflichten, die nicht unter äußeren Gesetzen stehen, allein zu übertragen (dem man im Deutschen den Namen Tugendlehre angemessen gefunden hat): so daß jetzt das System der allgemeinen Pflichtenlehre in das der Rechtslehre (*ius*), welche äußerer Gesetze fähig ist, und der Tugendlehre (*Ethica*) eingetheilt wird, die deren nicht fähig ist; wobei es denn auch sein Bewenden haben mag."

of right, or they are not 'fit for' external law-giving[6] (i.e. their enactment can be secured only by agents adopting and acting on the appropriate principle for themselves) and so are duties of virtue. On this reading, a dichotomy between duties of right (among them duties of justice) and of virtue looks plausible.

But in the Introduction to the *Metaphysics of Morals*, Section IV, titled *On the Division of a Metaphysics of Morals*, Kant says something rather different. He there uses the term *ethics* in the broader sense that he deems obsolete at the start of the *Tugendlehre*. In particular, he notes that some enactments of duties of right, which *could* have reflected external constraint, may in particular cases *actually* reflect internal laws, principles or self-constraint, and accepts that in such cases what is done should count as virtuous as well as right, or in relevant cases as both virtuous and just. On this view, it is only duties, and not their enactments that can be divided exclusively into matters of right and of virtue: the principled enactment of duties of right is both right and virtuous.

These thoughts (which are close to ones Kant had put forward in *Groundwork*) depend on distinguishing the *content* of duties, i.e. *what* they require, from the sorts of '*law-giving*' that can secure their enactment. It allows for at least *three* possibilities. We can enact duties of right in response to external constraint; we can enact them by making it a matter of principle to do so – by an 'internal' law-giving or self-constraint that leads to action that might have been, but in this case was not, enforced by others; and we can enact duties for which external constraints or requirements are impossible, in which case only 'internal' law-giving or self-constraint is possible.

This three-fold classification is spelled out in Section IV[7] of the Introduction to the *Metaphysics of Morals*, titled appropriately *On the Division of a Metaphysic of Morals*. There Kant writes, with fine disregard

---

[6] The terms *Gestezgebung* and *Selbstgestetzgebung* are often translated as *legislation* and *self-legislation*, rather than as *law-giving*. This seems to me misleading. A *Gestezgebung* is an action, literally a giving of law, not the product of an action, whereas legislation is the product of the action of legislatures. Translating *Selbstgesetzgebung* as *self-legislation* creates an illusion – and a puzzle – by suggesting that individual agents can *legislate*, or *give* or *make law*. Rather less mysteriously, what they can actually do is to adopt principles that have (or that lack!) the form of law. Individuals cannot literally legislate. I have discussed this issue in 'Self-Legislation, Autonomy and the Form of Law', in H. Nagl-Docekal and R. Langthaler (eds.), *Recht, Geschichte, Religion: Die Bedeutung Kants für die Gegenwart, Sonderband der Deutschen Zeitschrift für Philosophie* (Berlin: Akademie Verlag, 2004), 13–26, and in Onora O'Neill, *Constucting Authorities: Reason, Politics and Interpretation in Kant's Philosophy* (Cambridge University Press, 2016), 121–36.

[7] Which was section III in the Academy Edition: the page numbers have not been changed, but the order of the sections has been.

for the newer and narrower understanding of the term *ethics* to which he later pointed, that

> It can be seen from this that all duties, just because they are duties, belong to ethics; but it does not follow that the *law-giving* for them is always contained in ethics: for many of them it is outside ethics. Thus ethics commands that I still fulfil a contract I have entered into, even though the other party could not [i.e. could not in this case] coerce me to do so . . . All that ethics teaches is that if the incentive which juridical law-giving connects with that duty, namely external constraint, were absent, the idea of duty by itself would be [could be?] sufficient as an incentive . . . It is no duty of virtue to keep one's promises but a duty of right, to the performance of which one can be coerced. But it is still a virtuous action (a proof of virtue) to do it even where no coercion may be *applied*. The doctrine of right and the doctrine of virtue are therefore distinguished not so much by their different duties as by the difference in their law-giving, which connects one incentive or the other with the law.[8] (*MM* 6:219–20) [interpolations in square brackets OO'N][9]

On this view, some enactments of duties that *could* have been based on external coercion, may in fact be done on principle, and will reflect internal 'law-giving' or self-constraint, and the action will then count as 'a proof of virtue' and will be *both* right (in some cases specifically just) and virtuous.

Kant spells out the implications of this position very clearly, if with some asides and repetition, in the last paragraph of this section:

> Ethical law-giving (even if the duties might be external) is that which *cannot* be external; juridical law-giving is that which also can be external. So it is an external duty to keep a promise made in contract; but the command to do this merely because it is a duty, without regard to any other incentive,

---

[8] See also "The mere conformity of an action with law, irrespective of the incentive to it, is called is *legality* (lawfulness), but that conformity in which the idea of a duty arising from the law is also the incentive to the action is called its *morality*": "Man nennt die bloße Übereinstimmung oder Nichtübereinstimmung einer Handlung mit dem Gesetze ohne Rücksicht auf die Triebfeder derselben die Legalität (Gesetzmäßigkeit), diejenige aber, in welcher die Idee der Pflicht aus dem Gesetze zugleich die Triebfeder der Handlung ist, die Moralität (Sittlichkeit) derselben" (*MM* 6:219).

[9] "Hieraus ist zu ersehen, daß alle Pflichten bloß darum, weil sie Pflichten sind, mit zur Ethik gehören; aber ihre Gesetzgebung ist darum nicht allemal in der Ethik enthalten, sondern von vielen derselben außerhalb derselben. So gebietet die Ethik, daß ich eine in einem Vertrage gethane Anheischigmachung, wenn mich der andere Theil gleich nicht dazu zwingen könnte [. . .]. Die Ethik lehrt hernach nur, daß, wenn die Triebfeder, welche die juridische Gesetzgebung mit jener Pflicht verbindet, nämlich der äußere Zwang, auch weggelassen wird, die Idee der Pflicht allein schon zur Triebfeder hinreichend sei. [. . .] Es ist keine Tugendpflicht, sein Versprechen zu halten, sondern eine Rechtspflicht, zu deren Leistung man gezwungen werden kann. Aber es ist doch eine tugendhafte Handlung (Beweis der Tugend), es auch da zu thun, wo kein Zwang besorgt werden darf. Rechtslehre und Tugendlehre unterscheiden sich also nicht sowohl durch ihre verschiedene Pflichten, als vielmehr durch die Verschiedenheit der Gesetzgebung, welche die eine oder die andere Triebfeder mit dem Gesetze verbindet."

belongs to *internal* law-giving alone. So the obligation is assigned to ethics not because the duty is of a particular kind – for there are external duties in ethics as well as in right –, but rather because the law-giving in this case is an internal one and can have no external lawgiver. For the same reason duties of benevolence, even though they are external duties (i.e. obligations to external actions), still belong to ethics because their law giving can only be internal. – Ethics [. . .] has duties in common with right: what it does not have in common with right is only the kind of *obligation*.[10] For what is distinctive of ethical law-giving is that one is to perform actions just because they are duties and to make the principle of duty itself, wherever the duty comes from, the sufficient incentive for choice. So while there are many *directly ethical* duties, internal law-giving makes the rest of them, one and all, indirectly ethical. (*MM* 6:220–1)[11] [Note the 'one and all'!][12]

These passages sit uncomfortably with any thought that we should shift to the 'modern', narrow understanding of the term *ethics*, by restricting it to duties and enactments of virtue. Those who fulfil duties of right as a matter of principle (by self-constraint, from a 'sense of duty') also act virtuously, although what they do is (externally) indistinguishable from what they would have done in fulfilling the duty in response to some external constraint, such as coercion. This position is most naturally expressed by the thought that all duties are ethical duties *in the older and wider sense of the term*, including duties of right (among them those of justice). So we have reason *not* to narrow our understanding of ethics, and to see some action as both right and virtuous.

[10] Note that here Kant speaks of *duties* that are both duties of right and duties of virtue – not just of particular acts that fall under both.

[11] Cf. "the mere conformity of an action with law, irrespective of the incentive to it, is called *legality* (lawfulness), but that conformity in which the idea of a duty arising from the law is also the incentive to the action is called its *morality*"(*MM* 6:219).

[12] "Die ethische Gesetzgebung (die Pflichten mögen allenfalls auch äußere sein) ist diejenige, welche nicht äußerlich sein kann; die juridische ist, welche auch äußerlich sein kann. So ist es eine äußerliche Pflicht, sein vertragsmäßiges Versprechen zu halten; aber das Gebot, dieses bloß darum zu thun, weil es Pflicht ist, ohne auf eine andere Triebfeder Rücksicht zu nehmen, ist bloß zur innern Gesetzgebung gehörig. Also nicht als besondere Art von Pflicht (eine besondere Art Handlungen, zu denen man verbunden ist) – denn es ist in der Ethik sowohl als im Rechte eine äußere Pflicht, – sondern weil die Gesetzgebung im angeführten Falle eine innere ist und keinen äußeren Gesetzgeber haben kann, wird die Verbindlichkeit zur Ethik gezählt. Aus eben dem Grunde werden die Pflichten des Wohlwollens, ob sie gleich äußere Pflichten (Verbindlichkeiten zu äußeren Handlungen) sind, doch zur Ethik gezählt, weil ihre Gesetzgebung nur innerlich sein kann. – Die Ethik hat freilich auch ihre besondern Pflichten [. . .], aber hat doch auch mit dem Rechte Pflichten, aber nur nicht die Art der Verpflichtung gemein. Denn Handlungen bloß darum, weil es Pflichten sind, ausüben und den Grundsatz der Pflicht selbst, woher sie auch komme, zur hinreichenden Triebfeder der Willkür zu machen, ist das Eigenthümliche der ethischen Gesetzgebung. So giebt es also zwar viele direct-ethische Pflichten, aber die innere Gesetzgebung macht auch die übrigen alle und insgesammt zu indirect-ethischen."

Enactability: maxims and ends

This picture is complicated by Kant's later assertion (apparently, however, here relying on the narrower 'modern' sense of the term *ethics*) that: "Ethics does not give laws for actions (*ius* does that), but only for the maxims of actions" (*MM* 6:388; title of section VI).[13] This way of contrasting ethics and right elides a great deal. In prescribing or 'giving' a law for action, a duty of right too prescribes action on a maxim, although not on a maxim of ends, but nevertheless action on a maxim that unavoidably includes indeterminate act descriptions, so could be enacted or satisfied in various ways.

Indeterminacy is no barrier to enactment, but requires an exercise of practical judgement. Kant's view of the matter is that this is more demanding in the case of duties of virtue, because the relevant maxims specify no more than 'action for an end', so provide less indication of the specific way in which a principle should be enacted on any given occasion:

> if the law can prescribe only the maxim of actions, not actions themselves,[14] this is a sign that it leaves a playroom (*latitudo*) for free choice in following (complying with) the law, that is, that the law cannot specify precisely in what way one is to act and how much one is to do by the action for an end that is also a duty.[15] (*MM* 6:390)[16]

However, indeterminacy has to be resolved whether agents act on maxims that specify what must be done in some detail or on maxims that prescribe only ends to be pursued. Neither principles of right nor principles of virtue can *fully* specify what is to be done in enacting or instantiating them. Acting on duties of either sort requires agents to judge how to enact indeterminate duties in specific circumstances. There are better and worse ways of enacting principles of duty of both sorts, better and worse ways of judging practically, both in acting on duties of right and in acting

---

[13] "Die Ethik giebt nicht Gesetze für die Handlungen (denn das thut das *Ius*), sondern nur für die Maximen der Handlungen."

[14] Would this have been clearer if he had written "if the law can prescribe only the maxim of ends for actions, not actions themselves"?

[15] "[. . .] wenn das Gesetz nur die Maxime der Handlungen, nicht die Handlungen selbst gebieten kann, so ists ein Zeichen, daß es der Befolgung (Observanz) einen Spielraum (*latitudo*) für die freie Willkür überlasse, d.i. nicht bestimmt angeben könne, wie und wie viel durch die Handlung zu dem Zweck, der zugleich Pflicht ist, gewirkt werden solle."

[16] Similar passages: "there is no law of reason [for cultivating one's own perfection] for action but only a law for maxims of actions" ["Es ist also hier kein Gesetz der Vernunft für die Handlungen, sondern blos für die Maxime der Handlungen"] (*MM* 6:392); "The law [of beneficence] holds only for maxims, not for determinate actions" ["das Gesetz gebietet nicht diese [. . .] Handlung [. . .], sondern blos die Maxime der Handlung"] (*MM* 6:393); "ethical obligation to ends . . . involves only a law for *maxims* of actions [. . .]" ["die ethische Verbindlichkeit zu Zwecken [. . .] blos ein Gesetz für die Maxime der Handlungen enthält [. . .]"] (*MM* 6:395).

on duties of virtue. This may not seem obvious, because some duties of right are duties to *refrain from* or to *omit* certain sort of action, in which case it may seem obvious what is required ('Don't do anything of *that* sort'), and that such restraint could be enforced. But other duties of right require action of quite specific sorts. If I seek to comply with legislation governing business or professional life, or if I promise to provide someone else with accommodation, or an evening meal, what is required is more narrowly specified, but still leaves open many ways of living up to the relevant duty. In short, indeterminacy of principles has to be addressed in enacting duties of either sort, since maxims of right also do not fully determine their enactments.

Might Kant's underlying thought be that judging what to do in living up to maxims of ends is *more* demanding because they are *more* indeterminate? His comment at 6:390 that "the law cannot specify precisely in what way one is to act and how much one is to do by the action for an end that is also a duty"[17] could be read as suggesting this. But even if there is a quantitative difference, and maxims of ends are always *more* indeterminate than maxims of action, both sorts of duty require agents to address the indeterminacy of practical principles by judging practically in ways that are appropriate in the specific context. It does not therefore seem that the basic difference between duties of virtue and of right has to do with enactability.

Some limits of enforceability

This point is confirmed by the fact that the reason Kant gives for thinking that external law-giving *must* fail in the case of duties of virtue is not that they are more indeterminate, so harder to enact, but rather that they are not *enforceable*. Maxims of ends differ from maxims of action not because they eliminate the need for practical judgement, but because they do not specify *what* is to be enforced. In the Introduction to the *Doctrine of Virtue* Kant writes:

> Now, I can indeed be constrained by others to perform *actions* that are directed as means to an end, but I cannot be constrained by *others to have an end*: only I myself can *make* something my end.[18] (*MM* 6:381)

---

[17] "[. . .] das Gesetz [. . .] der Befolgung (Observanz) einen Spielraum (*latitudo*) für die freie Willkür überlasse, d.i. nicht bestimmt angeben könne, wie und wie viel durch die Handlung zu dem Zweck, der zugleich Pflicht ist, gewirkt werden solle [. . .]".

[18] "Nun kann ich zwar zu Handlungen, die als Mittel auf einen Zweck gerichtet sind, nie aber einen Zweck zu haben von anderen gezwungen werden, sondern ich kann nur selbst mir etwas zum Zweck machen."

The problem is not the (greater) *indeterminacy* of maxims of ends, but the *unenforceability* of requirements to pursue ends. Kant points out how hard it is to distinguish between action that genuinely seeks to secure an indeterminate end, such as the happiness of others or self-improvement, from externally indistinguishable patterns of action done with the very different end of securing a reputation for seeking others' happiness or self-improvement. (Remember Kant's example of the shopkeeper who gives the right change even to children, but whose honesty may be bogus.) Enforcement fails in such cases because enforcers cannot impose ends on others: "*coercion* to ends (to have them) is self-contradictory ... Another can indeed *coerce* me *to do* something that is not my end ... but not to *make this my end*" (*MM* 6:381).

However, while Kant shows that duties of virtue are not coercible or enforceable, he does not show that all duties of right are enforceable. Right is enforceable only if it is relatively clear what compliance with a duty of right would require, so clear what should be enforced. But clarity about requirements is necessary but not sufficient for enforcement, which also requires an enforcing agency, such as (but not necessarily) a state. It follows that there are some duties of right that cannot be enforced.

This is not merely because enforcement often fails in practice, although that is evidently true. Notoriously, law enforcement can be fragile and ineffective in many ways, even in well-ordered states and societies; and in less well-ordered states and societies things are worse. In addition the ambitious complexity of modern legislation, administration and adjudication often strains or overwhelms institutions and their office holders, and undermines enforcement. It is all too common to find that duties of right cannot *in practice* be enforced because institutions are lacking or ineffective, or because people routinely or sporadically breach or evade their demands.

However, I take it that Kant's appeal to enforceability sets a modal rather than an empirical test, and can bracket concerns about the actual limitations of various approaches to enforcement. His concern is with *enforceability in principle*, and is compatible with the reality that enforcement often fails, may have unintended consequences or may prove counterproductive. It is also compatible with the claim that sometimes duties of right that are enforceable *should not* be enforced.[19] The distinctive point is

---

[19] Examples that are often discussed include classical arguments for duties to tolerate wrongful speech, even wrongful action, and arguments against prosecuting wrongful action where doing so is 'not in the public interest'. However, these are not the cases Kant discusses.

that Kant evidently does not think that all duties of right are even *in principle* enforceable. For within the body of the *Rechtslehre* we find at least two discussions of duties of right that are explicitly said not to be enforceable.

The first is in a discussion of aspects of equity, which Kant sees as requiring forms of fairness that are unenforceable. He is emphatic that duties of equity are *not* to be seen as duties of virtue:

> *Equity* (considered objectively) is in no way to be seen as a basis for merely calling upon another to fulfil an ethical duty (to be benevolent and kind). One who demands something on this basis stands instead upon his *right*, except that he does not have the conditions that a judge needs in order to determine by how much or in what way his claim could be satisfied.[20] (*MM* 6:234)

Kant offers two examples of unenforceable claims in equity. The first is that of a partner in an enterprise who has contributed more than the others, although the deed of partnership provides for equal shares. Kant suggests that if the company is wound up, this partner has a claim in equity to more than an equal share, although the claim is not enforceable. The second example is that of a servant with a contract for a given wage, where its value is eroded by inflation during the period of employment. Again, Kant suggests that "he cannot appeal to a right to be compensated when he gets the same amount of money but it is of unequal value",[21] but only on grounds of equity and concludes that "a *court of equity* . . . involves a contradiction"[22] (*MM* 6:234); although a judge could hear such claims and perhaps act to meet them, this would not be an action of the court. He notes that the *motto* (*dictum*) of equity (*summa ius summa injuria*), has some truth in it, but insists that the claims of equity are unenforceable. But if these claims are, as he asserts, "in no way merely a basis for merely calling on another to fulfil an ethical duty"[23] (*MM* 6:234), then the distinction between enforceable duties of right and unenforceable duties of virtue cannot be exhaustive.

---

[20] "Die Billigkeit (objectiv betrachtet) ist keinesweges ein Grund zur Aufforderung bloß an die ethische Pflicht Anderer (ihr Wohlwollen und Gütigkeit), sondern der, welcher aus diesem Grunde etwas fordert, fußt sich auf sein Recht, nur daß ihm die für den Richter erforderlichen Bedingungen mangeln, nach welchen dieser bestimmen könnte, wie viel, oder auf welche Art dem Anspruche desselben genug gethan werden könne."

[21] "[. . .] er [. . .] kann bei gleichem Zahlwerth, aber ungleichem Geldwerth sich nicht auf sein Recht berufen [. . .]".

[22] "[. . .] ein Gerichtshof der Billigkeit [. . .] einen Widerspruch in sich schließe".

[23] "[. . .] keinesweges ein Grund zur Aufforderung bloß an die ethische Pflicht Anderer".

However, a second and more basic unenforceable duty of right is even more significant. One of Kant's most fundamental arguments in the *Rechtslehre* is that duties of right – in this context, specifically of justice – set enforceable standards *for everybody*, so must restrict action in the same way for all. But he also asserts that unrestricted freedom of action for everybody would prove self-defeating. Enforcement that is unsystematic cannot secure performance of duties – or protection of rights.

This is not initially apparent in Kant's most abstract formulation of the universal law of right (often referred to as the 'Universal Principle of Justice') as a demand that all should have the same freedom of choice and face the same restrictions on their freedom:

> Any action is *right* [*recht*] if it can coexist with everyone's freedom in accordance with a universal law, or if on its maxim the freedom of choice of each can coexist in accordance with a universal law.[24] (*MM* 6:230)

But if this is to be more than an abstract standard for the configuration of an ideal society, whose members are thought of as spontaneously respecting one another's freedom of choice, then systematic enforcement, and with it some coercive restriction of freedom, is required. Anarchy, i.e. the complete absence of enforcement and coercion, does not offer an adequate model for securing duties of right.

Kant concludes that duties of right that secure the same external freedom for all require coercion: "Right Is Connected with an Authorization to use Coercion"[25] (title of §D, *MM* 6:231). Consequently right "should not be conceived as made up of two elements, namely an obligation in accordance with a law and a separate authorization . . . to coerce"[26] (*MM* 6:232); rather these two elements are indissolubly linked.[27] If the same external freedom is to be secured for all, there must be authorised coercion that enforces common laws:

> coercion is a hindrance or resistance to freedom. Therefore, if a certain use of freedom is itself a hindrance to freedom in accordance with universal laws (i.e. wrong), coercion that is opposed to this (as *hindering a hindrance to freedom*) is consistent with freedom in accordance with universal laws, that is, it is right. Hence there is connected with right by the principle of

---

[24] "Eine jede Handlung ist recht, die oder nach deren Maxime die Freiheit der Willkür eines jeden mit jedermanns Freiheit nach einem allgemeinen Gesetze zusammen bestehen kann."
[25] "Das Recht ist mit der Befugniß zu zwingen verbunden."
[26] Das Recht "darf nicht als aus zwei Stücken, nämlich der Verbindlichkeit nach einem Gesetze und der Befugniß [. . .] zu zwingen".
[27] See Katrin Flikschuh, *Kant and Modern Political Philosophy* (Cambridge University Press, 2000).

contradiction an authorization to coerce someone who infringes it.[28] (*MM* 6:231)

Kant's modal claim that duties of right must be *enforceable* leads him to a more realistic view of right and justice than those advanced in much later, including contemporary, writing in political philosophy, which typically sees the definition of ideals and principles of justice as the fundamental task, treating enforceability as an ancillary matter, to be addressed only *after* principles of justice have identified.

The contrast between realist and idealist accounts of justice is stark. Some contemporary political theorists identify justice with securing specific *distributions* or *patterns* of resources (e.g. specific equalities, specific limits to inequalities), or of primary goods, which *cannot* be directly enforced. Others hold that justice includes rights to goods or services, which can be secured only if duties are allocated to specified agents or agencies, yet say little about the effective and acceptable allocation of the necessary obligations, leaving it indeterminate *who* has to do *what* for *whom*, hence unclear *what is to be enforced*. *A fortiori* they fail to link their claims about justice to an account of enforceability. Yet other contemporary approaches to justice identify it with achieving specified results or prescribed targets – whether maximal happiness or less grandiose states of affairs – which would require implausibly demanding calculations in order to identify either *what* should be enforced, or *on whom* the duties that are to be enforced should fall. Kant's insistence that enforceability is criterial for duties of right – and so of justice – leads him to a robustly realist political position.[29]

But while his appeal to enforceability has an attractive rigour and clarity, it comes at a price, about which he is clear. If duties of right – including those of justice – are to be enforceable, there must be agents or agencies to do the enforcing. Kant argues that enforcement is indispensable because human beings who inhabit the bounded terrain of the earth "cannot avoid living side by side with all others"[30] (*MM* 6:307), so are open to one another's depredations. Nor can they be sure that the vagaries of private

---

[28] "[. . .] der Zwang [. . .] ist ein Hinderniß oder Widerstand, der der Freiheit geschieht. Folglich: wenn ein gewisser Gebrauch der Freiheit selbst ein Hinderniß der Freiheit nach allgemeinen Gesetzen (d i. unrecht) ist, so ist der Zwang, der diesem entgegengesetzt wird, als Verhinderung eines Hindernisses der Freiheit mit der Freiheit nach allgemeinen Gesetzen zusammen stimmend, d. i. recht: mithin ist mit dem Rechte zugleich eine Befugniß, den, der ihm Abbruch thut, zu zwingen, nach dem Satze des Widerspruchs verknüpft."

[29] For more detail see Onora O'Neill, 'From Transcendental Idealism to Political Realism', in Nicholas Boyle, Liz Disley and John Walker (eds.), *The Impact of Idealism: The Legacy of Post Kantian German Thought*, 4 vols. (Cambridge University Press, 2013), 2:12–25.

[30] "[. . .] soll[en] im Verhältnisse eines unvermeidlichen Nebeneinanderseins mit allen anderen".

enforcement will protect them: private enforcement agencies may prove no more reliable than anarchy. He concludes that only public enforcement can secure a "rightful condition . . . under which alone everyone is able to *enjoy* his rights"[31] (*MM* 6:305) and that everyone has reason to take steps to secure the performance of duties of right by entering into a civil or rightful condition (*in einen rechtlichen Zustand*), in which a public authority – for example, a state – assumes the task of enforcement. Absent such a civil condition, there can be no assurance of others' restraint, and private enforcement would rule the day. Kant concludes "when you cannot avoid living side by side with all others, you ought to leave the state of nature and proceed with them into a rightful condition"[32] (*MM* 6:307).

However, this duty to leave the state of nature and to enter a civil society is necessarily *unenforceable*, since it is a duty to establish the possibility of enforcement. Yet it is not merely a duty, but a duty of right and Kant thinks that those in a state of nature would do wrong to refuse to join willing others in a civil condition, so insisting on remaining in a condition that is not rightful. So this most fundamental duty of right is *inevitably not enforceable*, since it arises in the absence of any enforcing power. A duty to enter and remain in a civil condition must therefore rest on force or agreement, rather than on enforcement by law, so escapes any presumed dichotomy between enforceable duties of right and unenforceable duties of virtue.[33]

In short Kant's distinction between duties of right and duties of virtue is *neither exclusive nor exhaustive*. It is not exclusive because duties of right are indirectly ethical, and their principled discharge counts as 'proof of virtue'. It is not exhaustive because neither the demands to leave the state of nature and to enter a rightful civil condition, nor the demands of equity, are enforceable. These duties do not meet either the criteria for being a duty of virtue, or the criteria for being a duty of right.

This incompleteness in Kant's account of the distinction between duties of right, including justice, and duties of virtue may not be any sort of failing. Just as there is reason to be circumspect about contemporary views that wholly separate the demands of justice and of virtue, so we may have reason to be cautious about Kant's tendency – even against the grain of some of his own arguments – to suggest that ethical requirements divide exclusively and exhaustively into duties of right and of virtue.

---

[31] "Der rechtliche Zustand [. . .] unter denen allein jeder seines Rechts theilhaftig werden kann".
[32] "[. . .] du sollst im Verhältnisse eines unvermeidlichen Nebeneinanderseins mit allen anderen aus jenem heraus in einen rechtlichen Zustand [. . .] übergehen". Kant labels this the 'Postulate of Public Right'.
[33] See Reidar Maliks, *Kant's Politics in Context* (Oxford University Press, 2014).

Index